The World of Constable John Hennigan

The World of Constable John Hennigan

Royal Irish Constabulary 1912-1922

Hal Hennigan

Cover design by Rose Finerty

Matador
9 Priory Business Park,
Wistow Road, Kibworth Beauchamp,
Leicestershire. LE8 0RX
Tel: 0116 279 2299
Email: books@troubador.co.uk
Web: www.troubador.co.uk/matador
Twitter: @matadorbooks

ISBN 978 1789015 256

British Library Cataloguing in Publication Data.
A catalogue record for this book is available from the British Library.

Printed and bound in the UK by TJ International, Padstow, Cornwall
Typeset in 11pt Minion Pro by Troubador Publishing Ltd, Leicester, UK

Matador is an imprint of Troubador Publishing Ltd

In Loving Memory of
John Hennigan 1891 – 1957
and
Eoin Hennigan 1973 – 2011

Acknowledgements

I must express my appreciation of the assistance given by so many individuals and institutions in facilitating my research towards the making of this book. While it's impossible to thank by name all those who contributed, some really must be mentioned.

My cousin John Callanan for the maps he skilfully prepared for me.

Lynn Nicks of Abu Dhabi, who found the time to scrutinise the manuscript, point out many errors and offer helpful suggestions. *Once an ELT...*

Máire Lohan of Galway, authority on Patrick Lyons, who meticulously read the manuscript, and helped me to see things from different angles.

Conor Brady for his wonderfully encouraging words when I needed encouragement.

Kevin Myers for his close reading of the manuscript, pointing out my most egregious errors and making very valuable suggestions.

Jim Herlihy, whose contribution to Irish police history is immense. He made time to talk to me and offer encouragement and suggestions.

All the staff of the National Library of Ireland, whose unfailingly cheerful helpfulness made my task easier.

The staff of Galway County Library, an institution of which I am a devout member, at St Augustine Street and Ballybane. They can never be replaced by robots.

Aisling Lockhart at the Manuscripts & Research Library, Trinity College, Dublin.

Sgt Martin Drew, former Curator of the Garda Museum, Dublin Castle.

The staff of the National Archives of Ireland, Dublin.

Bernie McMenamin of Fairwater Credit Union, Drumquin, Co. Tyrone.

Sister Dorothy of the Ursuline Community, Sligo.

Mairéad Treanor, Librarian, Met Eireann, Glasnevin.

Carmel Gilbride and her colleagues of the Eneclann team.

Greg Harrison of 100 Squadron (Royal Air Force) Association.

Most particularly, I am grateful to Colm Foley for his many comments and suggestions. I wonder if he'll recognise the ideas I've stolen from him.

And I want to express my special gratitude to Gerry and Lanna Foley for their kindness and support over the years. Sadly, Lanna is no longer with us and is sorely missed.

The staff of Irish Rail, Bus Eireann, Dublin Bus and Ulsterbus for helping me to make the most of my Free Travel Pass.

Contents

Preface

Readers will see that this book has neither an index nor references. These deficiencies are the result of a conscious decision. This is not a work of dispassionate historiography; it makes no claim to academic objectivity or detachment.

Born just twenty years after the foundation of the independent Irish state, I grew up in an Ireland where received wisdom was that the break from Britain was unquestionably positive.. To suggest otherwise was heretical. Nor was there any mention of the cost. The History schoolbook ended at 1916. Children knew they weren't getting the full story.

With one exception, my father never spoke of that tumultuous decade. Dying too young, he was gone before we ever had a drink together, and his memories remained unvoiced.

When I started to research this book my intention was to discover what I could about John Hennigan's police service and to learn more about the social and political conditions in which he then lived. As there are few details on record about a lowly Constable's life, the emphasis shifted to the RIC as a body of men, and I began to appreciate them as my father's comrades and friends.

Having been initially demonised and subsequently largely ignored, the men of the Royal Irish Constabulary are deserving of remembrance as Irishmen who did their duty as they saw it and, for the most part, did it honestly and honourably. I hope we all can claim as much.

Abbreviations

ADRIC	Auxiliary Division, RIC
AFC	Air Force Cross
AOH	Ancient Order of Hibernians (an organisation intended as a counter-weight to the Orange Order)
AIG	Assistant Inspector General
A/Sgt	Acting Sergeant
ASU	Active Service Unit (IRA); popularly called Flying Column in rural areas
BMH	Bureau of Military History. Military Archives, Cathal Brugha Bks, Dublin
BO	Barrack Orderly
CI	County Inspector
Con.	Constable
Col.	Colonel
CYMS	Catholic Young Men's Society
Det./Sgt	Detective Sergeant
DFC	Distinguished Flying Cross
DI	District Inspector
DMP	Dublin Metropolitan Police
DORA	Defence of the Realm Act

DV	Divisional Commissioner
F/O	Flying Officer (RAF)
Gen.	General
G Men	The political section of the DMP. The other Divisions, A – F, referred to the geograpical areas of the city's policing.
GS	Garda Síochana
HC	Head Constable
HR	Home Rule
IG	Inspector General
IP	Irish Party (in UK parliament) also IPP (Irish Parliamentary Party)
IRA	Irish Republican Army
IRB	Irish Republican Brotherhood
IV	Irish Volunteers
JP	Justice of the Peace (lay magistrate)
MC	Military Cross (British Army officers' award for bravery)
MM	Military Medal (other ranks' award for bravery)
NCO	Non-commissioned officer (Army)
NSPCC	National Society for the Prevention of Cruelty to Children
NWMP	North West Mounted Police
NUPPO	National Union of Police & Prison Officers
NV	National Volunteers
RCMP	Royal Canadian Mounted Police
RIC	Royal Irish Constabulary
RM	Resident Magistrate
RUC	Royal Ulster Constabulary
SF	*Sinn Féin*
Sgt	Sergeant
TC	Temporary Cadet (Auxiliary Division RIC)
TD	*Teachta Dála* (member of Dáil Éireann)
UVF	Ulster Volunteer Force

Royal Irish Constabulary Ranks – 20th Century

(with abbreviations used in the text)

Inspector General	(IG)
Deputy Inspector General	
Assistant Inspector General	
Divisional Commissioner	(1920 – 1922: Div. Comm.)
County Inspector	(CI) – equiv. to British Chief Constable
District Inspector 1st Class	(DI)
District Inspector 2nd Class	(DI)
District Inspector 3rd Class	(DI)
Head Constable	(HC) – equiv. to Inspector
Sergeant	(Sgt)
Acting Sergeant (until 1918)	(A/Sgt)
Constable	(Con.)

Pre-decimal Currency

The currency which served Britain and Ireland for several hundred years used both twelfths and tenths. The basic unit was the Pound which was made up of 20 Shillings. Each shilling contained twelve Pence, so that there were 240 pence in a pound. Each Penny was divided into two Halfpennies, or ha'pence. A penny could also be divided into four Farthings.

By the 20th Century, banknotes were used for denominations of One Pound and Ten Shillings. There was no longer a Crown coin to represent five shillings but the Half Crown was a substantial coin in both size and value. The shilling was the most important coin followed by sixpence and threepence. Then there was the penny, half-penny and little farthing which remained in circulation into the 1950s.

An anomaly was the Florin, a two-shilling coin resulting from an abortive move towards decimalisation in Victorian times.

A notional currency unit was the Guinea, or 21 shillings. It was used by the higher professions such as lawyers and medical specialists to lend a bit of class to their bills and gouge a bit extra from their clients. Ancillary services such as bespoke tailors and bloodstock dealers frequently emulated their patrons in this regard.

Pounds, shillings and pence were symbolised by £. s. d. Ten pounds, eight shillings and sixpence was written as £10/8/6. Five shillings was usually written as 5/=, five shillings and sixpence was 5/6, fourpence was 4d, and tuppence ha'penny was 2½ d. Simple indeed.

Glossary

CHIEF SECRETARY for IRELAND – The Government Minister responsible for Irish affairs.

DOMINION STATUS – The degree of independence enjoyed by former colonies such as New Zealand, Australia, Canada and South Africa. They were effectively independent, with their own armies and navies, but retained close links with Britain, acknowledging the Monarch as Head of State.

FÁINNE – A ring. In the public cultural context, it usually refers to a gold or silver lapel badge signifying the wearer's willingness to converse in Irish.

HOME RULE – Limited self-government in which a local parliament, subordinate to London, could make laws pertaining to local matters but where powers such as determining Foreign Policy, Defence and Finance were reserved to the Imperial Parliament.

IRISH REVOLUTIONARY BROTHERHOOD (IRB) – known as the Fenian Brotherhood in USA, a secret, oath-bound

Republican organisation dedicated to ending British rule in Ireland by force. Fenians launched four military incursions into Canada, and an abortive rising in Ireland in 1867. The instigator of the 1916 Rising, the IRB then drove the subsequent rebuilding of the republican movement. It appears to have died out after 1923.

LAND WAR – A period of major agrarian unrest after Irish tenant farmers, subjected to unaffordable rents, and arbitrary eviction especially by absentee landlords who had acquired land titles after the Great Famine of the 1840s, began to resist. Under the banner of The Three Fs – fair rent, free sale and fixity of tenure, the Irish Land League led by the tenacious Michael Davitt withheld rents when in dispute. The Constabulary was drawn into the conflict and became the target of obloquy through their presence during evictions.

POITIN – also Poteen, Irish *poitín* – illicit spirit distilled from time immemorial and target of much activity and eloquence by police and clergy.

PROPORTIONAL REPRESENTATION (PR) – Using the Single Transferable Vote, the elector can vote 1,2,3 etc. for a series of candidates in order of preference (or of those whom one dislikes the least). The proportion of seats won by a party more accurately reflects their support among the electorate than does the British 'first-past-the-post' system.

SHONEEN – Presumably a play upon the Gaelic *Seanín* (little John), the term ridiculed a 'little John Bull', an Irish person who embraced English ways.

UNDER SECRETARY for IRELAND – The most senior civil servant in the Irish administration.

NOTE ON GAELIC / ENGLISH LANGUAGE FORMS

When using the Irish language form of a word, I have used appropriate accents e.g. *Poitín*. However, where words have been assimilated into everyday speech in English e.g. Garda Siochana, Sinn Fein, I have dropped the accents.

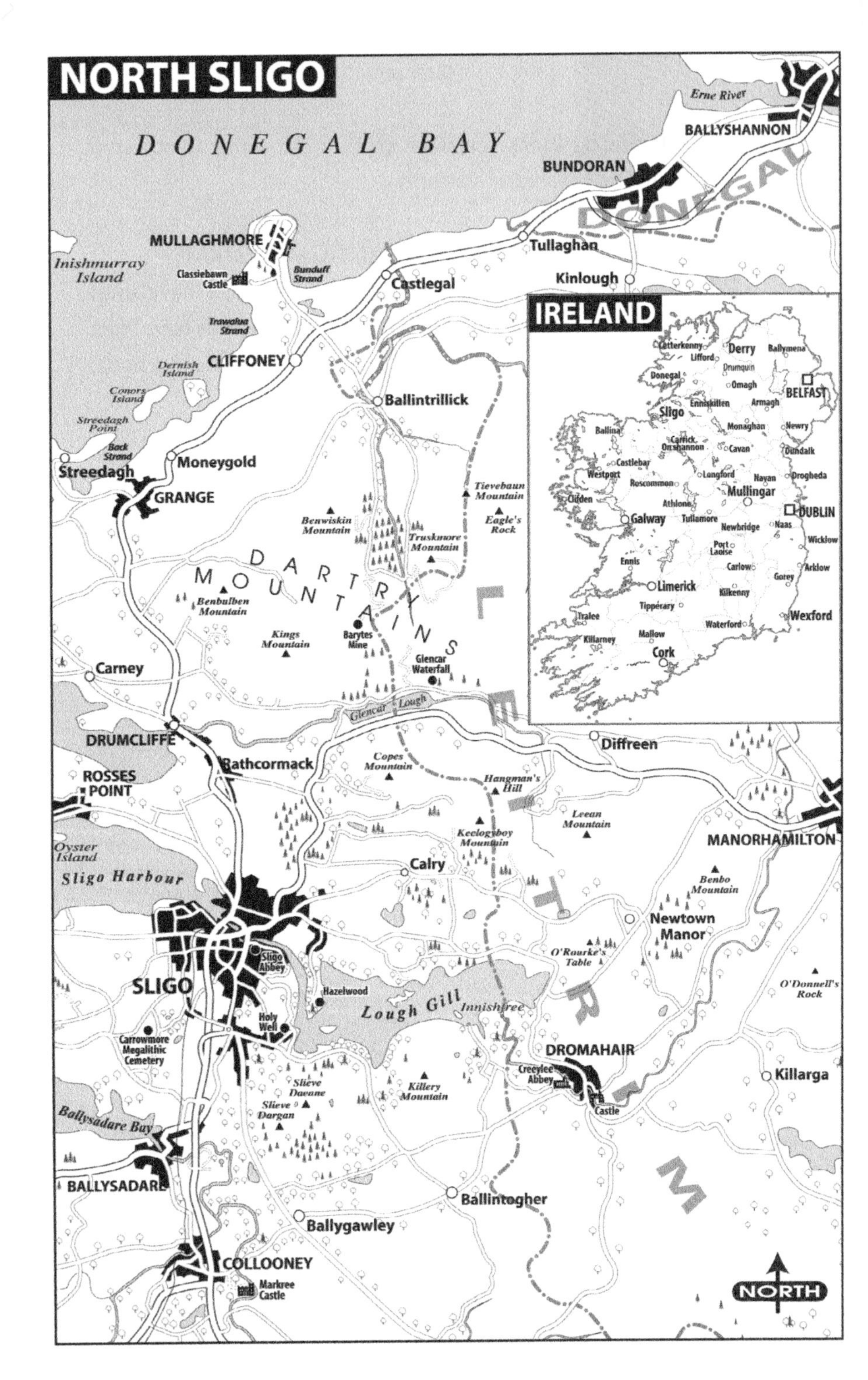

Prepared by John The Map Callanan.

The Road from Sligo

John Hennigan became a member of the Royal Irish Constabulary on 24th January 1912, recommended by District Inspector Moore. Aged 20, his previous occupation was recorded as postman. John's height was measured at 5'9" and his religion entered as Catholic. Shortly afterwards, on 23rd April, his friend John Gilmartin was appointed, also on the recommendation of DI Moore. His previous employment was listed as postman as well. Taller than his pal, young Gilmartin was a bigger man than most of his generation; though his height was scrupulously recorded as 5'11½", he was generally considered a six-footer. The nickname that would follow him throughout his life was "Wee John". Born and growing up close to each other, both the Sligo Johns would later serve in the neighbouring county of Donegal and remain life-long friends. As John Hennigan's mother was born Sabina Gilmartin and all were from the same area, it's possible that the two young men were related.

District Inspector Henry John Moore, a native of Longford, had entered the RIC as a Cadet in 1897. He had already earned BA and LLB degrees through Trinity College, Dublin. Moore would show himself to be a capable and ambitious officer. In

1913 he would receive a Recommendation for "good police work" during the Sligo labour strike. In the same year Moore, in practice competitions with the Webley revolver, proved to be the best shot in County Sligo with a highly creditable score of 45 out of a possible 48. DI Moore would grow in prominence over the next decade.

His superior, County Inspector Robert Ievers Sullivan, originally from Limerick was also a Dublin University graduate with MA and LLB degrees. He was described by one Constable as "a low-sized man with rather bulgy eyes and a peculiar accent which was hard to understand".

Membership of the police often recurred in families and as many as a third of recruits had relatives in the service. John's paternal uncle Bartley or Bartholomew served as a Sergeant in Mayo but had retired before John entered the Force. Common in the West of Ireland, the name Bartley was also given to John's younger brother. At the time of the 1911 Census, John's young sister Katie, aged 13, was living with the childless couple Bartley and his young wife, Mary Agnes, in Boyle Co. Roscommon. No doubt the example of Bartley's successful career would have been a factor in John's decision to apply, and having an uncle who'd been a Sergeant would have increased his chances of acceptance. Some familiarity with police culture was obviously seen as an advantage by the authorities.

Bartley was born in 1857 and joined the Force in 1880. Serving in Limerick, Mayo and Clare, he must have encountered some difficult situations during the Land War. He was promoted to Acting Sergeant in 1896 and got married the following year. In 1899 he was elevated to Sergeant. Although he'd been given a Reward in 1889, in 1900 he received a Caution for some unspecified transgression. His retirement on pension in 1905 was after a comparatively short career and may have been the result of ill-health. He was then only 48 years old.

Taking the road northwards from Sligo town to Donegal, travellers since time immemorial have had to pass through the narrow gap between Ben Bulben and the sea. Standing like the sharp prow of an inverted ship, the distinctive bulk of the mountain allows no passage otherwise. It's a landscape redolent of history, fraught with myth and magic. On Ben Bulben in pre-Christian times Fionn Mac Cumhail is said to have slain his friend Diarmad who had eloped with unfaithful Grainne. Here was fought the Battle of the Books in 561AD, resulting from the first legal expression of copyright in the Western World and causing St Columcille to go into self-imposed exile and make his mark on Europe's religious history. The round tower and high cross at Drumcliffe still remain to remind the passer-by of those Celtic Christian days. The schoolboy John Hennigan would have heard the stories in the village school and probably from his parents too. History was literally on his own doorstep. On the fearsome rocks at Streedagh three ships of King Philip's armada had perished in 1588 and there was talk of Spanish blood in the community.

There was no evidence of Spanish blood in the Hennigans. Typically, the men had fair, fine hair which thinned rapidly and complexions so fair as to be, in some cases, almost translucent.

By the turn of the century, as schoolboy John trudged to school, perhaps carrying the daily sod of turf for the schoolroom fire, the emerging poet W.B. Yeats had already celebrated much of the Celtic mythology and the North Sligo landscape in which his childhood imagination had been formed. His brother Jack peopled his paintings with the real characters he saw around him: determined jockeys at flapper meetings, fishermen, women spinning and deep-sea mariners at Rosses Point.

In the parish of Ahamlish the Hennigan family home stood within sound of the sea. In a small cottage of basically three rooms there lived ten persons at the time of the 1911 Census.

Patrick Hennigan, head of the household at age 55, spoke and was literate in Irish and English as was his mother Mary aged 90. Patrick's wife Sabina spoke only English as did the children. The eldest son James would inherit the little farm while 19 year old John and his siblings would have to make their own way in the world. In order of age, James was followed by P.J., Anne, John, Bartley, Thomas, Edward, and Michael Joseph then aged nine. Anne, two years older than John, was already a postulant nun in the Ursuline Order. Perhaps an added factor in her vocation was the custom which forbade an eldest son from marrying until his oldest sister was out of the house but the eldest child, Mary, had already gone to America. Teenage Katie, as we have seen, was then living in Boyle with Uncle Bartley and Aunt Mary Agnes. In rural Ireland it was quite common for children to be domiciled with childless close relatives; in many cases, if they were all in agreement, the child was adopted by the aunt or uncle and became their heir to farm, business, house or whatever they had.[1]

It's hard to imagine now but such little cottages were home to most of rural Ireland's large families. A common form was three rooms in a line with the front door opening into the kitchen, heart of the house. There, people washed, cooked, ate their meals and conversed. Baby chickens were hand-reared there and Indian meal and other animal foods were often prepared in the kitchen. The aroma of simmering maize mingled with the scent of fresh-baked bread. Generations were born, lived and died in these cottages and considerable ingenuity and craft went into making best use of the available space. Sometimes beds came out of the wall at night, sometimes a raised platform under the high ceiling increased the sleeping space. When children were still

1 The philoprogenitive tendencies of Irish small farmers, long a wonder to foreign travellers, were not discouraged by the Catholic Church but they brought large problems. Piety doesn't feed hungry mouths.

young, boys and girls could sleep in the same room but when they reached puberty some would have to sleep in the kitchen area. All the little cottages had thatched roofs but the thatching varied widely. Some used rushes, some straw. In its crudest form the thatch would simply have covered the space below but in more sophisticated houses tongued wooden planking lined a high ceiling. Despite their simplicity, such cottages were usually scrupulously clean. The lime whitewash which left the external walls brilliantly white also had anti-bacterial properties and could be used on interior walls, sometimes tinted with laundry-blue dye. When any degree of prosperity was attained, shop paint might be used inside. Above all, ease of cleaning determined the decor.

I have memory now of the Hennigan cottage only when my grandparents had passed on and it was home to Uncle Jim and his wife Mary. They had no children but she had flowers exploding all over the front and garden of their cosy cottage. Now I realise it was a remarkable achievement in the salt-laden air so close to the ever-growling sea.

Ten years after the Great Famine, the incredibly small amount of land they then farmed is a measure of how precariously the Irish peasantry survived. According to Griffith's Valuation of 1858 , the holding of one Patrick Hennigan consisted of 3 acres, 2 roods and 30 perches – roughly one and a half hectares – and theirs was not the smallest farm in the locality. It seems that in the decades that followed, the Hennigans maintained their foothold and increased their holding.

In the 1830s, before the Great Famine, the Gore-Booths of Lissadell undertook what may be seen as land clearance or an assisted emigration scheme depending on one's point of view. The family, paid off by Cromwell, owned thousands of acres in north Sligo. In evidence to the Parliamentary Inquiry into the famine, Sir Robert Gore-Booth offered grateful letters from former tenants whom he had helped to settle in Newfoundland. Among the emigrants were many Hennigans from the Maugherow area. Local tradition later had it that one famine ship had foundered with the loss of many souls but there is no evidence that this ever happened. The population of the area had certainly thinned out by August 1878 when Patrick and Sabina, born in nearby Lislary, got married in Ahamlish; there was only one marriage a month in the parish church that year. Sir Josslyn Gore-Booth, who succeeded to the baronetcy in 1900, supported the co-operative movement and was involved in setting up Drumcliffe creamery and others in the county.

It was a world of few opportunities in which English was necessary for advancement. There were few Irish poets in the official schoolbooks but the children learned by heart *The Ancient Mariner* and *The Wreck of the Hesperus*. Through Macauley's words they might have learnt of Brave Horatio's defence of the bridge at Ancient Rome, but possibly not of Sgt Custume's similar work at the Bridge of Athlone in 1691. Grey's *Elegy* was an enduring favourite. In the country school it really all depended on The Master, his personality, his scholarship, and his political inclinations. Ironically, the Big House of the area was Lissadell where the privileged Gore-Booth girls were developing radical ideas of nationalism and social justice. Further north stands Classibawn Castle, centre of Lord Palmerston's Irish estates which would eventually become a second home to Lord Louis Mountbatten through his wife, Edwina. The landed gentry – Percevals, Woodmartins, O'Haras, Coopers etc. – were almost entirely Protestant and most remained staunchly Conservative and Unionist. The same was true of the merchant class in Sligo town – Polloxfen, Midleton, Campbell-Perry and others.

Whether landlords were progressives like the Gore-Booths who improved their estates and promoted local industry or were more like the squireens who wasted the coin of their tenants and contributed nothing, it was still a world divided between the privileged and those without wealth. There was abiding resentment which often found a relatively harmless expression in the poaching of salmon or an occasional deer. For the rural poor, there was no education beyond the National Schools. Only in the larger towns and cities could limited post-primary schooling be provided free by such organisations as the Christian Brothers and Sisters of Mercy. For Catholics of means, there were fee-paying boarding schools. Sligo town had its Diocesan College and Ursuline Convent while for the poorer classes there was a Mercy Convent School and a Technical Institute for boys.

For the small farmers of North Sligo, politics took second place to survival. In the autumn their meagre incomes could be supplemented by the gathering of sea-rods to be sold for the extraction of iodine. The harsh landscape was punctuated by lime kilns for the production of lime to be spread as fertiliser. Seaweed too was used to enhance the soil. For them, politics was more about the land question than national independence but old grievances ran deep. When Cromwell came to Ireland he presented the Irish with the bill for England's emancipation from absolute monarchy, the confiscation of Irish land paying for British freedoms. By the end of the 19th Century some of those original families given land by Cromwell and in earlier plantations still survived in place. Others had been replaced after the Great Famine by speculative investors. Whatever their origins, the great majority of landowners seemed wedded to the British connection. When Charles Stuart Parnell, leader of the Home Rule movement, appealed to his fellow landlords to put their leadership skills and experience at the service of a self-governing Ireland, his call fell mostly on unreceptive ears.

But, in 1912 change was in the air. Wyndham's Land Acts had effectively created a new class of tenant farmers who tended to be socially conservative but politically ambitious. At the latter end of the 19th Century and into the 20th, government by the Tories had oscillated between Coercion and a policy of "killing Home Rule by kindness". The mass of the Irish accepted the kindnesses but remained wedded to the ambition of national self-government. Control of local government had passed from Grand Juries to County and Urban Councils elected on a democratic if limited franchise. An emergent Catholic urban middle class had found its voice and its mood was predominantly constitutional nationalist. The most important development was that Home Rule was about to become a reality after forty years of political struggle.

There was a resurgent cultural nationalism too. The Gaelic League was conceived as a non-political organisation to preserve and promote the Old Language but it inevitably attracted many whose nationalism was rather less genteel. Novelist George Moore memorably described young men "with Gaelic foaming on their beards like porter". The extraordinary upsurge in literary activity and achievements such as the establishment of the Abbey Theatre was another manifestation of this new spirit. The Gaelic Athletic Association offered less cerebral pursuits to those with energy and enthusiasm. But for the landless, especially in poorer western counties, there was little leisure or lucre to enjoy such activities.

When the land agitation was at its height the police were often called on for the hateful duty of "preserving the peace", i.e. protecting bailiffs during evictions. From the start of the new century there was a gradual running-down of the police establishment. The approach of Home Rule may have been an excuse for official inaction and a policy which has been described as "concealed abdication". Many police stations were closed and opportunities for promotion to Sergeant were reduced.

Since the bitter days of the Land War had been largely brought to an end by the Land Acts, the country was generally peaceful. Tenant farmers now had the security of tenure previously denied to them. However humble the circumstances, stability offered the prospect of betterment.

In editorial comment on 15th November 1913, the *Constabulary Gazette* put it: "Constables and Officers alike have been arriving at the conclusion that the Constabulary is an institution that has become unfashionable and unpopular with the political authorities, and that it is destined shortly to be thrown upon the scrapheap, and that, in the meantime, it is being allowed to rot".

Despite having had no increase in pay since 1908, and that increase being only the implementation of recommendations from seven years before, the Royal Irish Constabulary (RIC) was seen as a desirable option for those of limited education and opportunity. In practice it was becoming a civil force like the unarmed Dublin Metropolitan Police (DMP). It offered permanence and a pension and some status in the community. A policeman as prospective son-in-law could expect a welcome to many a family's fireside – but he had to have seven years' service before requesting permission to marry and the prospective bride's family would also be subject to official scrutiny.

It was often remarked that Police families placed great emphasis on education and advancement for their children. While "farmer" and "labourer" between them accounted for the former occupation of most recruits, it seems likely that both terms actually referred to farmers' younger sons. Landless, they had to be ambitious and hard-working to get on in the world. And there were indications that these were common characteristics. The proportion of policemen's sons entering the priesthood was well above the average. The phenomenon wasn't confined to Catholics; it was marked among the Church of Ireland community too.

By 1912, the Police were closer to the general population

than ever before. As one Galway observer put it "The Parish Priest and the Sergeant were the guardians of the parish". William Sterritt, a Donegal Protestant and son of a Sergeant recalled of his youth: "Oh they were well thought of, the ones in our area were all very nice, very nice. Of course that was their way to keep friendly with you because that's how they got their information". William himself went on to join the Royal Irish Constabulary (RIC) in its final years.

Although hardly an unbiased witness, Andrew M. Sullivan, "The Last Serjeant" writing in 1927, gave a description of the Irish Police which summarised a widely-held view:

> The subordinate officers of the Civil Power, whether in the Civil Service or the Constabulary, were all Irishmen. The R.I.C. was a body of men of whom any country would have been proud. For the most part they were young Catholic Nationalists, the younger sons of large farmers, and they represented the pick of disciplined intelligence, courage and character. They, of course, knew and understood their own brethren and countrymen, sympathised with their aspirations, and contrived their happiness, by the preservation of peace and order in the community.

The Depot

In January 1912, twenty year old John Hennigan joined the force. A candidate was accepted only after background checks revealed no evidence of criminal or subversive behaviour in his family background. He had to meet stringent physical standards – minimum height 5ft 8ins with chest expansion of 36 inches – and pass tests in literacy and numeracy at above school-leaver average. Many a country schoolmaster made a few extra shillings by tutoring those about to apply. In the village schools grown men would, on occasions, be seated scrunched up behind the little boys for a couple of weeks in preparation for the tests.

The physical examination at the Depot was crucial. Candidates had to be free from varicose veins and spinal curvature, without defects in sight, speech or hearing and with no disposition to illness. The Dublin Metropolitan Police was explicit in listing the main causes of disqualification: "swelled veins on legs, deficient chest capacity, decay of teeth, defective vision, want of muscle, skin diseases, chicken breast, and general physical weakness".

A contemporary journalist offered a stereotype of the Irish Catholic Strong Farmer. The first son would inherit the land. The second would become a priest and greatly please his mother. The third, usually not the brightest of the bunch but good-looking, strong and dependable, would become a policeman. Perhaps more to the point was the fact that younger sons had both the freedom and the necessity to leave the confines of their home place. The fierce parochialism exemplified by Matt the Thresher in Kickham's *Knocknagow* was a luxury they couldn't afford. Less academically-endowed adventurous spirits might join the Army or Navy to see the world; the Constabulary offered some mobility within Ireland as well as security of employment.

Training was done at The Depot in Dublin's Phoenix Park. This imposing set of buildings with its elegantly-proportioned central structure dating from 1842 must have imbued the new arrivals, used to country towns where the most imposing secular building was the bank, with a palpable sense of awe.

Recruits had to bring a suit and hat, 4 linen shirts and £2 – a considerable sum – for the purchase of necessities pending issue of pay. This was a big investment but not all recruits lasted the course. Some were dismissed within days, often for drunkenness. Many were let go after failing the Surgeon's examination but later readmitted when they had reached the required physical standards. The Depot was under the command of the Commandant, Assistant Inspector General Edward Humble Pearson, assisted by the Barrack Master and Head Constable Major. Conditions were Spartan: straw bedding was used for recruits right up to 1922; baths were a luxury with only three available for 500 men.

The RIC, known as the Irish Constabulary before 1867, was structured on quasi-military lines. The RIC was akin to a Continental-style Gendarmerie, a servant of government rather than the people. Its predecessors were the Revenue Police – "the Poitín Hussars" – and the Peace Preservation Force. (PPF). At its head was the Inspector General (IG); with one exception this was a distinguished military officer. The IG from 1900 to 1916 was Sir Neville Chamberlain, famous for devising the game of snooker whilst serving in India.

Michael Talbot has intriguingly suggested that the practice of wearing Sergeant's chevrons on the cuff derived from the mounted men of the PPF. As with cavalrymen, the rank insignia had to be visible below the edge of the short uniform cape.

Revealing the distinction between the RIC and other police forces in the United Kingdom, the Irish police served as a model for many of the colonial forces, most notably Canada and Australia. In 1858 RIC Sub-Inspector Charles Brew had been appointed Chief Inspector of the new police force in British Columbia. Former District Inspector Robert O'Hara Burke, who later led the ill-fated expedition which traversed Australia from south to north, had organised the Victoria Police. Officers from all over the Empire on which the sun never set were sent to the Depot for training; their presence must have been an exotic element in the Officers' Mess and a source of some pride to the Force as a whole. As Colonial officers, N.C.Os and Cadets had to wear their own distinctive uniforms, the whole assembly must have brought a vivid splash of colour to the Phoenix Park, tropical birds in the Irish mist. Occasional dark faces were reminders of the Empire's extent. A 1912 account published in the very month of John's arrival there, described the scene:

> All had to wear the uniform of their respective Colonies, and never was such a variety of uniforms seen at the Depot before; they differed in details, though there was a general sameness, particularly in their thinness and lightness, which was rather trying in the Irish winter months and rendered necessary the wearing of special uniform great-coats kept for the purpose. The sun

> helmets of some seemed very large and deep and the appearance, or rather disappearance, of the wearers in them, suggested the well-known line of the poet to his departed friend: "Though lost to sight, to mem'ry dear".

The Royal Canadian Mounted Police, as the North West Mounted Police became, and the Royal Irish Constabulary were the only police forces in the British Empire allowed the distinction of "Royal" in their titles. The original "Chief Mountie" and organiser of the NWMP was a member of the French family of Roscommon, a veteran of the RIC.

There is a multitude of references to connections between the RIC and colonial police forces but the connections should not obscure the differences. Across most of the far-flung British Empire, white British officers commanded rank and file policemen who differed from them in race, religion and culture. In the year 1912, the gap was in most cases unbridgeable. Also, when it came to recruiting native policemen, a particular ethnic group might be favoured to police the others. Even in post-colonial India with its kaleidoscopic ethnicities, religions, languages and castes, it was policy to recruit policemen separate from the community they were policing. None of these factors applied to Ireland where distinctions were mainly of class.

There was a clear distinction between Irish commissioned officers and the other ranks up to Head Constable. Police Cadets were also trained at the Depot, but separately. They lived in Mess with servants and their training laid great emphasis on horsemanship. Mess life entailed much drinking and horseplay and some ran up enormous Mess bills, all rather like the regular army. Ironically, like the recruits in training nearby, many were younger sons with few prospects, and, in the case of the Cadets, lacking the wealth needed for an army commission. The three grades of District Inspector – 3rd, 2nd and 1st Class – roughly corresponded to army Lieutenants, Captains and Majors. County Inspectors were equivalent to Army Colonels and British Chief Constables. When Cadets left the Depot to take up their first postings as DIs, 3rd Class, they knew little of the law or policing and had to be trained on the job by long-suffering Sergeants and Head Constables – the highest non-commissioned rank and equivalent to Inspector today. But DIs did have social status and like army subalterns they would be welcomed into the homes of the gentry. The RIC structure mirrored not only the military caste system but that of society at the end of the previous century. In a statement to an 1882 enquiry, amongst the reasons offered by officers against reform of the system, County Inspector Maguire stated of the promoted ranker, "he would be left isolated by the Magistrates and gentlemen whom he ought to mix with". The distinctions of class and religion which divided "the two Irelands" were clear.

It seems that rank and file policemen generally preferred officers of Cadet background rather than those who'd come up through the ranks themselves. The latter knew all the tricks and dodges whilst the former probably had a generally broader outlook and were easier to hoodwink.

But it was now the 20th Century and change was happening, although slowly. By 1910, 80% of recruits were Catholic. Up to 1890, three-quarters of officer cadets were Protestant. From 1891 half of DI places were reserved for promoted Head Constables. The system was moving towards denominational balance in the upper ranks and some modification of the class bias. Most Catholic District Inspectors came up through the ranks and by 1910 were on average 40 years old as opposed to Protestant DIs' average of 28 years old on appointment. That thwarted change in the upper ranks and almost all the County Inspectors were Protestants who had entered as Cadets.

The real hurdle for a Head Constable (HC) was the age

of 48 after which he could not be promoted further. Many a competent and ambitious Head Constable had to serve out his years at that level while "beardless boys ... are placed over the heads of men... grown mature, grey or white in the service of their country". In 1872 the pay of a HC had been £101; by 1914 it had risen to £104. While DIs and CIs had to retire after 40 years' service, quite elderly Sergeants and HCs were often allowed to remain on even after reaching full pension entitlement.

The bottleneck created by these practices affected policemen all down the line. Of promotions to Acting Sergeant, two thirds were made on the basis of seniority. Constables had to have seven years' service and pass qualifying exams conducted by the County Inspector in Arithmetic, Orthography, Handwriting and Police Duties. Such promotion generally came after 21 – 23 years of service. There were many complaints about elderly Sergeants and Head Constables who justified their existence by harassing their subordinates.

The P List, introduced by the reform-minded Sir Andrew Reed, IG from 1885 to 1900, was a route to accelerated promotion by competitive examination. For successful candidates there was still the problem of too few vacancies. Promotion from Sgt to HC was Byzantine and four different lists were used.

Andrew Reed, it's worth noting, was the only RIC Cadet Officer to reach the top job, the other IGs all having a military background. He was a practical policeman and his publications, especially *The Constable's Guide* were essential handbooks. The procedures and quotas he introduced opened the way for Catholics to achieve real promotion. His more humane and civil approach to discipline reduced the rate of dismissals over the RIC's last 30 years to 5% of attrition from a previous level of 30%.

That said, it must be acknowledged that Reed's successor, Neville Chamberlain, a military man, contributed to the developing civil character of the force. He put a forceful emphasis on civic courtesy:

> Every policeman who desires advancement in the Royal Irish Constabulary should make courtesy and politeness to the general public his special study. These qualities are as important for study and improvement as drill and police duties.

However, institutional inertia and resistance to innovation still seem to have pervaded the system. Management showed no interest in improving efficiency by the provision of bicycles and motor cycles for instance. Probably too many Officers were satisfied with doing things the way they always had been done. Employment was scarce so Constables should have been grateful to have a steady job.

A contemporary of John Hennigan at the Depot was William Herbert Bodley. Three years older than John, Bodley was a Cadet. As revealed in his official diary, in many respects his training mirrored that of the ordinary recruits; in many important ways it differed. On Monday 19th February 1912 Bodley was attested in the Commandant's office. The following morning he turned out on Parade in Marching Order from 9.30 until 11.00. Then there was School from 12.00 to 1 pm. At 2 pm it was time for Drill until 3.00, followed by School again from 3.15 to 4.15. That routine didn't change much during the month, except for the introduction of Fire Drill. In April Riding School began, not a requirement for the other ranks but becoming progressively more important for the Cadets in training. There were also Gym, Swimming and Ambulance lessons. In May musketry training began; sometimes there were trips to the Army firing ranges fifty miles away at the Curragh and to the Magazine Fort in Phoenix Park for revolver practice. Cadets began to attend the Orderly

Officer of the day as he undertook his inspection tours and they practised performing the duties of Orderly Officer. Having taken a Finance examination at Dublin Castle, William Bodley was promoted to District Inspector 3rd Class on 11th September and on 1st October took up duty in Portlaw, Co. Waterford. John had gone from the Depot a month before him.

Àfter leaving the Depot, their paths seem never to have crossed. William was discharged from the Constabulary on gratuity, i.e. without a pension, on 31st July 1918 having apparently suffered from prolonged periods of ill-health. His service was shorter than John's, and much less onerous and dangerous as things turned out.

Despite the institutional arthritis, by the first decade of the 20th Century the social barriers between the ranks were no longer impermeable. Young officers depended on their men and, if they were to win respect, had to engage with them and respect their knowledge and wisdom. The farmers' sons who filled the ranks were at close quarters with young men of the Anglo-Irish small gentry class and learned to judge them as men and as officers. They could themselves acquire some sophistication and start to aspire to a better quality of life than their forbears.

It should be emphasised that the Dublin Metropolitan Police was a separate entity, a blue-clad civil police force funded by civic revenues much like city police in Britain. Its uniformed members were unarmed and promotion was through the ranks. It was finally incorporated into *An Garda Síochána* (Guardians of the Peace – the new Irish Free State police) in 1925.

For the RIC recruits in training, however, there was still inordinate emphasis on foot drill and musketry. Like the dark green uniforms, much of the training and drill was based on that of the Rifle Brigade. One tradition, for example, was the practice of carrying rifles at the trail – held horizontally in the right hand. While it seemed to have nothing to do with policing, the rationale for drilling was that it instilled discipline and cohesion among the members of a unit. At least Rifle Brigade drill and training differed from that of ordinary infantrymen in that it was designed to promote individual alertness and self-reliance rather than mechanical responses.

Despite the military trappings, it's important to remember that policemen were not subject to military discipline. Under the Police Code the most common punishments for errant members were fines. The heaviest penalty which could be imposed was Dismissal.

Recruits did study basic law and had to commit it to memory. Also there were lessons to improve their Reading, Writing and Accountancy skills. It was said long afterwards that RIC men always wrote a good hand. There were lessons on detective work but no instruction on intelligence or political work. Adding to the military aspect of the Depot, the mounted section and the band were also based there as was the Reserve Force of 400 men under the Inspector General's direct command. They could be deployed anywhere as and when needed. To qualify for the Reserve at that time, policemen had to be at least six feet in height and have fewer than eight years of service. One drill instructor, Tom Shannon, was six feet, seven inches, well over two metres tall. When they marched to Mass in Aughrim Street on Sundays, spiked helmets in place, they must have been an impressive sight. It's no wonder that both the RIC and DMP were renowned for their tug of war teams.

The six months of training included foot drill, practice with revolver and carbine, PE, swimming, rope-climbing, ju-jitsu, first aid, fire-fighting, criminal law and police duties. They also learned stringent lessons of discipline, order and personal hygiene to a standard well beyond that common in the day. The concept of "intelligent judgment" was instilled into them along with the art of "eliciting information" from a populace notoriously reticent when talking to the authorities. The value of keeping a policeman's own mouth shut was taught and the importance of "courtesy to the general public" was heavily stressed.

The notion of the prying Peeler putting talk on an unguarded rustic over pints of porter was an abiding one, especially among people of a revolutionary disposition, but it was a caricature. Any elicited confidences were more likely to do with poaching or *poitín* than with politics. And drinking held more perils for the policeman than for the public.

One of the researcher JWR Goulden's correspondents leaves us a glimpse into training at the Depot:

> The Detective training was lectures 'ad lib' on the qualifications necessary to become a good detective; be it understood that the RIC was a detective force from the Inspector General down to the youngest "park pigeon". I still have a lively recollection of District Inspector Bodely's animated lectures, and lessons imparted with such seriousness. He was known by us as "Old Pro". His pet phrase, when one of us would give him a foolish answer, was "Remember lad you are here only on probation" hence the soubriquet "Old Pro". I'd simply revel in repeating some of our idiotic answers... Pro put the question – "You lad on the top seat. What would you do if, when on patrol, you found a man lying on the roadside having been seriously assaulted?" Answer: "I'd ax him who bate him" and so on. Pro – "Next boy – if the man, instead of being seriously wounded, was actually dead, what should you do?" "I'd ax him who kilt him, Sir." Pro – "Come down out of that, my lad – remember you are only here on probation." And so on and so forth, yards of it.

From Reveille at 6 a.m. until 5 p.m. the recruits were constantly busy. In the evening they had access to both a dry canteen and a wet canteen in which pints of stout from a nearby brewery were available. No doubt recruits were soon informed of the charitable aspect of having a pint. The RIC maintained a burial plot in Glasnevin Cemetery and in the case of any member or former member dying without family to bury him, the cost of a decent interment would be met from the profits of the wet canteen.

The first thing a recruit noticed was the impeccable order of the Depot, everything spick and span, creased and polished. The barrack square was spotless, without even a discarded matchstick to mar its proud surface. When inspected at 9.a.m. each morning, every bed was folded to a precision no hospital matron could fault, personal kit correctly stowed and floors immaculately swept. Saturday mornings were given over to a routine of scrubbing and disinfecting until every room in the barracks shone. "The change which the six-month course of training effected in a young, country boy was almost unbelievable" wrote one of them. A veteran remembered: "The first appearance in public in uniform is a very important event in a policeman's life and whilst in many cases bashfulness is in evidence, the majority display great eagerness and pride in their new attire."

Once the uniform had been issued, after four to six weeks, they could go out only in uniform rather than civvies. The cane, or "swagger stick" was obligatory and those without it would be turned back at the gate. In winter black leather gloves were issued.

Another wrote "The day I donned my first uniform was one of the happiest of my life, and I felt that 'Dublin belonged to me' as I swaggered down Grafton Street with my black cane-stick, gloves neatly under my shoulder strap, and my whistle-chain across my breast." One year after Constable Mee stepped out of the Depot, it is likely that Con. Hennigan in his turn shared the same feelings of bursting pride and youthful excitement. The perception of Dublin which remained with him for life was of its more fashionable and salubrious areas: Grafton Street with its carriage trade and a DMP man at the bottom diverting the less presentable citizens around to the parallel Dawson Street, the bracing seafront at Clontarf and, of course, the broad leafy expanse of Phoenix Park.

Barely two months into his training, John Hennigan probably didn't have opportunity to attend the great rally held in O'Connell Street on 31st March to celebrate the passing of the Home Rule Bill. Imagine the scene. At least sixty-four special trains have brought people from all over Ireland to hear John Redmond speak; attendance is estimated somewhere between 100,000 and 150,000. It is a great festive occasion for Nationalists, a triumph for constitutionalism. A noted baritone sings from the main stage *A Nation Once Again* and the chorus is taken up by thousands. On a minor platform at the corner of Abbey Street a radical schoolmaster also speaks. "Let us unite and win a good Act from the British, I think it can be done." he says, "If we are cheated once more there will be red war in Ireland". It's unlikely that many on that day were taking the views of Patrick Pearse too seriously.

In April 1912, trainee policemen as much as the general public must have been thrilled at the developments in technology evidenced in Ireland. On the 11th, the Belfast-built *RMS Titanic* called at Queenstown, the last port on its maiden voyage westwards. On the 14th, word of the disaster reached Ireland and those in the Depot would surely have heard the news before the mass of the public did. They must have shared in the general feelings of disbelief and horror at the loss of life. That month also saw the first attempt by pioneer aviators to fly from Britain to Ireland. It was less than three years since Harry Ferguson of Co. Down had made the first powered flight in Ireland. On the 17th, Irishman Damer Leslie Allen attempted to make the crossing from Holyhead to Dublin in a Bleriot monoplane. He crashed into the sea and his body was never found. On the 22nd, Englishman Denys Corbett Wilson, also in a Bleriot, made the crossing from Wales to Crane near Enniscorthy in 1 hour, 40 minutes. On the 26th, Welshman Vivian Hewitt flew from Anglesea to Dublin in 90 minutes. Interpret it as one might, the water barrier between the two islands had narrowed: a new era had begun.

The Rifle: The Heaviest Cross a Policeman Had to Bear

Despite the government's unwillingness to disarm the Force, the weapons issued to the RIC were not even close to military standard. At the turn of the century the Snider rifle which had been in use for nearly forty years was replaced by the Martini-Henry carbine, a cut down version of the rifle which had been in use with the British Army since 1871 but a step up from the Snider which had been around since the Crimean War. A single-shot rifle with a lever-activated dropping block, its barrel was now reduced from 32 to 21 inches.

In an 1899 Commons debate the Chief Secretary stated that many Sniders were rusted and unreliable and a danger to their users. He said that in the previous decade the Police had been obliged to fire their weapons 14 times: twice at evictions when fired upon, seven times during Moonlighting episodes, three times during affrays between water bailiffs and poachers, once during a riot and once when a land agent and his escort were fired at. Their infrequent use substantiates the Police claim that rifles were redundant.

The Martini-Henrys were replaced by cavalry carbines – Lee

Enfield Mk 1 or Lee Metford from 1904 onwards. These also had a 21 inch barrel but were 6 shot magazine repeaters of 0.303 calibre. The sword bayonet had been replaced years before by a short knife bayonet for crowd control. In 1920 the RIC, by then thoroughly militarised, replaced these with standard war-surplus Lee Enfield point 303 rifles with 10 shot magazines.

The standard sidearm was the Webley RIC.44 calibre revolver introduced in 1868. The flamboyant Col. George Armstrong Custer is said to have owned a pair. They could possibly have come to him through his second-in-command Major Myles Keogh, formerly of the Papal Army. Presumably ownership of the pistols passed to the Native Americans who defeated the foreigners at the Little Big Horn battle.

Actually, by the time John Hennigan joined the Force it probably didn't matter what sort of weapons were issued to them. Once they'd left the Depot most policemen rarely fired full-calibre rifles again. A Morris tube allowed small-calibre pinking practice indoors as well as out – and it was much less noisy.

A Sergeant's son, Patrick Shea remembered watching the annual practice using Morris tubes. Each man was required to fire twenty-one shots from three different positions. "We saw indifferent marksmen manufacture evidence of competence by putting their cardboard targets on the ground and piercing them with the sharp end of a bullet so as to produce results which the sergeant in charge of the party could sign and confidently place among the district archives".

Firearms were unfamiliar at best. A former Constable said that he'd never fired a rifle in six years of service between 1912 and 1918. "I just carried it. It was used for the purpose of training and deportment. We went through the form of loading and unloading the magazine. I cannot recall ever having put a bullet in it."

In view of what happened during the final years of the RIC, it's worth remembering why the police came to be armed in the first place. In the 1830s, Ireland was still a very violent place, over-crowded and seething with discontent. It was only thirty years after the uprising of 1798 had been brutally suppressed. Since then there had been the rising of Robert Emmett in 1803 and in Wicklow the guerrilla leader Michael Dwyer had not surrendered until December of that year. Catholics seethed with anger and indignation at having the unjust and insulting burden of Tithes to the Anglican Church imposed on them. Faction fighting was still a common sport, secret societies were still in evidence and lawlessness was widespread.

At any time, in any country, the military are the wrong people to deal with civil disorder; in that situation they are at best a crude instrument of the state. Soldiers are trained to deal with external enemies and their methods are usually lethal. But police taking over from the military could not be sent out unprotected on dangerous duties. In December 1831 a party of thirty-eight policemen under Sub-Inspector Gibbons and a process-server called Butler were ambushed while collecting tithes. Despite having firearms, soon Butler, Gibbons and twelve Constables were dead and another fourteen severely injured. Three of the attackers also died.

In 1848, the skirmish – the battle of Widow McCormick's farm – that was the hopeless New Ireland rising took place. The Police dealt with the insurgency without the aid of a single soldier and with very little bloodshed. Exhausted by the Famine, the country was quiet for almost two decades. In 1857 General Lord de Ros put the case that the force should be essentially disarmed. Policemen should carry truncheons and perhaps small pistols only. Inspector General Brownrigg argued that batons alone for policemen would be seen as an invitation to draw them into stick fights, a favourite sport for many especially after a few drinks on a Fair Day.

We should remember too that the British experiment of putting unarmed constables on the streets was a brave and unique one. Throughout Continental Europe it was normal for a policeman to be issued with at least a pistol even if his duties did not always require him to carry it, much less to use it. But in Britain, if policemen found themselves facing seriously armed lawbreakers, soldiers had to provide firepower as had happened during London's Siege of Sydney Street in 1911. The pistols and shotguns specially issued to the police were inadequate on that occasion.

In 1867 the much more serious Fenian uprising was also dealt with by the police without the aid of the military, with minimal loss of life – and at minimal expense. That could not have been suppressed without firearms. Perhaps the very efficiency of the Irish Constabulary in coping with political violence was to work against them in that the government remained reluctant to change their status from gendarmerie to purely civil police.

In summer, RIC members were often seconded to, and retired members temporarily employed by, the Manx police to help them cope with the seasonal influx of visitors from Great Britain. That clearly demonstrated that Irish policemen were perfectly capable of carrying out policing duties without dependence on firearms.

The animosity towards the Constabulary during the Land League's "Plan of Campaign" subsided quickly. A look at policemen's claims for compensation for injuries sustained on duty is revealing. Between 1880 and 1900, there were two cases in Galway West Riding; both were 'Ordinary' common assaults, not political. The figures for Galway East Riding were precisely the same. In County Tyrone, by contrast, there were eight cases relating to political disputes and a further four assaults.

By the start of the 20th Century, events such as those of 1867 belonged in a distant country. Post-Famine Ireland with its declining and increasingly prosperous rural population was a much more settled place. When people at large complain of the police being under-employed, it's an indication that society is fairly law-abiding. It was a perennial complaint of Dublin rate-payers, annually ventilated in City Hall, that Dublin had far more policemen per head of population than comparable English cities. In a squib "What to do with our police", published in *The New Ireland Review* in 1907, Arthur Synan showed how the government, disregarding economic principles, generated a supply of policemen without consideration of demand and offered suggestions as to how it could get better value for the £1½ million annual expenditure on the RIC. Among the ideas were policemen becoming schoolmasters – as they were already liberally educated in shorthand, the laws of evidence and other matters – and going into food production, e.g. "RIC Potted Oxtail" with the Constabulary badge guaranteeing quality and promoting an Irish product superior to imported competition. Policemen running modelling classes, village orchestras and cross-roads dancing would help to "relieve the deadly dullness of rural Ireland". Such whimsy shows no sense of concern about threats to the fabric of society.

After the Passing Out parade, when they marched in review to Moore's sprightly melody The *Young May Moon*, newly-minted Constables were dispatched to stations somewhere outside their home county. Altogether there were about 1,400 stations or barracks, some large and some quite tiny.

Barracks and Police Stations: A Place to Live

In the RIC context, use of the military term "barracks" is misleading. Constabulary Rules and Regulations of 1908 stated that: "The Constabulary should as far as practical be lodged in houses hired from private individuals". Requirements were issued to County Inspectors:

- Houses should be slate-roofed, free from damp, chimneys to draw well and a sufficient supply of good water on the premises or near at hand.
- The number of rooms should be proportionate to the size of the party, including space for a Sergeant's family.
- There must be a strong room with a fixed bench for a prisoner to sit or lie on.
- It is indispensable that there be a privy and a shed for fuel.
- If possible it should be detached and well enclosed with garden and walled yard. Windows should have wooden shutters. There should be eave shoots and downpipes, with a cistern or large water butt.

While the official guidelines sound reasonable, in practice Constables had to share the living space and privy with the Sergeant's family if he was married, and share their sleeping quarters with each other. If they brought in an involuntary guest in inclement weather their problems were compounded as regulations stipulated that prisoners had be dried out by the fire. There were some Board of Works purpose-built police stations especially in larger towns. Some major landowners built barracks and leased them to the government for a peppercorn rent thus ensuring their own security, but most police stations were far from being imposing barracks.

There were exceptions, one being Errismore Barracks beyond Clifden in furthest Connemara. This imposing turreted and walled structure was popularly believed, not least by its occupants, to have been intended for the North West Frontier but that the plans had been mixed up in London. The other side of the story was that somewhere on the edge of Britain's Indian Empire, Pathan tribesmen were gazing upon a structure designed for the soft grey days of *Íar Connacht*. The barracks at Caherciveen and Ballinamuck were two other examples of imposing edifices.

Most of the 1,400 or so posts around the country were small, rural stations manned by a Sergeant or Acting Sergeant and three or four Constables. In his notes for a history of the force, JWR Goulden evoked an image of the more typical police station:

> Actual buildings were nearly all rented houses neither designed for defence, spaciousness nor comfort. Flagged floors which have been almost standard have been boarded except in the kitchen which retained their old austerity. On each door in the house was a number and over each bed in the dormitory hung the name and

> register number of each member. … The day room was ascetic in its cleanliness and whitewashed regularly. The short Lee Enfield carbines in the arms rack shone as did all belts, sword bayonets.

Police personnel were not evenly distributed around the country. In 1913, with a policeman for every 783 inhabitants, loyal Co. Down must have been the most peaceful county in Ireland. At the other end of the scale there was a policeman for every 202 Galway people and one for every 214 who dwelt in Clare. Probably it was agrarian unrest rather than political disaffection or serious criminality which merited these numbers. The figures for Sligo and Donegal were 365 and 488 respectively. The rule which prohibited policemen serving in their native county was not absolute, at least where some native Irish speakers were concerned.

As early as 1907, in a pamphlet entitled *The RIC: A Case for Reform* the editor of the *Constabulary Gazette* dealt with "The Constabulary Rifle" amongst other issues. "If it is considered advisable to arm the RIC with rifles, they ought not to be obsolete weapons and the men ought to be able to use them. If, on the other hand, the rifles are not necessary they ought to be taken away and all that appertains to the pomp and circumstance of war taken with them… When the Constabulary Rifle disappears, promotion from the ranks will follow as a natural consequence. The Constable will cease to be a half soldier, and the gap that exists between him and his masters will disappear." He deals with another, related, issue, the officer's horse. The officer had to buy the horse himself. Thereafter he received an annual allowance of £50 for the animal's upkeep plus another £45 p/a for a groom. Unlike the allowances paid to the rank and file, these allowances were pensionable. Despite being mandatory, the horse was not used for duty apart from rare ceremonial occasions. For official duties, e.g. inspection tours, officers received a rather generous allowance of ninepence per mile for car-hire. (In 1907, this would still have meant horse-drawn vehicles rather than motor cars.) The Officer's horse was purely for show, to maintain the military façade just like the rifles.

The RIC and Sport

As part of Sir Andrew Reed's innovations, getting away from the military image, he encouraged young policemen to become involved in sports. Being a career police officer, he knew what he was talking about when he urged them to resist the temptations of alcohol and gambling. He stated "every policeman should be able to swim well". Novice policemen had to learn life-saving. In that connection it is worth noting the high number of awards to RIC members by the Royal Humane Society. In a ten-year period they were credited with saving over 100 lives from drowning, nearly half of those resulting in awards. Thousands of members also held first-aid certificates from the St John Ambulance Corps and there were also frequent newspaper reports of policemen risking their own lives by bringing runaway horses under control.

Reed wrote, using italics for added emphasis, "*It is my desire that every encouragement should be given to the men of the force to take part in athletics and manly sports in their leisure time*".

Sir Neville Chamberlain, who succeeded Reed as Inspector General in 1900, continued his sports crusade. The popular craze for cycling was eagerly embraced by Constabulary members, and manufacturers and agents quickly recognised a lucrative and influential market. One advertiser in the *Constabulary Gazette* asserted "Irish miles are shorter than English on Kelly's Special Cycles".

All sporting activities were popular with police. Patrick Shea recalled the Athlone barracks being constantly the scene of all sorts of athletic exercises and training by off-duty policemen. The year 1904 saw the all-Ireland RIC Championships with inter-County competitions including those in swimming, cycling, rifle shooting, weight throwing, foot racing and step-dancing.

Success in competitions on a United Kingdom scale, especially in tug-of war, made celebrities of some RIC and DMP men. Such achievements boosted internal morale and fostered *esprit de corps.*

Officers had far more opportunity to engage in sporting activities than did the rank and file. They had more leisure, more opportunity, and more money. In a quiet district a young DI could live the life of a country gentleman, riding to hounds and steeple-chasing if the fancy took him. Officers could have access to tennis, golf, football, and cricket. Game shooting was seasonal. Fishing was popular with all ranks.

The RIC's relationship with the Gaelic Athletic Association (GAA) was difficult. District Inspector Thomas St George McCarthy, rugby international and hurling enthusiast, was one of the acknowledged founders in 1884. Despite his being a friend of Michael Cusack, Father of the GAA, not everyone was happy about McCarthy's participation. He withdrew from any management role in the GAA but remained a life-long spectator at its matches. Retiring in 1912, the old athlete drew his pension for a further thirty years. In 1887, the Central Committee imposed a ban on policemen's participation which was ratified the following year by Convention. In 1893, with the tensions of the land agitation eased, the ban was lifted. However, the Irish

Republican Brotherhood's influence was growing behind the scenes in national organisations. In 1906, annual Convention re-imposed the ban on policemen participating in the GAA, and extended it to soldiers. Disapproval was also aimed at those who were friendly with the Police. The people of Doonbeg bought a wagon load of turf for Sgt Jones as a farewell present on his transfer. They also asked him to be a judge at the local GAA sports. This was excoriated by Arthur Griffith's *Sinn Féin* newspaper as a "display of captive slaves licking their chains".

There is also a report of a match played under GAA rules in the Phoenix Park during the Great War between teams from the RIC and the Royal Dublin Fusiliers, the "Blue Caps". The policemen won by 4 goals and 2 points to 2 goals and 2 points.

1912: The Road Northwards, and Routine for Ordinary Roberts

JWR Goulden's notes for his projected history of the RIC contain the opinion that "the year 1912 was the last nearly normal year in the history of the Royal Irish Constabulary". In New York, a new song "When Irish Eyes Are Smiling" was published. Its sentimental, romanticised view of Ireland would prove durable among Americans. Back home, many an Irish eye would cease to smile in the coming decade.

On the first day of August 1912, John Hennigan found himself in County Tyrone. With the population to police ratio at 577 to one, it was a generally peaceful county. Nonetheless it is easy to imagine that John may not have been best pleased by his posting. Although Omagh was relatively near to his native Sligo and had a rail link to it, a young Catholic policeman might have preferred to have been sent to a Nationalist area. Across North East Ireland the police were not in favour with the Protestant and Unionist majority of the people and were frequently referred to as "Papist Peelers". The province was in ferment. The Third Home Rule Bill had been introduced in the House of Commons in April and Unionists were becoming increasingly vocal in their opposition to it. The police rank and file, being Catholic and apparently Nationalist in outlook, were looked on with suspicion and hostility. On the 28th of September nearly a quarter of a million men signed the Solemn League and Covenant opposing Home Rule and almost as many women signed a supporting document. The Peelers watched nervously.

Still, the Ireland of 1912 was a generally settled and increasingly prosperous land with an economy more advanced than much of Europe, and still traditional in social matters. The most common female names, according to the Census of the previous year, were Mary at 16%, followed by Bridget at 8% and Margaret at almost 6%. John was the most common male name at over 10%, followed by Patrick at over 9% and James borne by 7%.

Galway town, not "city" officially, was the largest in Connacht with a 1911 borough population of 13,255, down from 13,426 in 1901. The total population of County Galway was 182,224, down 5% from 1901. It was a city much declined; while its business had a vast catchment area, the hinterland was impoverished. The coming of the railway had destroyed much local manufacturing and most of the boastful late-Mediaeval buildings had fallen into ruin. Galway needed development, and Home Rule, with its links to Britain and the Empire, offered the best promise of that.

Sligo, Connacht's second town, was doing quite well. Its port was busy, and local shipping such as the Sligo Steamship Company linked the town with Glasgow and Liverpool. The Borough's population was just over 11,000 but the hinterland included south Donegal, north Leitrim and Roscommon, and part of Mayo. The Midland Great Western Railway linked Sligo to Dublin and the Great Northern Railway ran to Enniskillen,

Omagh and Derry. The Sligo, Leitrim and Northern Counties Railway, the local narrow-gauge line colloquially known as the Slow, Late and Never Comes Regular, puffed its way up and down gradients from Ballysadare to Enniskillen and served the rural community. The problems of the Borough were social and political, with apparently never-ending confrontation between Nationalist and Unionist interests. Corruption at Municipal level seemed to be endemic.

Omagh, the County Town of Tyrone, was then a small market town sitting on the confluence of two rivers, about 40 miles from Derry, the nearest port. Its traders served the agricultural community, supplying their needs and marketing their produce. The population of Tyrone was less than half of its pre-Famine total and it was predominantly rural with Catholic and Protestant small farmers coexisting, but glowering at each other during the marching season. The 19th Century industrial development of the North-East had taken place to the east of the River Bann. Only three towns in the county – Omagh, Dungannon and Strabane – had more than 2,000 inhabitants and even in them the fields closed in upon the streets.

Opposition to Home Rule was not simply a question of ethnic identification, still less of religious prejudice. Beneath many an Orangeman's hard hat sat a hard business head. The North-East, centred on Belfast, was the locus of manufacturing industry in Ireland and a centre of importance in global terms. Belfast boasted the world's biggest factories in the production of ropes, biscuits, mineral waters and many other products. The economy of the North East area was integrated with that of Great Britain and its markets were not just imperial in extent but worldwide. There were fears that a Dublin Parliament, favouring the agricultural economy of the South, would impose protectionism and destroy this hard-won prosperity.

In his early years of service John Hennigan may have been

moved around a bit in the Omagh district but by the fourth year he was definitely located in Drumquin, a neat little Plantation village on the road between Castlederg and the county town. Founded in 1617, Drumquin is at the conjunction of several minor roads and became a staging post for travellers to and from Derry City. This led to the establishment of a hotel and some shops. In 1912 the population was about 200, most of whom were Catholic. Across the road from the police station, there stood and still stands O'Cahan's public house, in that same family since the 1820s. A Constable would not have been wise to pay social visits to licensed premises so close to work and home. As Felix Kearney's emblematic song put it: "Drumquin, you're not a city".

In 1912, Acting Sergeant R.B. Tilson was in charge there; the following year he received his third stripe. In 1914 he was replaced by A/Sgt T. Kemp. Two years later, Kemp too was promoted to full Sergeant. Omagh Station was in the care of Head Constable Lockhart who reported to District Inspector Bernard Conlin.

Wherever located, a novice Constable would not have been expected to show initiative but to do what his Sergeant told him and keep his opinions to himself. He might appear in Court but only to give supporting evidence in a prosecution brought by a Sergeant or Head Constable. On the 12th December at Castlederg Petty Sessions, Con. John Hennegan (sic.) gave corroborative evidence in a drunkenness case.

A policeman may have been trained much like a soldier but when he took up duty he became effectively a civil servant with an extraordinary range of administrative duties. The carbines sat in locked racks in the barracks while the police busied themselves with agricultural statistics, crime statistics, meteorological observations, reporting on persons of interest politically, observations on the harvest and fish catches, and gathering all the information which government needed. He also had to escort patients to asylums, prevent wakes for those who had died of infectious diseases, help the Coastguard to protect wrecks, and maintain order during elections. While he wasn't expected to personally supervise sheep dipping, he had to satisfy himself that farmers were doing it and that cases of bovine tuberculosis were being reported to the authorities. He had to be informed about Foot and Mouth regulations and prepared to enforce them. Every month each County Inspector sent a detailed report to the Inspector General. With Cork, Galway and Tipperary divided into East and West Ridings and Belfast reporting separately, that made 36 reports in total. The IG's office then made a national summary which, along with the County Reports, went to the Lord Lieutenant and the Secretary for Ireland (the Government Minister responsible for Ireland) and to the Under-Secretary (chief civil servant).

As there was little enough ordinary crime in Ireland, the Government could impose all those administrative tasks on the Constabulary. But many observers commented on a general lack of respect for the law. "The Irish seemed to lack the civic spirit of the English" was the view of an Irish Catholic senior officer. This attitude manifested itself in never giving evidence against neighbours especially relating to land or family disputes. Vendetta law occasionally erupted. And unfortunate tramps were often made scapegoats.

Many may see this as alienation from the law which was imposed by the colonial power, a quasi-patriotic reaction to the constraints imposed by British rule. But the attitude didn't change with the establishment of an independent Irish state. In his revealing story *In the Train* (1936) Frank O'Connor puts the defendant Helena, the prosecuting Gardai and the witnesses together on the train coming back west after her acquittal. All know each other well: they all know that Helena, desperate for her lover, was responsible for the death of her unloved husband, but the witnesses were never going to say so in the big courthouse up in Dublin.

In western counties especially, agrarian outrages continued to express land hunger. Since August 1907, Counties Clare, Galway, Longford and Roscommon had been "Proclaimed" as being "in a state of disturbance" and needing extra police. Hay-burning, animals driven off or maimed, walls knocked down, shotgun cartridges hidden in turf for the fire, graves dug, and shots through windows persisted. Prosecutions failed due to the absence of witnesses. Sometimes the Justices of the Peace who accompanied paid Resident Magistrates were not inclined to convict their own neighbours and friends. The JPs were no longer appointed just from the gentry but from people of substance, merchants and such, and might be quietly petitioned by a defendant to sit on The Bench on a particular day.

The comment of Richard Adams, a County Court judge in the previous century, seems apposite: "You have been acquitted by a Limerick jury and you may leave the dock with no other stain upon your character".

In 1912 the foot patrol was a key element in the policing system. It was an everyday duty for Constables, Sergeants and Head Constables. Day patrols were conducted between 6am and 6pm, generally by one man armed with a baton. One policeman recalled it as a daily stroll with a blackthorn stick, made official by the belt with baton and handcuffs, as he chatted with the local people. Night patrols consisted of two or more men, half of them carrying unloaded firearms. Particulars of what was observed during the patrol were noted afterwards in the barrack's Day Book. The reasons for the training in walking at a measured pace of 2½ mph, and the emphasis on good handwriting become clear. Still, in an isolated station during inclement weather it's not unlikely that many patrols had reality only on the page.

As far as weather was concerned, 1912 was a relatively benign year in which to learn the business of patrolling. While it was a very windy year, it was fairly dry with an unusually high number of days without rain. It also had a cooler summer and milder winter than usual.

There were also "Meet Patrols" where policemen from neighbouring stations were supposed to meet and exchange important information. They met all right but it was more to exchange gossip and have "a good grind" – moaning about anything and everything. Meet patrols between districts were a different matter, with the respective DIs present.

In a small station it really depended on the sergeant in charge. In Kesh, Co. Sligo, where Galwayman Jeremiah Mee found himself, the regime was relaxed. Each man had to do at least two "Rising Patrols" each month during the hours of midnight and 8 a.m. In Kesh the men detailed for these patrols went to their beds. But in the morning no entry was made in the Day Book until someone had cycled the route and confirmed that all was well. Then the entry would be made "Found all regular". The sergeant was aware of the value of details for credibility and the wording would vary. Noting the wind direction was useful. He would also make special notes such as "saw a light in the window of Ruane's licensed premises. Inspected the premises and found all regular". All members of the patrol signed the report.

It's hard to see what practical purpose could be served by most of the nocturnal patrolling. Outside of towns and villages, the roads and fields must have been pitchblack. As most roadways were unpaved, the crunching of Peelers' big boots on gravel would have reached the ears of any competent burglar or poacher and any lights they carried must have been easily visible. Only on a moonlit night could patrolling policemen enjoy any natural illumination. Even in built-up areas, public lighting was limited. Regulations stated that policemen should walk on the grassy part of the roadway. When the Constabulary was landed with the additional responsibility of protecting historic structures, members could easily persuade themselves that sheltering in important ruins at night was doing their duty.

Kesh's avuncular sergeant confided the unwritten rule of the Constabulary: "keep sober and shaved and keep the diary and patrol book up to date and you can't be sacked". In a peaceful district there was little policing to be done. On the western island of Inishbofin, local lore has it that the RIC party enjoyably stationed on their peaceful island were reduced to committing the occasional petty crime themselves in order to justify to the distant hierarchy their presence there. Of course the tyranny of the telephone did not then rule people's lives.

The more remote the station, the more scope for individual initiative. On the island of Arran off Donegal the government was amply represented by a Sergeant and four Constables. It is said that the Sergeant decamped on a Norwegian fishing boat for two weeks. When he returned from his holiday in Norway, the official books were all properly filled in and the secret well kept. That little island garrison maintained its security by an arrangement with the ferrymen from the mainland. If the ferry Captain found himself carrying any RIC Officer intent on inspection, a prearranged signal warned the island policemen and gave them a chance to look busy.

Younger policemen made use of the daily foot patrols to meet and make friends with people, especially the young women of the district who were happy to converse with clean, fit and presentable young men. Off-duty, the bicycle allowed policemen to attend dances, sports and race meetings in their limited free time. "Patterns" or Patron Days which entailed some religious service at the shrine of a local saint were also an occasion for general festivities. With four Justices of the Peace living locally at Kesh, it was an unwritten rule there that at least once a week a policeman would walk or cycle past each of their houses to show officialdom how diligently the Constabulary attended to their duties.

Policemen were required to have high standards of personal hygiene and many photographs attest to confident pride in their appearance. Describing his Sergeant at Ballintogher, Co. Sligo, Jeremiah Mee wrote: "Sgt Flynn was rather small for an RIC man being five feet ten – the average height being around six feet. He kept himself very neat and tidy and wore a very large moustache, curled up at each end like a drake's tail. The RIC were noted for the big, twisted moustaches which were a relic of the 10th Hussars of Napoleon's army. The waxed ends were called the Maringo Twist."

Life in a small country station could be placid and relaxed – but boring, especially in the long dark nights of winter. One policeman relieved the tedium by writing an ode to "A Barrack Pet", not unlike the mediaeval monk addressing his pet cat "Pangur Bán":

In a mountainy station both cosy and dry
No Peeler in Ireland so happy as I
And I envied no man from Moville to Portlaw
While my favourite friend lived – my pet jackdaw…

Proud Jack had eccentric pragmatical ways
For I once decked him out in a suit of red baize
Such pride and such antics you never yet saw
And I laughed till I cried at my pet jackdaw….

And Jack was so cute, such rare instincts he had
He knew when my spirits were light and when sad
In his whole composition he had only one flaw
A too sensitive heart had my pet Jackdaw….

Another anonymous Constable wrote in his personal notebook – alongside notes of sheep-dipping and the bulling of heifers – drafts of lyric poems centred on comely young women:

> Charming little Kitty went walking down the lane
> To visit Auntie Betty who lives in Ballymain.
> The morning rays were glancing on Kitty's yellow hair
> And roguish lights were dancing in Kitty's eyes so fair.
> I met her at the turning beyond the holly tree
> And she wished me a good morning as friendly as could be.
> But my heart made such a flutter that I could scarcely hear
> And I could only mutter Oh yes 'twill rain I fear
> Rain! Oh such an arrant fool! How could it rain today?
> The brightest day by any rule that ever shone in May.
> And Kitty smiled and left me standing in the lane.
> Had love of sense bereft me? Oh, how I wished 'twould rain.[i]

There were no patrols on Sunday mornings when policemen were required to attend Divine Service of their respective denominations. (Presumably enterprising miscreants were well aware of that.) With the exception of the Freemasons, policemen of all ranks were forbidden to join any secret society, and religious tracts were prohibited in the barracks. Only in notoriously sectarian Belfast was there a policy to balance the numbers of Catholic and Protestant members of the Force.

Apart from the onerous routine of inspection tours, Officers were largely desk-bound. Once they'd left the Depot, police duties were more clerical than soldierly. A County Inspector had to keep 22 books, A District Inspector had to cope with 18 books plus 51 returns to the CI, and Sergeants and Head Constables had to maintain 13 records.

The frequency of inspections probably varied in relation to a barrack's distance from County Headquarters. The inspection books for Killylea, Co. Armagh, have survived. The Station party consisted of Sgt Hall and four Constables, a common establishment. Mrs Hall and a five-year-old child also lived there. On the 10th January 1912, DI Mulhane found the "Barrack very clean and neat and well-kept". On the 20th CI Oulton inspected. In February there was only one inspection, by DI Mulhane on the 6th. Inspections continued at a rate of one or two a month by one or other officer. This frequency can hardly be a consequence of any dissatisfaction with the policemen: on 7th October the District Inspector wrote "Sgt Hall is much above most Sergeants. In the month he did 31 day patrols and 21 night patrols". Nonetheless, on 19th November the County Inspector was a little concerned about revolver practice: "Hall is a little hasty in firing words of command". Revolver practice seems to have been about handling the weapons; there's no indication that the things were actually fired.

Throughout 1913 the CI seemed to be particularly interested in the military aspects of the job. His subordinate, a lowly DI 3rd Class, could hardly do other than emulate the CI's enthusiasms. Every inspection seemed to involve revolver practice and grips. The theory of drill was tested and in May it was reported "Con. Smith made two bad mistakes in resisting cavalry". That conjures up an image of Irish policemen stoutly standing up to invading Hussars. Percy French could have written the song.

In what free time he had, the young Constable was expected to familiarise himself with a multitude of laws requiring enforcement. *The Irish Constable's Guide* in its 627 pages offered a digest of the legislation from Abduction to Wrecks by way of Affray, Bawdy Houses, Conspiracy, Embrocery, Larceny and Lotteries, Pedlars and Piracy, Riot, Sedition and Vagrancy.

There were occasional emergency duties. In smaller towns and villages without a Fire Brigade, it was policemen who manned the mobile pump, carried out rescues and administered first aid in the event of a fire.

Discipline was strict. If there were allegations of misbehaviour a hearing was held before senior officers. Punishments were varied: a fine of £3 to £5 could be imposed, a policeman could be transferred at his own expense and repeat offenders could be dismissed. Alcohol was the most common source of problems.

The welcoming atmosphere of a public house could be seductively dangerous to a policeman's career. Here, with a few coins jingling in his pocket, a Robert – as Irish policemen liked to call themselves – could escape to a wider world of social intercourse than the barrack could provide. On cold winter days, a poker might be kept constantly in the turf fire and its glowing tip plunged into a glass of the black beer to provide a warming draught of mulled porter. But the uniformed policeman had to be moderate in his consumption and guarded in his speech.

At Killylea in February 1914, the DI reported: "A day patrol on 7th inst. performed by Con. Leonard is very badly filled but the constable was drunk and is reported for same."

A Sergeant who was over-indulgent to his men could find himself in trouble too. In December 1912, DI Culhane reported "Con. Smith said Sgt Leonard of Keady induced him to report on paper that he had been relieved of Barrack Orderly duty at Armagh and Killylea…whereas no such thing ever occurred. On the occasion in question, I found Con. Smith absent from his post as BO and Sgt Leonard stated that he released him to go to the Post Office".

To John Hennigan or any other young "Robert" entering the service in the year 1912 his career must have looked a bit uncertain. Although he'd attained an apparently permanent and pensionable position, there was no clarity about future prospects for the service itself. In October, Chief Secretary Birrell, harried by Unionist leaders Carson and Craig and others, told the House of Commons that the provisions of the Home Rule Bill allowed for the establishment of local police forces throughout Ireland and that the RIC could gradually be reduced and eventually cease to exist. In any case the RIC would remain under Imperial control for six years after HR was brought in.

In The House some MPs became mightily exercised on the topic. Sir John Rees asserted that the new Irish Government would be in the grip of the Ancient Order of Hibernians and that the RIC would become the obedient servants of the AOH. Viscount Castlereagh – not a title likely to inspire affection in Nationalist Ireland – invoked the shibboleth of "no finer force" and demanded that it be taken out of Ireland altogether and made an integral part of the British Army.

The members of this fine force were also and primarily concerned about the fact that they – and the DMP – were underpaid as demonstrated by comparison tables showing pay rates for police forces in Britain. The problems of recruitment in Britain which had led to pay increases could be attributed to the easy availability of well-paid civilian employment but recruitment difficulties in Ireland were not so readily explained. The *Constabulary Gazette* identified two causes: poor pay and poor promotion prospects due to the RIC's archaic structure. When it referred to the cost of "the Decorative Branch" of the service it pointed out the absurdity of having 36 County Inspectors and their retinues for Counties so disparate in size and population. Even in 1912 the journal was already publishing informative and laudatory articles about police pay and conditions in Queensland and NSW, Canada and Shanghai.

In its editorial of 21st August, the *Constabulary Gazette* stated that "There is no doubt that the semi-military, and entirely unnecessary semi-military equipment of the RIC, is altogether to their detriment". Advertisements in the Police journal addressed the non-military, everyday concerns of Constable Patrick Plod.

The "Service" boot for country roads was offered at 14s 6d per pair. The Midland Rubber Company offered "The RIC Tyre" with extra heavy tread, beaded-edge cover, "practically puncture proof" with two-year guarantee for 15s. And, among the bicycles for sale, the "RIC Rover" was a bargain at just £9.10s. With a machine like that under your bottom, you could indeed be a flyer on the tar road. Other makes were available from just £6.

In the unlikely event that a young Constable had a few shillings to spare, he might indulge in some purchases from A.W. Millar of Ellis's Quay, Dublin. Shirts, plain and fancy, cost between four shillings and seven shillings, tailor-made flannel drawers cost four shillings and sixpence while tailor-made swans-down drawers could be had for just two shillings and ninepence.

A weekly feature of the *Gazette* was the advertisments offering postal tuition to members of the Force who wished to study for advancement. Sample questions concentrated on Arithmetic, Composition (essay writing), Geography, and Orthography and Handwriting. Questions of law were dealt with in frequent articles. Promotion to Sergeant was either by seniority – leading to the coronation of many a "Bog Kaiser" – or through the "P List" by competitive examination and limited to 30 places per annum.

In Omagh and throughout the county *The Tyrone Constitution* was widely read. It reported on 1st February that the Presbyterian Convention had expressed opposition to Home Rule. Readers' letters expressed concern about the recent Papal decree of *Ne Temere* which ordered that in cases of "mixed marriages" all the children were to be brought up as Catholics. Up to then the common practice had been that sons followed their father's religion and daughters that of the mother. Interestingly, the Decree had never been implemented in Germany, the Catholic bishops there advising the Pope that it would bring the

Church into conflict with the civil power. Another Papal edict *Motu Proprio,* forbidding priests from being tried in civil courts, also caused disquiet even though it never applied to Ireland. To a Protestant Unionist such interventions offered evidence that Home Rule would indeed be Rome Rule. In January 1911 a large meeting of Protestants in Dublin had protested against the promulgation of the *Ne Temere* Decree and challenged the HR politicians to ask the Pope that it be withdrawn. Archbishop Peacocke said that "the dividing wall between Protestants and their Catholic fellow-countrymen was high enough already and they should not want to make it higher".

The notorious "McCann case" had incensed much Protestant opinion. In November 1910, Rev. William Corkery of Belfast had published a letter from one of his parishioners, Mrs Agnes McCann. She had married Catholic Alexander McCann in a Presbyterian ceremony some years before *Ne Temere* came into effect. The couple had agreed to continue attending their respective churches. The arrangement continued happily until the family moved to Belfast. Then, Mr McCann's priest advised him that the marriage was invalid due to *Ne Temere* and that they would have to marry in a Catholic ceremony. She refused and he subsequently deserted her, taking their children. These revelations led to large protest meetings in Belfast, Dublin, Edinburgh and London at which all Protestant denominations were represented. The anger so generated fanned the anti-Home Rule flame.

The political pot was being blatantly stirred by opportunist British politicians, most notably Bonar Law the Leader of the opposition Conservative Party. In a speech delivered in July 1912, he said there was "no length of resistance to which Ulster can go in which I shall not be prepared to support them". A contemporary Unionist slogan expressed a profound rejection of the democratic will: "There are stronger things than parliamentary majorities".

While the prospect of allowing a part of Ireland to opt out of the Home Rule arrangement was being considered behind the scenes, the North-East was not homogenously Protestant and Unionist. The 1911 Census reveals that the land area of Tyrone was almost evenly divided between Catholic and Protestant with Omagh being in a predominantly Catholic district. Prime Minister Asquith referred in a private letter to "that most damnable creation of the perverted ingenuity of man – County Tyrone". But then, had he ever visited the place or met its people?

Of course, opposition to Home Rule was not confined to the North-East. The Unionist *Sligo Independent* published a number of short political verses in 1912. One such from "A.D." was "The Union for ever!":

Ulster now shall decide
And will not be denied,
Whether Ireland and England in friendship abide.
Or let Devlin and Redmond the countries divide.
No, the turn of the tide
Will soon see them defied,
And the will of the electors no more set aside.
Better men who have tried
To pass Home Rule have died,
But the Union we'll keep to whatever betide.

The *Tyrone Constitution* was a typical contemporary provincial newspaper in its mix of local and national news with snippets from further afield. Of course this was a time when most rural people had neither opportunity nor money to take a daily paper, nor the time to read it. The local weekly paper – a conduit to the wider world – brought news and promoted discussion.

In early 1913 it reported a bizarre attack on a man in Dublin by a cheetah. Advertisements offered a new bicycle for sale at

£3.10s and a used one for only 10 shillings. For many a young policeman, a bicycle was his first purchase and gave him the chance to make the most of his limited leisure time. On the 14th March, a court case at Sixmilecross introduced an ingenious "Bona Fide" defence which must have entertained many a pub and police station. The definition of a bona fide traveller was "a person who has travelled 3 miles measured by the nearest public thoroughfare, whether such thoroughfare be by water or by land, from the place where he lodged the previous night to the place where he demanded to be supplied with liquor."

The short cut from the defendant's residence to the licensed premises was 2 miles, 3 furlongs making the drinker "found on" after hours liable to penalty. However the official route by road was 2 miles, 7 furlongs, 32 perches, plus another 12 perches to the defendant's house making him entitled to a late-night drink. The case was referred to a higher court. The same legal arguments would be resurrected in courts of the Free State and Republic, with policemen and defendants "chaining" routes, and the principle of Bona Fide traveller would be extinguished only in the 1960s. As the concept of bona fide traveller contained the requirement that the purpose of the journey should be something other than just to get a drink, what profitable fun the lawyers must have had!

In the early years of the 20th Century, much of rural life still moved to ancient rhythms and the police, along with priest and parson, were part of a social system which guarded against excess. Young Cecil King had been born into a police family; his father was one of five Roscommon brothers who entered the RIC. Growing up around police stations, Cecil saw the policemen as well-disciplined men upholding Christian and family values, notable for the proportion of their sons who entered the priesthood. Cecil remembered them as busy monitoring family disputes, keeping the peace on fair and market days, compiling tillage statistics and dealing with poachers on land and in the rivers.

After spending two years in Sligo as Acting Sergeant in charge of the No.2 Barrack in Wine Street, James King received his third stripe in charge of Grange Station. It was his seventh station in 14 years. Duties of the Sergeant and four Constables seemed largely to be dealing with wandering cattle, drunks, and prosecuting farmers for cruelly leaving their donkeys unshod.

Fair Days were held monthly. The buying and selling would conclude by noon and the village's three pubs soon filled. Family grudges were unwrapped and settled by ashplant fights. Tests of prowess occurred. Police tactics were to let the combatants go a distance before collaring them as they tired. They were shoved into the detention cell, "The Black Hole", and released when sober. As the Black Hole had no sanitation other than a drain in the corner, fumigation followed the release of the prisoners. These fairday scenes and scents of man and beast would have been familiar to John Hennigan growing up nearby.

On the first day of each month, Sgt King walked to Sligo to collect the pay for the barrack. It was a round trip of 8 to 10 hours walk. It doesn't seem to have occurred to officialdom that giving the man a bicycle would have resulted in a better use of his time.

From the days of the Revenue Police, the detection of illicit distillation was a responsibility of the Constabulary. Being cheaper than "Parliament whiskey", the local untaxed product was always popular. With the addition of a drop of tea to colour it, the mountain dew might be sold over the pub counter especially on a busy day. Grange was a key station in the ongoing struggle. Once a month Police were sent across by boat to Innismurray. This small island, some five miles offshore, was famous for its ancient monastic ruins and in more recent times was a renowned centre of *poitín* distillation. The islanders would leave a few jars of the spirit where they could easily be found. Lest the precious still be accidentally discovered it was often put in a boat and spent the day at sea. Duty done, the Police party brought the jars back to Grange where they were officially sealed. On his monthly inspection the DI presided over the destruction of the contents by pouring the spirit down the water vennel in the backyard. One jar was set aside for the DI "for his own use". But sometimes kegs had been gimleted and the poitin replaced by water. One day the DI was given the wrong keg. Sgt King was called before DI Russell. Despite his protestations of innocence, the Sergeant lost his stripes and the family had to vacate the barrack accommodation and move to a rented house at Moneygold. The culprits were never discovered. But six months later Sgt King was transferred to Collooney and his stripes were restored.

Constable Jeremiah Mee in his memoirs gives a delightful account of poitín-searching on Innismurray. He depicts it as a choreographed charade where policemen played their assigned roles, probing with official steel rods into potential hiding places for stills and their produce. The islanders gave them a warm welcome and the policemen brought letters and parcels to and from the island. Some parcels undoubtedly contained yeast and treacle for the business. "Having failed to destroy the sole industry of these friendly people we returned to the home of Mrs Harte who always provided tea for the police and revenue officers." The government paid for the meal but it wasn't invoiced for the drop of poitín which followed the food. Mee's manuscript is more explicit in regard to collusion between the poitin-makers and the police than the published version: "These people had imagination and brains and it would have been a thousand pities to hurt or harm them in their splendid effort to snatch a living from the barren rocks of their wind-swept island".

"Poteen-hunting at Innismurray was reduced to a very fine

art by the RIC and with the co-operation of the good Island people." Mee goes on to tell how a still no longer fit for purpose could be of benefit to the policemen. They would occasionally receive an "anonymous" letter telling them precisely where a still might be found. The next raiding party dispatched to the island would start their search as far away as possible from the spot indicated so as to make a find more credible. When the still was found, the policemen celebrated their success with great enthusiasm as such a capture meant a welcome bonus to their salaries. A still being found on a farmer's land meant prosecution for the farmer, so the discovery would invariably be made on the seashore with nobody identified as responsible.

On his next visit to the barrack, the District Inspector would inspect the captured equipment before completing the paperwork. While he was being entertained in the station, two policemen were detailed to destroy the still in accordance with regulations. This was supposed to be witnessed by the officer but he had confidence in his men who had just given him a success for his records. The still was carried into the back garden and hidden in a safe place. Banging the zinc roof of the lavatory with a heavy club produced noises "loud enough to convince the DI that the destruction was in progress[2]."

As a boy looking across the water at Inismurray, John Hennigan must have heard the stories, such as Mr Power from the great Dublin distillery visiting the island and being so impressed by the local product that he had commissioned a small pot still to be constructed and discreetly delivered to the islanders. John probably heard too about the policemen who'd been stationed over there but who'd been drawn into the seductive ways of the community and had to be withdrawn. And tradition dies hard:

2 The next page of Mee's m/s is missing but it seems logical to suppose that the understanding between policemen and poitin-makers could extend to the still being discreetly repaired and finding its way back to the island. Everybody would benefit.

there was a complete still cached underground on Inismurray in the 1950s; I saw the photographs.

There was continuity in police practice also. In later years a Garda who'd been stationed at Grange told me about the disposal of poitin after it had been shown in evidence in the District Court. No longer poured into the Constabulary's outside drain under the eyes of a superior officer, the newer technology allowed the spirit to be poured down the inside sink where, following the moral precept 'Waste Not, Want Not', an enterprising policeman could uncouple the S-bend and divert the outflow into a sufficiently large, clean receptacle.

1913: The Political Temperature Rises

Judging from the editorial comment in the *Constabulary Gazette,* the main concerns of policemen at the start of the year remained the vexed issues of pay and promotion, and uncertainty about the survival of the Force after Home Rule was implemented. To restructure the RIC as a normal civil force on the British model would clearly entail disarmament and democratisation of opportunity. On 4th January the journal stated: "Our cry to social and political reformers to take in hand the reconstruction of the RIC on a modern basis has fallen on deaf ears". It stated bluntly that "useless rifles, useless swords, useless trappings, useless horses and a huge surplus of officers continue to burden the public purse and make impossible the cry of the worker for a living wage". It also lamented that improved pay and conditions had been conceded "for every Police Force in the UK except the RIC". Even their brothers in the DMP had got an extra £104 per annum.

Again, on the 18th January, the *Gazette* referred to "the old traditions as to the character of the RIC organisation. Is it military or is it civil? ...How much it would mean to the RIC to secure recognition as civil servants, students of the clauses of the Home Rule Bill can well appreciate."

A year later the same idealistic attitude was set out explicitly:

> As a matter of fact, the Constable might be made immensely valuable to the nation. Suppose that the following changes were made, for example
>
> 1. Swords and rifles removed.
> 2. Promotion from the ranks introduced and applied to all except the highest officers.
> 3. Pay, promotion and pension so adjusted as to make the Force attractive to Irishmen.
> 4. Duties extended to include a variety of work done at present by the Inland Revenue, and Old Age Pensions duty, Insurance Commission inspection work and, in fact, everything of a civil nature that they are fitted to do for the State.
>
> It would then happen that the Irish people would love the Constabulary as a calling; the standard of recruiting would rise; first-class young fellows would join and there would be no going into the highways and the byways to find recruits by persuasion. Moreover it would be an inexpensive department of immense value and importance.

However, another obstacle stood in the way of evolution towards a civic police model but was not mentioned in these debates. The RIC had responsibility for gathering intelligence on political matters which was then passed up the line and kept the Government informed. The Government saw political activity as not only the conspiracies of armed subversives but National associations such as the GAA and the Gaelic League. They also had to keep an eye on organisations such as the Ancient Order of Hibernians and Foresters as well as the burgeoning Trades Unions. While the DMP had its G Men, the RIC had no Special Branch. An individual policeman might be given the part-time task of collating political information in a district and reporting to his DI, but there was no specialised agency dealing with revolutionaries. Given the image of the Peeler with his notebook at political gatherings it was hardly surprising that the Force would be regarded with dislike and suspicion by many moderate as well as radical Nationalists. If it came to a confrontation between people and government, the Police would always stand by The State.

Songs and jokes can reveal social attitudes. In some societies the police are uncompromisingly repressive and the jokes which denigrate them will be cautiously whispered. Possibly the best jokes are indeed to be found in repressive societies but it's not easy for outsiders to access them.

In a society where the police are seen as generally benign, there can exist a sort of amiable disdain for them – until they're needed. A classic image of the policeman emerges from the old Dublin chestnut about the DMP man on night patrol who found a dead horse in Westmoreland Street. He hauls out his notebook and pencil to record the incident but realises that he's uncertain of the spelling and it's too dark to read the street nameplate . Knowing that he'll catch hell from his Sergeant for yet another spelling error, he drags the horse around the corner into Fleet Street.

A popular song for decades was "Moriarity".

When first I came to Dublin town
'Twas in Eighteen Eighty Three,
I went direct with me head erect
For to join the DMP.
Me majestic feet woke Kevin Street

As I walked up proud and free;
For well I knew, they could not do
Without me, Mor-i-ar-i-ty.

Chorus:

I'm a well-known Bobby of the stalwart squad,
I belong to the DMP
And the ladies cry, as I pass by,
'Are you there, Mor-i-ar-i-ty?
With no delay I drew me pay
And began for to study too
A polisman I soon became
Prepared for me job to do
Thieves far and near I filled with fear
Gaol birds avoided me
Malefactors trembled when they heard
'Here's Mor-i-ar-i-ty'

Chorus

A rather more acerbic attitude towards the RIC was shown in the 19th Century song "The Peeler and the Goat" in which a Tipperary policeman mistakes a goat for a vagrant. The belief that he is stupid or drunk, or both is explicit in the satire:

A Bansha peeler went one night
On duty and patrollin' O,
And met a goat upon the road
And took her for a stroller O
With bay'net fixed he sallied forth
And caught her by the wizzen O,
And then he swore a mighty oath

'I'll send you off to prison, O'.
'Oh, mercy, Sir!' The goat replied,
'Pray let me tell my story O!
I am no rogue, no Ribbonman,
No Croppy, Whig, or Tory O;
I'm guilty not of any crime
Of petty or high treason O,
I'm sadly wanted at this time,
For this is the milkin' season, O'

And, after several verses:

'The consequence be what it will,
A peeler's power I'll let you know,
I'll handcuff you, at all events,
And march you off to Bridewell O.
And sure you rogue, you can't deny
Before the judge or jury O,
Intimidation with your horns,
An' threatening me with fury, O'.

'I make no doubt but you are drunk,
With whiskey, rum or brandy O,
Or you wouldn't have such gallant spunk
To be so bould and manly O,
You readily would let me pass
If I had money handy O,
To treat you to a poteen glass –
Oh! 'tis then I'd be the dandy O.'

The Authorities were not amused. Holding the song to be disrespectful towards the Police and the State, it became an offence to sing it or whistle the tune.

In the new year the weather became more aggressive. On the 7th February there were widespread gales with winds of up to 80 mph / 130 kph. One result was the highest tide in the Shannon estuary for fifty years and resultant flooding in Limerick.

The politically quiet interlude was not to last either. In January 1913 the HR Bill was passed by the House of Commons and rejected by The Lords. On 31st January the Ulster Volunteer Force was founded. In April 1913, labour unrest occurred at centres outside Dublin. Riotous scenes occurred at Sligo Docks and one man was killed. Thirty Ship Federation men were brought in from Liverpool as strike-breakers. Omagh, being a county town serving a rural community was not directly affected by industrial disputes. Unrest there remained centred on Home Rule.

On the 2nd May the *Tyrone Constitution* newspaper published a piece by "Peggy", perhaps more for its sentiments than any poetic merit:

> The shamrock with its three little leaves close together
> From the one little stalk extend
> Says plainly that England and Scotland forever
> Should always old Ireland befriend
> And let no Home Rule Bill them sever
> An Irish Parliament in Dublin, never!!!
> As long as an Orangeman has his breath
> Let him fight for this, till the very death
> For it would be a crying shame to see
> Great Britain severed for ever from thee!

In May, also, the delightfully eccentric Willie Gibson became Lord Ashbourne. Clad in Neo-Celtic garb including a green kilt, he would be continually ejected from the House of Lords for his refusal to speak there any language other than Irish or French.

He was later associated with the Anglo-Irish committee from which sprang the plot to import rifles for the Irish Volunteers. His sister Violet would later attempt to assassinate Mussolini. She really could shoot: her first shot hit the Duce's proud nose, the second failing only because the pistol jammed.[ii]

On the 30th May the *Morning Post* protested about "Home Rule RIC". It pointed out that the original proportion of Protestants had fallen from 34% to 18% and was expected to fall to 15%. It asked if the police were members of the Ancient Order of Hibernians, a Nationalist equivalent to the Orange Order.

In June there were seizures of arms in Dublin and London. In July the HR Bill was again passed by The Commons and rejected by The Lords. In August, there were riots in Derry. In the same month the Transport Union dispute began in Dublin and escalated into a widespread lockout. There was conflict between Union members and police. In the worst incident, Dublin Metropolitan Police baton-charged a crowd assembled to hear Jim Larkin speak: two people died of their injuries. Some participants were "country police" brought in to bolster the DMP. A British witness, Handel Booth MP, wrote "The noble street was in the hands of the most brutal constabulary ever let loose on a peaceful assembly". The police showed no sympathy with the "Socialists" unlike in 1907 when Belfast policemen themselves went on strike. Still, an unpleasant editorial reference in the *Gazette* to "Dublin scum" may reveal more of the Countryman's contempt for "Jackeens" than ideological bias. Neither of the police forces showed restraint under provocation and injuries inflicted by them were long and bitterly remembered.

In this context it may be useful to look at the suggestion in Liam McNiff's book that DMP men did not generally have a close relationship with the less well-off Dublin citizenry. Over the entire history of the DMP from 1836 to 1925, fewer than 14% came from County Dublin. Drawn largely from the same small farmer class as the RIC, albeit mostly from midland counties, they had little instinctive understanding of those who lived in the overcrowded tenements of what were often called "the worst slums in Europe". As so much of their duty lay in protecting the property of more prosperous classes, the potential for conflict with the poor was always present. The big, burly constables with country accents were outsiders. Beyond Dublin, at least in 'normal' times without agrarian or political conflict, RIC men moved and worked among people with whom they innately identified.

In September, Sir Edward Carson announced the intention to set up a provisional Ulster government in the event of HR becoming law. In November, the Irish Citizen Army, a force to protect workers, was set up. In Dublin a week later the Irish Volunteers were established. The gun was being reintroduced to Irish politics.

Sectarian forces were at work. There was indignation among the Constabulary at a suggestion in the *Morning Post* that Protestant policemen would have problems implementing government policy. "Are Protestant members resigning at the prospect of Home Rule? Are Protestant recruits not coming forward?" The *Gazette* ridiculed the idea that Catholic and Protestant colleagues might see their duty differently. The RIC took pride in its non-sectarian character.

The labour troubles and street battles of the summer still resonated. A Dublin crowd celebrated Christmas Day of 1913 by throwing Sgt Kiernan and another DMP man into the Liffey. They were saved from drowning by two passing RIC men. In the far north-west, DI Moore left Sligo on transfer to Raphoe, Co. Donegal.

Even as the ship of state was entering choppy waters, the concerns of the ordinary Robert were more mundane. On 13th February 1914, at Castlederg Petty Sessions the fines for drunkenness were set out. First offence merited 1 Shilling fine, second offence 10/=, third offence 20/=, fourth offence 40/= (£2). Drunk & disorderly/ abusive behaviour: first offence 10/=. Singing and making a noise cost 5/= for first offence, 10/= for a second, 21/= for third offence which seems excessively harsh even if the singer were out of tune.

Meanwhile the Ulster Volunteers were building up their strength. On 11th February the 2nd (Mid-Tyrone) Battalion paraded: about 1,000 men plus cyclists and some cavalry. On the 18th, the 1st Battalion paraded in Newtownstewart. All the marching and manouvering was made easier by 1914 being a drier year than usual in the northern half of Ireland; foul weather tends to cool political ardour.

In March 1914 the Inspector General's report makes serious reading. He wrote that on the 19th it was rumoured in Belfast that the government was sending troops to disarm the UVF and seize its leaders. A mobilisation was called in Belfast, "picture palaces were used for circulating the order". "Unionists of every sort are still firmly convinced that military operations against their movement were really ordered and only averted by the actions of the officers at the Curragh." A sinister omen for the RIC was the report that a proportion of the UVF had been detailed for police work; truncheons had been ordered. Rifles were still being imported.

Constable John and his colleagues had real cause for apprehension. The Tyrone County Inspector reported that it was freely being stated that one of the first acts of the Ulster Provisional Government would be the capture of the police and their arms, and that a captured policeman was to be shot for every Unionist who died in an attack on a barrack.

On 24th April the situation intensified. The steamer "Mountjoy" (a.k.a. "Clyde Valley") arrived at Larne and transhipped about 100,000 rifles with ample ammunition. Lord

Dunleith told the District Inspector that any police interference would be resisted by force. Some senior Constabulary Officers colluded with the organisers. The arms were distributed across the province by hundreds of motor cars. According to the IG, "Party feeling across the province could scarcely be more bitter...it is stated that Nationalists at Belfast are apprehensive and anxious to have military in the city".

In truth, the powers of the Police regarding arms importation seem weak and unclear. The repeal in 1903 of the Arms (Peace Preservation) Act which controlled the importation and possession of weapons was done against the advice of the RIC, the DMP and the Resident Magistrates. Sir John Ross described repeal of the Act as bringing "a lighted candle into a powder magazine".

The IG's report for May noted that Irish Party approval for the Irish Volunteers had boosted their membership from 25,000 to 69,000. Gen. Chamberlain astutely observed: "In Ireland the training and drilling to the use of arms of a great part of the male population is a new departure which is bound in the not distant future to profoundly alter all the existing conditions of life". And again, "Each county will soon have a trained army far outnumbering the police"

Far from the realm of politics, the everyday cycle of life and death continued to turn. During May the *Gazette* informed its readers about one of their former colleagues:

> The County Mayo Force will be sorry to learn of the death of Bartley Hennigan, ex-Sergeant RIC, which occurred at the close of a mission given in Boyle RC Church on Sunday 3rd inst. The poor man was seen to faint immediately after the ceremonies were over and he expired outside in about five minutes after, surrounded by clergymen who each in turn pronounced the words

> of absolution over his head. His remains were borne on the shoulders of the local Constabulary to the local churchyard and the funeral was one of the largest seen in Boyle for many years. The references to his death in the *Roscommon Herald* and *Western Nationalist* bear ample proof of the respect the deceased was held in by the people of Boyle. He served for 17 years in Mayo and retired in Newport about four years ago. To his sorrowing wife we offer our sincere sympathy.

The death certificate for Bartholomew Hennigan stated that he was 56 years old and that the cause of death was Cardiac Disease from which he had suffered for four years. It's clear that his early retirement had been due to ill health. Probably Constable John was given leave to attend his Uncle Bartley's funeral. Then, as now, police officers turned out to honour a deceased colleague. John could have taken the Sligo train from Bundoran and then the Dublin train to Boyle.

If Bartley was a sincere Catholic, and it's reasonable to suppose that he was, the circumstances of his death must have offered great consolation to his relatives. Not only was his wife Mary Agnes present when he died but he was surrounded by priests. In the years ahead many a policeman would be without benefit of clergy as his lifeblood leached into the dirt of an Irish road.

As well as offering comfort to the afflicted, religion could also be a divisive and malevolent influence. In June the IG reported from Tyrone "distrust and hatred between Catholic and Protestant never half so deep within the memory of the County Inspector (himself an Ulsterman)." That same CI noted that the example of the UVF had given immense stimulus to the physical force party on the Nationalist side and feared that the Irish Volunteers, formed to uphold the law at least concerning Home Rule, would be subverted by the separatists. Business continued to suffer, with a great reluctance to invest in a climate of such uncertainty.

In a June editorial the *Gazette* astutely commented: "The raison d'etre of the Cadet system in the RIC is the rifle, a fact which has been continually referred to in this journal. An armed force is assumed to require officers recruited from a superior class to that from which the rank and file come". It went on to state that "the use of the Constabulary rifle has become nominal" and referred to the rise of Volunteer movements with up to date rifles:

> One sees no sign or token in any quarter that Volunteering is to be discontinued, but on the contrary, there is every indication that the movement is only in its infancy. This, in our opinion, adds a powerful argument to the claim for abolishing the rifle and making the Force a purely civil body, like that of London and other forces in Great Britain. It is inconceivable to us that in its present condition the Constabulary could be used against any armed force, especially in numbers and equipment.
>
> We suggest that the moment is appropriate for the final abandonment of the Constabulary rifle and all that its possession entails as a hindrance to promotion.

Sadly, the result of an official Pay Commission was again a disappointment. Many grievances were not addressed and the question of reform was avoided altogether. However, in a minority report the Treasury Remembrancer Mr Headlam offered three observations and recommendations:

The whole organisation was antiquated, not having changed since its inception.

The Cadet system should be abolished, with a superior class of Head Constable taking over the duties of officers. Promotion should be from the ranks.

The rifle should be abolished.

The Home Rule Bill continued its painfully slow progress towards becoming law. Regarding the Irish police nothing, as usual, continued to be done. One Arthur Trew said in a letter "the police are the only part of this rotten government they will keep as you could not get message boys in the "island" for the same pay as these peelers are getting".

While reinforcements from southern counties had been drafted northwards during May in anticipation of trouble with the 3rd reading of the Home Rule Bill, in less divided areas of the country policemen were able to bring their children to celebrations marking its passage and participate in the singing of "A Nation Once Again".

During July Tyrone remained "peaceable". Senior policemen noted that the discipline imposed by the respective volunteer organisations had contributed to "temperance and preservation of the peace generally". The Twelfth of July celebrations had passed without drinking, rowdy conduct or 'party expressions' from either UVF or IV members.

There were, inevitably, some disturbances. On foot of an assault case in Newtownstewart near Omagh, a mob abused the "Fenian police".

But events continued to move forward. On 26th July 1,500 obsolescent German rifles, a small but significant consignment, was unloaded by the Irish Volunteers at Howth with the RIC powerless to intervene.

On the way into Dublin 20 rifles were seized by DMP and military (but were later returned). Later that evening, soldiers of the King's Own Scottish Borderers fired on a hostile but unarmed crowd, killing four civilians. This was a bitter contrast to the impunity with which the UVF had imported arms and one can only guess at the feelings which beset John Hennigan and others like him. The fact that Assistant Commissioner William Vesey

Harrel of the DMP had been forced to resign over the incident led to dark suspicions that the Police had been made scapegoats. Harrell, a barrister and magistrate, had held the rank for fourteen years, in succession to the famous detective John Mallon, his father's protégé. But that day William Harrel had indeed blundered and allowed his zeal to exceed his authority. Returning to barracks, the soldiers were still nominally under his authority. Ordinary DMP Constables had been unjustly disciplined.

Experienced members of the Police watched events with measured judgement. Thomas Fennell saw Sir Edward (later 'Lord') Carson and Galloper Smith (later Lord Birkenhead) "preaching sedition and inciting mutiny over Home Rule. Instead of trials they were promoted, one to the Lords, one to the Lord Chancellorship of England." Mutinous Army officers were not censured.

John McKenna was a capable and ambitious policeman. In 1906 he'd made it to the P List (listed 19th out of 100) and was appointed Sergeant. The following year he earned his certification as a Weights and Measures Inspector and was posted to the seaside village of Carnlough, Co.Antrim. There he came under pressure from his DI to fabricate evidence of UVF activity; the idea was by exaggerating opposition to Home Rule it would put pressure on Asquith to bow to the demands of the anti-HR party.

In 1914 he was abruptly transferred to Larne. There, both his District and County Inspectors attended the landing of UVF rifles and the DI even lent his car for their transportation. This would not be McKenna's only experience of political and sectarian pollution within the RIC but the seeds of future conflict were being sown. "Carson rekindled the Fenian flame".

Many of the difficulties faced by the British state in Ireland originated with institutional and cultural deficiencies. From its inception with the Act of Union in 1800 the United Kingdom of Britain and Ireland was patently incomplete. It was a constitutional arrangement brought into being by a perceived military necessity and pushed through the unreformed Irish Parliament by bribery and chicanery. Rather than direct rule from Westminster, a subordinate government was put in place, centred in Dublin Castle and with a Lord Lieutenant as representative of the Crown. The Chief Secretary was a Minister at Westminster and there was never clarity as to which office was subordinate. The Castle became a byword for jobbery and intrigue as the old Protestant Ascendancy sought to cling to its privilege and power. London's policies were never consistent, veering between regarding Ireland as just like England and, on the other hand, ruling the two islands quite differently. Sometimes, as in Balfour's policy of killing Home Rule with kindness, London combined largesse with coercion. Remaining unchanged until 1921, the Government of Ireland with its many Departments and Boards was inefficient and unaccountable to the people of Ireland. The Under-Secretary, or chief civil servant, was normally the most powerful man in the system, aided by the fact that he lived in Ireland and usually had longer tenure than his political master.

In a letter to the historian G.H. Orpen[iii] in September 1931, former RIC Head Constable Patrick Lyons[iv] wrote about relations between Britain and Ireland during the Union: "It was assumed that Ireland ought to assimilate itself to England – that oil ought to mix with water. Legally we were brothers to the English – but really only step-brothers. They hated and despised the common Irish and they were grieved when the Irish returned – at least – the hatred"

It seems to have been axiomatic among the British ruling class that the Irish were incapable of ruling themselves even in the limited form of Home Rule. Lord Salisbury, recurrent Conservative Prime Minister in the 1880s and '90s, set out his views when responding to the proposition that "We are to have confidence in the Irish people:"

> Confidence depends on the people in whom you are to confide. You would not confide free institutions to the Hottentots, for instance. Nor, going up the scale, would you confide in the Oriental nations whom you are governing in India, although finer specimens of human character you will hardly find than some who belong to those nations, but who are simply not suited to that particular kind of confidence of which I am speaking… This which is called self-government by the majority, works admirably well when it is confided to the people who are of Teutonic race, but it does not work so well when people of other races are called upon to join in it.

Unsurprisingly, he also opposed votes for the working class.

In the years 1912 to 1914 the prospect of imminent civil war in Ireland and of a politically divided British Army officer corps being preoccupied with coping with domestic violence must have had some influence on the strategic thinking of the German General Staff. While they probably knew little and cared less about Ireland, it may have been a case of England's difficulty being Germany's opportunity. (With Carson having dined at least once with the Kaiser, the Germans were aware of the British problem in implementing HR.) Britain's Regular Army was tiny by Continental standards but was acknowledged as highly professional; however, a large proportion of the regular Tommies were actually Irish. The troops themselves may have been apolitical, with unswerving loyalty to their respective Regiments, but who knew what might happen in a civil war situation once their officers began playing politics.

In a letter to the *Gazette,* one policeman offered a mordant opinion: "Between wars, rumours of war, next year the boys of the finest Force (moryah) and the worst paid will have a hot time".

August 1914: War Comes to Europe

Then the guns of August spoke. The United Kingdom of Britain and Ireland was officially at war from 4th August and the general feeling as noted by the police was anti-German and pro-British. Both UVF and Irish Volunteers turned out to escort troops off to war. A further 500 rifles arrived in Omagh for the UVF but already many of its members were enlisting for war service. There was talk of the UVF as an entity being incorporated into the Army. In Omagh a Nationalist band played 100 RC soldiers to the Catholic church and later played Protestant soldiers to their church, put the instruments in the porch and waited outside. After Divine Service they played the soldiers back to barracks. One can imagine policemen of all ranks breathing a sigh of relief and quietly giving thanks to the Kaiser for averting civil war in Ireland.

The *Constabulary Gazette* had no doubt about the righteousness of the war in Europe. Germany was clearly the aggressor and the barbaric behaviour of the Kaiser's forces in Belgium served to reinforce that view. The burning of Louvain's famous library and massacres of civilians were widely reported war crimes. The sense of outrage provided an emotional context for Redmond's declaration in Parliament that Nationalist Ireland would stand with Britain against German aggression.[v]

The Nationalist *Sligo Champion,* supporting the IPP, said in its editorial of 8th August: "From the Irish point of view the war is likely to result ultimately in much good. England, let us hope, has learned the lesson that the situation teaches that if Ireland is to be her friend in time of stress she must treat Ireland with confidence and justice in times of peace".

The Unionist *Sligo Independent* commented: "It is something to know that Ireland is the one bright spot in such a time of gloom and suspense...Mr Redmond's magnificent offer in the House of Commons on Monday ... has shown to Germany and the world that while Irishmen may have their differences and acute differences, they are bound together inseparably on one point and that is a passionate love for their native land and today they are joined together in one common brotherhood prepared if needs be to sacrifice their lives in defence of their country".

An undated memo to Lord Kitchener, probably from Percy Illingworth[3] in August 1914, offered some observations: "At the present time the Irish Volunteers of the South are a collection of independent bodies of men – under no discipline, and under self-appointed so-called officers acting without any cohesion and for the most part unarmed... The material is good if about 30% are eliminated, this 30% consisting of the 'corner-boy' element and 'ne'er do wells' of the towns. The country lads, the farmers, the farmers' sons, labourers and the like are excellent stuff, and of the same class as go into the RIC."

Redmond's offer was that the Irish Volunteers would co-

3 Percy Illingworth, a Yorkshireman, was a Liberal politician who had served under Asquith as Parliamentary Secretary to the Treasury from 1912 to 1915

operate with the Ulster Volunteers in the defence of Ireland. The quid pro quo was Home Rule. One interesting response was the improbable willingness of some Unionists to involve themselves in the IV movement.

Redmond received an immediate telegram from Major Bryan Cooper of Markree Castle in Sligo: "Your speech has united Ireland. I join National Volunteers today and will urge every Unionist to do the same." He joined the local Company, took charge of a section and offered use of his family's demesne for drilling purposes. As a trained officer with experience in the Boer War he had much to teach the Volunteers.

In a letter to the Unionist *Irish Times* Bryan Cooper made his views clear. "Sir. Our response to Mr Redmond's magnificent speech must be an immediate one. I am this day joining the National Volunteers and I urge every Unionist who is physically fit to do the same and to show the world that Irishmen can forget their quarrels and stand united against a common danger. Bryan Cooper"

This Eton-educated former Unionist MP, whose ancestors came to Ireland with Cromwell, went on to serve with the Connaught Rangers in the Gallipoli campaign. After the establishment of the Irish Free State he was elected as a TD in 1923 and re-elected in 1927. When he died in 1930 his coffin was draped with both the Tricolour and Union Flag.

The *Sligo Independent* reported the setting up of a "Corps of Sligo Unionists who will be enrolled as Irish Volunteers" with Col. Wynne in charge. The Police report for August mentioned a "Unionist Volunteer Corps" with about 70 members. The grounds of Sligo Grammar School may have been used for drilling. But by May 1915 about half of them had enlisted in the Army.

On the 9th August, Maj. Hillas of Templeboy offered his services to Col. Maurice Moore who led the Volunteers. He was appointed County Sligo Inspection Officer and immediately stressed the importance of protecting the coastline.

Not all the Volunteer leadership or rank and file were happy with the new Unionist members. Seán O Cinnéide of the Tubbercurry company complained that IV officers had not been consulted about the appointment of Maj. Hillas and demanded someone who shared their ideals. A *Champion* editorial warned: "We cannot allow our new friends to collar the organisation and shape it to their own ends... Our interest should be in Ireland first, last and all the time".

Acutely aware of the need for experienced soldiers as instructors, Col. Moore and others took a pragmatic view. Alec McCabe, Volunteer officer and IRB member, wrote to Hillas, welcoming his appointment. Other leaders who co-operated with Hillas were Owen Tansey and Seamus Devins on the Republican wing of the Movement and apparently more concerned with the Major's military skills than his political views. However, the Major's less than enthusiastic reception prompted him to resign soon afterwards.

The whole episode of Sligo's Loyal Irish Volunteers demonstrates that political convictions and party affiliations were more complex, less clearly defined and more fluid and evolving than post-Independence dogma would have us believe.

Regarding the impetus towards the de-militarisation of the police in the early 20th Century, a Commission of Enquiry reported in 1914 "...with the special emergency of the moment, the police is not sufficiently military to cope. For normal times it is unnecessarily military". Recognising the demands being made on the available manpower, in August the physical criteria for RIC recruits were slightly relaxed.

Unfortunately for the RIC the movement towards disarmament was arrested by the outbreak of war. It was inconceivable that the wartime government would disarm the Irish Police, at least for the duration.

Considering the overall situation, the Inspector General was careful to point out to his political masters that hostility to Home Rule had not declined. When the King gave the royal assent to the HR Bill in September his picture was hissed in Belfast picture houses and in some Protestant churches people walked out during the National Anthem.

The weather that autumn was "exceptionally fine" and the harvest was above average. Rainfall in northern areas was less than usual, with drought in some areas between 18th September and 12th October. It was already apparent that some people were going to make a lot of money out of the war. The Army was paying handsomely for horses of all kinds: farm and draught animals to pull wagons and guns, and hunters to become officers' chargers.

In November, in a less than coherent account under the headline "Remarkable Scenes at Drumquin" the *Tyrone Constitution* told its readers of events leading to John Toland being charged with attempting to rescue Thomas McCanny, presumably from police custody. Con. John Hannigan (sic.) gave evidence that before the row commenced several respectable people complained to him about the conduct of McCanny. He cautioned McCanny and warned him to behave himself. A/Sgt Kemp and and Con. Kinsella also gave evidence as did several others. We are without the full story but the result was Toland being bound over to the sum of £20 with two sureties of £10. The default penalty was three months.

In January 1915 the Tyrone County Inspector reported that "at no time in living memory has there been such good feeling between Catholics and Protestants". In February he said "party feeling is asleep". In Coalisland the Parish Priest directed that the Nationalist band should not parade the streets until in celebration of a German defeat. In April a concert organised by Unionists in Dungannon in aid of the Serbian Relief Fund was hosted by the Nationalist Hall.

Police duties now included enforcement of regulations under the Defence of the Realm Act. There were also occasional patrols of strategic structures such as railway tunnels, waterworks etc. Loitering near a bridge or tunnel was prohibited as was the lighting of bonfires. Foreign nationals had to be checked. An official circular told the Police "It is to be borne in mind that Germans or parties of German extraction will frequently speak English without a foreign accent".

Licensing hours for public houses were enforced and it became an offence to buy a drink for another person. Treating a soldier or serving him a drink outside the restricted time allowed were serious breaches of the law. A proposal to raise taxes on beer and spirits was "universally resented" while the Tyrone CI worried about the "increase of drinking among women whose husbands are at The Front". On the economic front, the flax industry, so important in Ulster linen production, was suffering from a lack of imported raw material.

The Separation Allowances paid to the wives and children of men on active service were considerable. A wife received 12 shillings and sixpence per week. With two children it became 21 shillings per week. A private soldier received a shilling a day. For very many women it represented their first taste of economic independence and some of them certainly set out to enjoy it.

Concerns about excessive drinking were not just the expression of middle-class puritanism. Branches of the NSPCC, with their paid inspectors, had been established only in cities and large towns; elsewhere it was the responsibility of the Police to protect children from neglect and abuse. In rural areas neglect tended to be an effect of dire poverty; in towns, alcohol abuse was a major cause. Unwanted pregnancies frequently resulted in a charge of "Concealment of Birth", a euphemism for infanticide. Among single women at least, such cases were usually resolved by the offender being sent to a Magdalene Laundry.

In February "Woman Patrols" similar to those in Britain were set up. Members of the nineteen patrols were given a semi-official status and allowed to wear an armband with white and navy blue stripes. The patrols were organised "for the safeguarding of girls from the results of the excitements aroused by the war". Welcomed by the Police and Military hierarchies, the movement was ecumenically against sin: its chiefs included the feminist pioneer Mary Hayden MA and Mrs Haslam of the Society of Friends.

Perhaps it was reaction to such female activities which prompted a joke of the day: "The courage of the Turk is explained by the fact that a man with more than one wife is more willing to face death than if he had only one."

A letter-writer to the *Constabulary Gazette* waxed eloquent about the petty regulations inherited from the previous century. One example was The Box which was required to be maintained by every Constable. It contained knife, fork, spoon, scissors, razor, webbing brush, blacking tin, hairbrush and comb, two pairs of socks, shirt, towel and a set of brushes. It was only ever opened for inspection by officers; all the functional items were available in the police station.

Another archaic inheritance from the Military was the Marching Order kit. This was a valise with similar items to the Box. It never went anywhere beyond the backyard for monthly inspection by the Member in Charge and quarterly by the District Inspector. The correspondent asked, plaintively and reasonably: why?

While the police were aware that Sinn Fein and the IRB were continuing to organise, they don't seem to have taken the threat very seriously. In Tyrone it was noted that Dr McCartan appeared to be active on behalf of the IRB but there was no attempt to arrest him, possibly because he was a naturalised American citizen. As the Nationalist volunteers had split into National Volunteers who followed John Redmond and Irish Volunteers who did not, there seemed to be no threat there. By this time many of the NVs had joined the Army and the NV movement continued to decline. The IVs continued to gain adherents but their numbers were still few. In fact the upper echelons of the police seemed to have dismissed the Republican threat as ephemeral because it contained few "people of consequence". Some more prescient police officers realised that it doesn't take a university degree or private income to become an effective revolutionary.

In mid-1915 many Nationalists worried about the implications of Carson becoming Attorney General while Redmond had declined a Cabinet post. It was also noted that there seemed to be inordinate delay in sending the 36th (Ulster) Division into action while other formations, recruited later, were already engaged with the enemy. The Irish 10th Division was being shredded at the Dardanelles.

The contrasting treatment by the War Office of volunteer soldiers from the respective traditions was niggardly and partisan. While the 36th Division was allowed to keep its UVF character and even retain many of its own officers, the Southern 10th and 16th Divisions of the "New Army" were denied official national symbols and insignia. Political and sectarian prejudices seemed to lead to a perception of untrustworthiness of the Irish especially in formations larger than a battalion. From the 17th Century there had been Irish Brigades in armies across Europe but this was the first time that the Irish had taken to the field in Division strength. In Nationalist eyes, two divisions made an Irish Army to be proud of as they marched with their British brothers to oppose the forces of tyranny. But were they trusted by the military hierarchy? Kitchener may have been born in

Kerry but it's unlikely that he'd have gone to Croke Park to support The Kingdom.

In the Dardanelles Campaign the 10th was used piecemeal with battalions detached to reinforce other divisions rather than being deployed as an entity. As losses mounted, instead of being reinforced by Irishmen from other divisions the national character of the 10th and 16th was diluted by the addition of British and Indian battalions.

Inspector General Chamberlain reported in July 1915 that there was "no reason to believe that there is any general enthusiasm for insurrection among the Sinn Feiners, beyond its opposition to recruiting for the army". In August, the crops of County Tyrone were "looking splendid". In September the county recorded only two indictable offences, both concerning defilement of girls under 16. It was an "absolutely uneventful month as regards politics". This remained the situation until the end of the year, notwithstanding the continuing activities of the energetic Dr McCartan and his fellow "extremists".

In July, Constable Thomas Hennigan, a native of Mayo, who'd been brought into the area for special railway protection duty was patrolling the line near Dungannon. In trying to avoid an approaching engine he stepped in front of a goods train. Knocked down, the engine went over his foot, reducing it to a pulp. At the District Hospital the limb was amputated.

Policemen, just like all the others on small incomes who weren't making money out of the war, were increasingly feeling the rise in the cost of living. Official Board of Trade figures showed the price rise in basic commodities from July 1914 to June 1915: sugar up 68%, fish up 64%, flour up 50% and bread up 40%. Unlike British police and other government departments, the RIC did not receive a war bonus. Not least among the deprivations for ordinary folk was the price of beer. From the 1914 price of 4 pence a pint, the cost of Guinness stout in Dublin rose to its wartime peak of 10d in July 1918, an increase of 150%.

In that summer of 1915 a good-natured debate about the relative superiority of Irish Roberts to British Bobbies sporadically exercised letter-writers to the *Constabulary Gazette.* One of the points made was that the relative poverty of Ireland meant that police recruits were drawn from higher educational and social levels than in more prosperous urban England. It was claimed that English policemen, coming from an urban trades background would readily abandon policing when skilled jobs became available. On the opposite side it was argued that while Irish policemen were impressive in their physique and educational attainments, they lacked experience of dealing with "real crime" and the skills to deal with it. It was pointed out that in Ireland but not in Britain the inspection of Weights and Measures, entailing certification through rigorous Board of Trade examinations, was the responsibility of the Constabulary. Perhaps the most telling point was that the very existence of the Cadet system led to the implication that the ranks of the RIC did not contain men of sufficient ability to occupy its higher positions. That inference damaged the prospects of Irish policemen not only at home but when applying for supervisory positions in Britain and the Colonies. It was also pointed out that the exigencies of war offered an excellent opportunity to change the system.

A contemporary joke illustrated the rustic sagacity of the Irish policeman. A "Jarvey" or horse-cab driver had been paid twopence by his Fare. The Jarvey demanded more – for carrying luggage – in this case a dog. The Fare contended that the dog was a passenger and that 2d was the correct fare for two passengers. The matter was put to a Constable: "How was the dog travelling?" "Sitting up." "Then it was a passenger. If it had been lying down it would have been luggage."

Two incidents three weeks apart illustrated the diverse

challenges of normal policing. At Newry on 28th August a man was found roosting in a tree. On being called down he said he was a bird and in his nest. More persuasion elicited a protest that he was asleep and not to be disturbed. When finally talked down he was found to be a local character in the condition known as "the horrohs". If his name was Sweeney, it wasn't recorded.

On 11th September a charge of attempted murder was preferred against Christopher Callan. Acting Sergeant Kiernan of Castlebellingham told the court that the accused fired two shots towards him, the pellets hitting the ground in front of him. The A/Sgt was armed only with a baton. He shouted to Con. Thompson to draw his revolver although the Constable didn't have even a baton with him. The ruse worked. Having expended his ammunition, Callan surrendered his shotgun and was taken into custody.

Despite the exigencies of the day job much of the Roberts' ire was directed towards officialdom. The Gazette editorial in October vented frustration: "But anyhow the fact remains that the Constitution of the Constabulary is probably the nearest approach extant to the laws of the ancient Medes and Persians, whose chief characteristic was that they altered not."

On the 4th December the *Gazette* offered editorial comment on the economies which would undoubtedly be needed after the war. "The semi-military police of Ireland may at one time have had a *raison d'etre*. Now that it is becoming more and more clear that the Constabulary are not going in any large numbers to the war, the semi-military training will automatically cease to have any justification, and the highly expensive embroidery which accompanies it will disappear. The Ulster boys and the Munster boys and the Faugh a Ballaghs who are fighting side by side in the trenches of Flanders will come home to Ireland to sing songs of peace, and woe to the politicians who endeavour to make discord." That was essentially the same sentiment more eloquently expressed by Tom Kettle, Nationalist MP, who would lose his life on the Somme battlefield: "Used with the wisdom which is sown in tears and blood, this tragedy of Europe may be and must be the prologue to the two reconciliations of which all statesmen have dreamed, the reconciliation of Protestant Ulster with Ireland, and the reconciliation of Ireland with Great Britain".

A new police grievance had been added to the many accumulated over the years. Some 2,000 RIC had volunteered to join the Colours and participate in the war. After about 200 had enlisted the authorities imposed a ban on policemen joining the military. Hopes of forming a distinctive RIC Battalion were dashed; the majority of those who went to war were absorbed into the elite Irish Guards and a distinctive identity was denied them. Meanwhile news that four young men of military age had been taken on as RIC Cadets while experienced Constabulary Officers had gone to the war was incendiary information. There was an inevitable interpretation, if a very guarded one, that these young men were "dodging the column". The Guinness Brewery, one of the most desirable employers in Ireland, had already made clear that it had suspended new First Class Clerkships for the duration. When hostilities ceased, preference would be given to war veterans.

Only 5% of RIC rankers and 10% of their officers went to war, proportions well below those of British police forces. One factor deterring enlistment was that the ordinary Roberts couldn't afford it. If they went into the Army, they were no longer paid as policemen but simply as private soldiers on a shilling a day. Normal practice in British police forces was to continue police payment less the seven shillings a week. Post Office employees got both. Another option was to induct RIC men into the Army as NCOs (who were desperately needed), given that they'd been trained in Musketry and basic military skills. Although not generous, a NCO's wages were more than the daily pittance an untrained soldier received.

Despite all that, over 2.000 volunteered to join the Colours though most were not allowed to go. As with so many aspects of British government attitudes and actions in Ireland during those years, the rationale behind policy is barely discernible and not at all comprehensible.

There were also disquieting indications that the government was preparing for the possible introduction of conscription in Ireland. A new task was about to be imposed on the Constabulary. Whereas in Britain completion of forms for the new National Registration Act was a task for householders, in Ireland it was to be a job for policemen. Given the extent and detail required to complete the fifteen questions for each individual registered, it was an impossible task. But the implication was that in the event of conscription being introduced it would require policemen's local knowledge to implement it, a task they did not agree with or relish. Discussion in the *Gazette* conceded that while conscription might be fair in principle, introducing it in Ireland would be divisive and cause animosity and unrest. It would be better to encourage volunteers.

In the mud of winter 1915 the trenches of the opposing armies were largely static from the North Sea to the Swiss border. The Dardanelles expedition was a debacle and the surviving invaders were evacuated in December. Thousands of Irish soldiers would remain forever in Turkey alongside British, French and Anzacs, and their Turkish opponents; Johnny and Mehmet were at peace together in their graves.

Apart from the many families whose loved ones had gone to The Front, most people in Ireland were unaffected directly by the war and life generally continued at its usual sedate pace. There were exceptions, for example a case of "Furious Driving" in November. Two motor lorry drivers appeared in court accused of "recklessly driving their cars". It was reported that "the defendants were apparently racing each other and were "covering about 20 miles an hour". Driver Mitchell was fined 20 shillings and costs, Egan ten shillings and costs, "both licences being endorsed".

1916: Transfer to Donegal

Under the headline "Maimed on Active Service" the *Constabulary Gazette* in January carried the story of a young Constable who'd suffered the loss of a lower limb while patrolling the railway line near Dungannon in November. He was still in hospital in Dungannon, facing a very difficult future. He'd already been categorised as disabled on an annual pension of fourteen pounds, five shillings and fourpence "a wholly inadequate pension in the circumstances". The *Gazette* made a couple of points. If there had been any question of contributory negligence, Constable Thomas Hennigan would have received only a gratuity, i.e. one month's pay for each year of service. His character was above reproach and he was a lifelong abstainer. If a soldier lost a limb at war his pension was 10 shillings and sixpence a week, drunk or sober. Constable Hennigan, by contrast, was fobbed off with 5 shillings and eightpence. However, it is recorded elsewhere that Thomas Henegan (sic.) subsequently received a grant from the Royal Bounty Fund for the purchase of an artificial foot.

The *Gazette* suggested a better alternative: provide the man with an artificial limb and employ him as a clerk on full pay, a solution in line with modern practice. It hoped the authorities would reconsider the case. Clearly, they didn't. At 24 years old, young Thomas found his career ended on 22nd June 1916, less than a year after his accident.

The shabby treatment given to Thomas Hennigan was a foretaste of what was to come for many members of the Constabulary and their families.

The new year brought change for John Hennigan also. On 1st February 1916 he was transferred to south Donegal. That must have pleased him and by implication he must have pleased his superiors sufficiently to have been given such a desirable posting. As regulations required, he was in a different county but in fact less than twenty miles from his home place. It was within easy cycling distance of his parents on the family farm. An additional pleasure was that his friend John Gilmartin had already been transferred to Donegal the previous April. The angry passions of Belfast would have seemed far away.

The 19th February edition of the *Gazette* noted:

> In County Tyrone, much to the regret of his comrades and a wide circle of friends, Constable Hannigan (sic) has been transferred from Drumquin to County Donegal and allocated to Duleek. During his service in Tyrone he made hosts of friends and his transfer from Drumquin is much regretted both by his comrades and civilians. John was certainly a good comrade and a good policeman in every sense. On the eve of his departure he received some very suitable presentations showing the esteem in which he was held by both police and civilians. Good luck, Jack, is the sincere wish of your comrades.

He was then 24 years old and back on familiar ground, but an area with its own peculiarities. In Sligo town the visitor might be struck by oddities in the speech of working men, with its flat vowels and dropped H, clearly the legacy of generations as a garrison town. A few miles beyond the town limits in any direction the accents were typically rural Connacht. Going northwards into Bundoran, the cadences of Donegal began to be heard, and were clearer still in Ballyshannon. Bundoran had been a seaside resort since the 1890s where people came to breathe the bracing air or avail themselves of hot and cold seawater baths. Some came to play golf on the clifftop links. Since the railway opened in 1866, Bundoran could provide convenient access to South Donegal and hotels and guesthouses sprang up along the single street. Busy in summer, the village must have needed little policing in the darker months.

In the north-west, 1916 had started quietly. While the *Donegal Vindicator* reported on 59 deaths in Britain from German aerial bombing, the most immediate evidence of war was the barrels of petroleum and lubricating oil washed up on the beach at Bundoran. Flotsam in such a public place was immediately collected by the authorities but in more remote locations might prove a boon to the impoverished.

Ballyshannon was a town of close to 4,000 people, similar to Donegal's administrative centre, Letterkenny. The County Inspector was based in Letterkenny so the authority of Ballyshannon's District Inspector was more immediate. In early 1916 the *Vindicator* was calling for the waters of the River Erne to be harnessed to provide power for war factories. The technology existed; enterprising hotel owners were generating their own electricity at nearby Dromahair. But it would be 1952 before the hydro-electric station at Catherine's Falls was officially opened. Desperately short of paid employment, a town like Ballyshannon would have been transformed in 1916 by a munitions factory. The *Vindicator* sourly observed "But perhaps our rulers conclude that Ballyshannon's three and only industries – cards, billiards and dancing – command all the available labour".

In truth, Ballyshannon is a picturesque little town, located where the mighty Erne tumbles into the sea and frenzied salmon fight the weir. It owes its existence to the bridge that spans the river after a sharp turn on the Sligo road and brings the traveller to a steeply-climbing street of shops, the heart of the place. William Allingham, of course, is the Bard of Ballyshannon whose poem "The Fairies" was known to every schoolchild. James C. Mangan may have prophesied the Erne running red "with redundance of blood" but it was Allingham's gentler vision that was quoted more readily by aged men drinking porter. However, he was no gentle dilettante dandling airy visions; Allingham was a strong journalist and penetrating diarist who excoriated the ignorance on Ireland of his own friends Tennyson, Rosetti and Carlyle of whom he wrote "He knows nothing of Ireland except what feeds his prejudices". Allingham's long, epic poem *Laurence Bloomfield* shone a harsh light on the system of land tenure in Ireland and the evils of rack-renting.

Despite reports of shipping losses such as the P & O liner *Persia* to torpedoes, such disasters seemed far away and the Sligo Steam Navigation Company advertised its weekly sailings to Liverpool carrying passengers, cargo and livestock. War news in Ballyshannon's *Vindicator* consisted of some reports of deaths at the front but rather more space was given to congratulatory reports on the successful evacuation from Gallipoli, "an achievement without parallel". While the Conscription Bill seemed assured of passage through Parliament, the newspaper didn't believe it would ever be implemented. The Irish Party, given assurances that it did not apply to Ireland, did not support but was not opposing it. The *Vindicator* quite clearly took the IPP and National Volunteers approach to national aspirations. Ireland's martial traditions were lauded through a series of weekly articles on the origins and exploits of the Irish regiments in the 18th Century French army. The German assault on Verdun was also noted and the progress of the battle monitored. Clearly, once again France needed *les Irlandais* marching beside her.

The war was a factor in everyday life, even if only occasionally irksome for many. A young man called Hugh Sweeney was arrested in Rathmullen for a breach of the Defence of the Realm Act, accused of eliciting information likely to be of use to an enemy government. He'd been caught writing in a notebook, presumably shipping details, when apprehended. Young Hugh was remanded on bail while the document was examined. For many others at home, though, the war was the reality of a blunt telegram from the War Office or Admiralty telling them that a son, brother, husband or father, would never be seen or touched by them again. A lover's loss would not be communicated directly. In the extraordinary symbiosis of the trenches it could be the most and the least, so different in their short lives, who were closest; the younger sons of great families found themselves in command of youngsters like themselves. Lacking in formal education, some uncouth youths may have had skills of survival that the privileged possibly lacked. In Ireland, the strong farmers and the merchants of the town sent few enough sons to the war. It was the gentry, the landless and the urban unemployed who followed the colours.

The War had other unprecedented consequences. The Ballyshannon newspaper *The Donegal Vindicator* in its Peripatetic Pressman column offered an opinion on the effects of separation allowances: "the plain truth is that women of a certain class are simply revelling in luxury and liquor and some steps should be taken to end the saturnalia. 'When the boys come home' there will be no fires burning, but on the contrary empty houses and bare cupboards. Probably some of them are counting on the boys not coming home at all, and that a grateful nation will keep on filling up the porter jar out of gratitude".

At the Ballyshannon Petty Sessions one man was fined ten shillings for buying a pair of boots from a soldier of the Royal Irish Fusiliers. A soldier who was charged with the larceny of a pair of lady's corsets – the property of Ellen Carty and valued at one shilling and eightpence – was given the benefit of the First Offender's Act and released from custody. The circumstances of the theft were not reported.

Finner Camp was situated between Bundoran and Ballyshannon and must have been a constant nuisance to the police. Given that it mostly contained men of the 36th (Ulster) Division, the customary ebullience of soldiers had here a hard sectarian edge. True, the Military Police would deal with trouble-makers but it could often be the Constabulary which had to first intervene when disturbances arose.

On 4th March the *Gazette* welcomed a circular from the IG which invited 100 RIC rankers to apply for training at Portobello Barracks allowing them to enter the Army with the rank of Sergeant.

The same edition carried the less generally important news that "Constable Hannigan (sic) who was recently transferred from Drumquin in County Tyrone to the County Donegal , has been allocated to Duleek". The *Gazette's* error regarding John's new posting persisted. In both the Constabulary Lists and in the 1911 Census the only Duleek Station recorded is in County Meath, outside Slane. It is likely that John was posted directly to Bundoran in the Ballyshannon District.

While it seemed strange that the *Gazette* should expend so much indignation on the issue of RIC men being denied opportunity to go to the war, its reasoning became clearer in April. In effect, it expressed the perception that the reluctance to free up policemen to join the army was due to a fear that if many were commissioned from the ranks (as seemed likely with well-qualified RIC men) the old Cadet system would be shown up as utterly indefensible.

April 1916: War comes to Dublin

The relaxed complacency of the RIC, its management and its political masters was shattered in 1916. Official reports stated that up to the latter part of April the country was "quiescent".

It may not be peculiar to Ireland but there is a pervasive if gloomy optimism on that island which is perhaps fostered by the weather. It's a passive optimism: better times are coming but we needn't do anything to hasten them. Since the call to arms in August 1914 the police may have succumbed to a feeling of relief that the Kaiser and his allies in Vienna and Constantinople had defused the Irish powder keg. After the shared sacrifices of Flanders and Asia Minor, it could have been hard to imagine that Green and Orange could ever again be at each other's throats. The National Volunteers had gone to the War in large numbers.

However, in secret, other agenda were being shaped. We now know that as early as 1912 Britain's decision makers had begun to accept that Irish Home Rule would entail the partition of the island but that was not something Redmond and the Irish Party were yet prepared to publicly concede. But behind the scenes some ultra-nationalists were becoming ever more frustrated by the slow pace of constitutional progress towards even a limited independence. The physical force tradition claimed lineal descent through the Fenians from the republican United Irishmen of 1798. Dismissive of parliamentary politics, they plotted a different route.

On Good Friday 21st April, Sir Roger Casement, former star of Britain's diplomatic service, was arrested on a Kerry beach after landing from a German submarine. On Saturday, Casement was brought to London and Eoin McNeill cancelled the Irish Volunteers mobilisation order for Easter Sunday. On Sunday night Bailey, Casement's companion, disclosed to his captors the insurrection plans including a German arms shipment. But the arms ship, the *Aud*, had already been intercepted by Britain's Royal Navy and scuttled by her Captain. According to the Police IG, "It seemed unlikely that the intended rising could take place". But on Easter Monday, it did.

It's an open question how many of the Irish Volunteers who turned out on the streets of Dublin knew that they were being mobilised for revolution, or thought they were carrying out manoeuvres. As for the seven signatories of the Proclamation of the Republic, there was no unanimity of aims, their ideals varying from socialist republic to pastoral paradise. The Proclamation itself was stronger on rhetoric than realism.

According to the BMH testimony of the revolutionary Leslie Price (the future wife of Tom Barry), the SF leader Fr Michael O'Flanagan denounced the rebels as murderers. She diminished his credibility by saying that the priest had passed by a wounded tramp before kneeling to attend another man.

During the Rising, precipitated by "a conspiracy within a conspiracy", 14 RIC members were killed and 23 wounded, a small proportion of the approximately 200 dead and 2,500 wounded in total. Of course most of the violence took place in Dublin, outside the RIC's jurisdiction. At Ashbourne, Co.

Meath, a group of over sixty police racing to the relief of the besieged barracks was ambushed by Irish Volunteers under Thomas Ashe and Richard Mulcahy and suffered eight fatal casualties, the dead including a County Inspector and a District Inspector. The fifteen police wounded were treated humanely. Con. Bratton who was driving the rearmost car, unarmed and in civilian clothes, was allowed by Ashe to take the CI's body back to his widow. She'd had no knowledge of her husband's death till Bratton, with another policeman's wife for support, brought the body to her door. Appropriately described as a battle, it was, apart from the confrontation at Mount Street Bridge, the only really successful military action by the Rebels that week.

Patrick Shea was then the eight year old son of an Athlone Sergeant and later recalled hearing the news. "We had a visit from a big ruddy-complexioned sergeant in the police whose brother, also a policeman, had been killed at Ashbourne where a party of police reinforcements had been attacked and I had to leave the room because he was crying and the sight of an adult shedding tears was too much for me".

Three unarmed DMP Constables were shot dead. James O'Brien was on duty at the gate of Dublin Castle when he was murdered by Sean Connolly of the Irish Citizen Army, himself shot dead shortly afterwards by an Army rifleman. Michael Lahiffe was shot down at St Stephen's Green by another member of the Citizen Army, possibly Countess Markievicz. Was the ICA, led by James Connolly, expressing a particular animus against the DMP, perhaps a legacy of the labour conflicts in 1913? William Frith was in Store Street Station when he was shot through the window by a sniper. Six other DMP members were seriously injured that week.

A hundred years later, we heard the testimony of his family regarding the fate of Constable Edward Dunphy. He had been on duty in Sackville Street when taken prisoner by Michael

Collins. Inside the GPO he was later spotted by James Connolly who enquired as to his identity. Told he was the policeman who'd been on duty at Nelson Pillar, Connolly's response was "Take him out and shoot him". The O'Rahilly took him away but did not countenance a war crime. He brought Dunphy to the GPO's side door on Henry Street and ushered him out saying "I couldn't shoot a fellow Irishman", and wished him luck. Dunphy ran for Henry Place but was hit by a sniper on the roof. Tended by street traders he was brought to hospital. Unfortunately, his injuries led to his death three years later, having first gone blind. His family, however, down the generations would honour The O'Rahilly for his decency. As for Connolly, the story could lead one to have diminished sympathy with him in his execution while tied to a chair.

There was also trouble in East Galway where about 650 rebels turned out, but without the arms from the *Aud* they had little hope of being effective. The Galway Rising had a clear agrarian impetus, an extension of the Land War. In Galway town, the atmosphere was loyal – to Redmond if not necessarily to King and Empire. A Committee of Public Safety was formed and Special Constables were appointed. Drawn from the National Volunteers, they were armed by the military and were on hand to assist the RIC; they were referred to in the press as Galway's own Citizen Army. The shooting affray at Craughwell in which Con. Patrick Whelan, aged 36 and a native of Kilkenny, was killed was to some extent a battle between Irish Volunteers and opposing National Volunteers in the role of Special Constables. According to a Volunteer's statement to the BMH, Whelan was shoved up onto a low wall by DI Heard and called out to the rebels. "Surrender, boys. I know ye all". He was instantly shot fatally. That foolish exposure seems improbable. A more likely explanation is that the former Irish Guards Corporal simply didn't manage to find effective cover, being six feet, three inches (almost 2m) tall, and suffered wounds to face and neck. The inquest heard that the wounds were caused by No.4 shot, a heavy gauge used for hunting large game. In any case, Patrick seems to have been a thoroughly decent young man who had defended his mother from his abusive father. Very unusually for a Catholic family, his mother had obtained a divorce from the Courts on grounds of cruelty. It's also quite probable that Patrick had previously socialised with the man who shot him; the family of Whelan's girlfriend, Mary Kyne, owned the pub in Castlegar.

No official blame attached to DI Heard. He was soon afterwards promoted to CI and in 1920 was elevated to become Commandant of the Depot. As County Inspector for Kerry, he was present on the momentous day when Jeremiah Mee and his fellow Constables defied the authority of Divisional Commissoner Smyth at Listowel Barracks.

The town of Galway remained solidly supportive of the status quo but, cut off from the world beyond, rumour abounded. Under Martial Law, with pubs and shops shut and the populace subject to curfew, a siege atmosphere gripped the urban dwellers. It was said that a peasant army was marching on the town.

Galway Town had actually long been regarded by ultra-nationalists as a West British stronghold but was probably typical of most towns in the country. Its middle-class inhabitants had already been mocked as Shoneens – little John Bulls – by D.P. Moran in a 1903 ballad :

> We are just come back from our English schools
> To Irish dirt and Irish fools
> Dear God we were born beneath your frown
> When you let us be born in Galway town….

Our collars are high, our hair is short
Our swagger canes are the latest sort
We are most genteel from heel to crown
For we are the shoneens of Galway town.

Yet we'll do our best for the poor fools there
We'll swing our canes, we'll crop our hair
We never will talk like a Claddagh clown
We'll remain the shoneens of Galway town.

With the impoverished hinterland, the Military was a major economic influence on the town. The Connaught Rangers was very clearly the local regiment. More than 400 of the Irish-speaking men in the Claddagh fishing village at the river mouth, and from Connemara, had volunteered for the Royal Navy or, as reservists, had been called back to the Fleet.

With the Navy becoming involved in shelling the rebels at Oranmore and 4 inch shells exploding in unpredictable locations, the inhabitants of the coastal villages fled towards the relative security of the town. The refugees were not always received with enthusiasm.

At Moycullen it was said that local insurgents refrained from attacking the RIC barrack because the Sergeant's wife was ill. As in Dublin, the Rising had little popular support. At Craughwell National Volunteers occupied the barrack to assist the police should it be attacked. Despite a lot of marching and countermarching by the IV, dashing about by the Military, and four Royal Navy ships busying themselves in Galway Bay, the only fatality in the East Galway uprising was the unfortunate Constable Whelan.

In Wexford, fearing attack by the Irish Volunteers, the National Volunteers under the command of Col. Jameson Davies turned out to assist the police. (Enniscorthy was in Rebel hands from Thursday 27th until Sunday 30th.) The NV at Callaghan's Mills in Co. Clare took up guard duty on the Post Office and were later officially thanked by Army and Police chiefs.

One of the ugliest acts of the week was in Castlebellingham, Co. Louth, where Constable McGee and Army Lieutenant Dunville were callously murdered whilst being held prisoner.

The editorial line of the *Gazette* was understandably condemnatory: "Easter week of the year 1916 will, we venture to say, mark a historical period in Ireland's history, and one that all true friends of this unhappy country will bitterly regret."

Its assessment of the leaders was dismissive but probably in tune with much of contemporary opinion: "A revolution led by the Larkinite demagogue, the Rathmines Schoolmaster and the Sligo Adventuress with the Russian title, is after all, very little more than a glorified street riot". Nor was *The Gazette's* call for severe punishment out of line with views expressed in the public press.

Given that the centre of Dublin had been reduced to a burnt-out shell, looking like a town in Flanders after the Huns had wreaked havoc, there was little popular sympathy with the perpetrators. There was outrage among the more cultured citizens at the destruction of a magnificent street with the Post Office as its centrepiece, and the nearby Royal Hibernian Academy with the hundreds of paintings in its annual exhibition. But attitudes quickly changed and people began to remember that Britain had used artillery against the Empire's second city.

At Ballyshannon, first news of "The Dublin Rebellion" prompted an editorial response in the *Donegal Vindicator* : "It is a deadly blow to Ireland, as bad or perhaps worse, than the assassination of Sir Frederick Cavendish. They will pay the penalty, many of them with their lives, but that will not wash away the stain from the fair name of Ireland". Expressing a widely-held opinion, the newspaper saw the Rising as the product of "Larkinism and German gold"; its leaders were referred to as "the Mad Mullahs of Dublin". Such views were widespread among constitutional nationalists, not merely the judgement of the Unionist persuasion.

Although Tyrone and Donegal remained peaceful the country was overall in an "unsettled condition". There was Nationalist anger when it became clear that north-east Ulster was to be excluded from Home Rule. That encouraged growing sympathy with the Sinn Fein insurgents. The protracted series of executions during May disgusted many moderate people. Had they been carried out immediately after the Rising there might have been less revulsion but strung out as they were through May they seemed the product of cold and vindictive revenge. One observer described it as a slow trickle of blood from under the cell door. In a heartfelt speech to the House of Commons John Dillon cried: "You are washing out our whole lives' work in a sea of blood… it is not murderers who are being executed; it is insurgents who fought a clean fight, however misguided". The violence on both sides was destroying the achievements of the parliamentarians. Amongst ordinary people, resentment at the executions grew. It cannot have helped if word seeped out from the military prison at Arbour Hill that, on his arrival to take charge in Ireland, Maxwell had ordered the preparation of burial pits large enough to accommodate several hundred bodies in anticipation of mass executions.

The editorial response of the *Donegal Vindicator* encapsulates what was happening to opinion across nationalist Ireland. On 12th May, it expressed the view: "That a rebellion can be put down without some bloodletting is probably too much to expect, but with the precedent of South Africa before our minds, we may be pardoned for believing it should be of the smallest possible quantity". Of the arrests in Derry of prominent Sinn Fein members, the editorial noted: "their Sinn Feinism is of the academic order, rather than militant". And it ominously continued "a continuance of the reign of terror will cause a revulsion of feeling".

By failing to distinguish between Sinn Fein and the Irish Volunteers, Dublin Castle obscured all difference between militant and non-violent separatism, extremists and moderates. The crude reaction by the Military authorities alienated much moderate Nationalist opinion and strengthened the physical force Republicans. Incidentally, the myth that the RIC were wonderfully efficient spies is clearly exploded by their failure to predict the Rising until it was upon them.

A week later, the Nationalist *Donegal Vindicator* could state: "... today, thanks to the great and good generalship of Sir John Maxwell and Kildare Street Club, we are Sinn Feiners to the last man". It wasn't only the executions that caused such an extraordinary swing in opinion. The heavy-handed tactics employed under Martial Law alienated many law-abiding people. The journalist who contributed to the *Vindicator* as Peripatetic Pressman was warned not to "bring the administration of martial law into contempt" as an article of his was judged by the Military "to foster sympathy with those who have taken up arms or plotted to do so". This journalist, in fact the editor, had consistently supported Ireland's involvement in the War and had a son serving with the Highland Light Infantry. He was warned by the Military Authority on 22nd May of the possible "seizure and destruction of your printing plant". The Defence of the Realm regulations provided such powers.

Himself a long-time supporter of Home Rule who described the insurrection as "ghastly", George Bernard Shaw expressed the unpopular view that "The men who were shot in cold blood after their capture or surrender were prisoners of war". Of course, being Shaw, he had to annoy his compatriots as well as the British. "Let us grieve, not over the fragment of Dublin city that has been knocked down, but over at least three quarters of what has been preserved. How I wish I had been in command of the British artillery on that fatal field! How I should have improved my native city!"

Inveterate jester he may have been, but Shaw saw the executions through unsentimental Irish eyes: "It is impossible to slaughter a man in this position without making him a martyr and a hero, even though the day before the Rising he may have been only a minor poet. The shot Irishmen will now take their places beside Emmet and the Manchester Martyrs in Ireland, and beside the heroes of Poland and Serbia and Belgium in Europe; and nothing in heaven or on the earth can prevent it".

Whatever one's views on the morality of the enterprise it is beyond question that the Rising had enormous impact. Described by some as the poets' rebellion, it found in the words of W.B.Yeats an eloquent epitaph. He evoked the patronising attitude with which urbane citizens like himself had viewed the zealots:

I have met them at close of day
Coming from counter and desk among grey,
Eighteenth century houses
And passed with a nod of the head and polite meaningless words
Or have lingered a while and said polite, meaningless words
And thought before I was done
Of a mocking tale or a gibe
To please a companion
Around the fire at the club
Being certain that they, and I
But lived where motley is worn
All changed, changed utterly
A terrible beauty is born.

With the immodesty of the true poet, he wonders if he himself does not bear some responsibility: "What if words of mine sent out / certain men the English shot".

Using the name Dermot O'Byrne, the musician who became better known as Sir Arnold Bax, Master of the King's Music, wrote in angry verse about the executions:

And when at last the golden bell
Of liberty was silenced
He learned to shoot extremely well
At unarmed Irish gentlemen.

"A Dublin Ballad" was promptly banned as seditious. O'Byrne, in a rather better poem "Shells at Oranmore" evoked the conflict in Galway.

Across the threatening tranquillity
Where are but ice-grown rock for pasturage
Strange lumps of death came shrieking from the sea
And still the earth's cold entrails quake with rage
That such a thing could be.

A terrible beauty may have been born but the birth wasn't universally welcomed. Support for Sinn Fein was growing, but at first only slowly. In the words of Patrick Shea: "This was still a minority movement; the revolutionary implications of republicanism were unwelcome to god-fearing people who were making money as never before".

In his Witness Statement to the BMH, J.R.W. Goulden, son of Sgt Henry Goulden, recalled the atmosphere of the time in Tourmakeady, Co. Mayo. Although a Protestant, young Goulden attended the local Catholic school.

> In the months following Easter Week, the police going on patrol carried their carbines but they still went about singly and, beyond this small display of force, life went on much as before. The district was very free of crime except an occasional petty theft or a row at a fair. There was one meeting about the time of conscription. The people around were all small landowners and they were receiving good prices for their cattle and other produce owing to the war and were better off than they had ever been before.

In the year 1970, police veteran Pat Mahon looked back: "The vast majority of the RIC were nationalists e.g. they envisaged a measure of Home Rule coming into operation by constitutional means. They shared this belief with their countrymen but they and the general population were overborne by the advocates of physical force." And again, "But as the gnomes of the Celtic Twilight had lauded the Rebellion of 1916 without the knowledge (or approval) of the Irish public, one should have assumed that a minority group would again take it upon themselves to make decisions affecting the fate of the country".

In June there was an ominous development for the police. It was reported that "several hundred" DMP members were being given musketry training at Dollymount. They were to be armed with Lee-Metford carbines. While during the Fenian uprising of 1867 they had been issued with Sniders and members had carried cutlasses on night duty during the Land League days, the DMP had been unarmed for thirty years.

There was indignation at this regressive step. The *Gazette* called on the Government to ascertain the views of the police. Arming was unpopular with officers and men and the DMP Chief Commissioner was asked to make clear whether rifle practice was intended only for members who volunteered or was to be imposed on the whole establishment.

The general DMP view was that becoming semi-military would alter their relationship with the citizens and expose them to greater danger. Questions were asked in the House of Commons.

In July the Home Secretary told the House that it was "not proposed that this force should carry rifles on duty or otherwise, except in cases of gravest necessity". It is difficult to understand government thinking. The fact remains that while two defenceless DMP Constables had been brutally murdered face-to-face during the Rising, others who had been made prisoner by the rebels had been treated decently. The DMP had been withdrawn from the streets by 3pm on Easter Monday. Had they been armed and ordered to fight the insurgents, it could have meant a massacre of the police.

Overall, wrote the IG that month "The country is singularly free from ordinary crime", Farmers were prosperous. Times had never been as good. Young farmers showed little inclination to join the Army, or the Irish Volunteers for that matter. It was reported that some dealers and retailers were making fortunes. Ordinary labourers were getting £2 – £3 per month in munitions factories. But fractious behaviour was always in evidence: there was a riot between civilians and military at Bundoran on 16th June. The soldiers were Inniskilling Fusiliers of the Ulster Division. It was reported that civilians playing handball were abused by drunken soldiers "using party expressions" no doubt disparaging to Nationalists and the Pope. Sticks and soldiers' belts were used in the fight. Bundoran Police, possibly including John Hennigan were quickly on the scene and nearby stations were called on for reinforcements. A strong military party with fixed bayonets arrived from Finner Camp but the affray was over. Several soldiers were reported as seriously injured.

In Donegal some people joined an anti-partition league. The county would be isolated and clearly suffer economically if an internal border were imposed in Ireland. There was no industrial development in Donegal and any chance of it would disappear with a frontier between Derry City and its natural hinterland. Many in the county depended on migratory labour for a cash income, going to Britain – especially Scotland – during the summer as "tatie hokers" helping to harvest potatoes. In the summer of 1916 many returned empty-handed, having failed to find work due to anti-Irish prejudice in the wake of the Easter Rising. Their "frigid reception" was partly explained by John Pimbley, a large farmer in Lancashire: "I have refused to employ young Irish labourers who have asked me for work because I don't think it's right for our young men to have to go and fight and these young men left".

Also, migratory labourers were fearful of being conscripted while temporarily resident in Britain. Donegal's County Inspector pointed out that the only way to stop Sinn Fein from engaging with the impoverished was to provide work for them e.g. in munitions factories.

It may have been in recognition of Galway's loyalty that the town became the location of one of the five National Shell Factories in Ireland, rather a long distance from the products' point of use. Employing almost entirely women, the factory was a huge boost to the urban economy. The first 18 lb shell was produced in February 1917. Galway Woollen Mills won a contract to supply uniforms, and a branch of the War Hospital Supply Depot produced 100 yards of gauze per day.

Bundoran's seaside Pierrot show was being continually interrupted by a rude member of the audience. The manager rebuked him: "Were you brought up in ignorance?" The reply was instant: "No, sir. I was brought up in Ballyshannon".

Ireland and the Wider World of 1916

Traumatic as the deaths of April and May were on this small island, they were numerically insignificant compared to what was happening in Continental Europe and on the seas that year. The Battle of Verdun lasted from 21st February until 20th December and took the lives of some half a million men, French and German, their flesh and bone pulverised into mulch. France was fighting here for its very existence, as the German strategy was simply to kill as many Frenchmen as possible. There was no tactical objective.

At the end of April, as the Easter Rising in Dublin flared and was snuffed out, the rebels' compatriots in the 16th Irish Division were suffering excruciating deaths by that most vile of the new weapons: poison gas. (Although the scientist who developed the weapon for Germany saw it as no worse than other ways of killing people his wife, herself a scientist, shot herself.)

The only fleet action of the war was the Battle of Jutland at the end of May, involving 250 ships. In a few hours ten thousand men died, a thousand at a time as great ships blew up and vanished.

What we now call the Battle of the Somme began on 1st July 1916. British and French forces were to smash through the German lines along the River Somme and break the stalemate in the war. Things did not go to plan. On the first day the British Army suffered the worst casualties in its history. In the first few hours the 36th (Ulster) Division alone suffered 5,500 casualties of whom almost 2,000 were killed. Across the province of Ulster from Antrim to Donegal, as news of the disaster came through families drew down the blinds in whitewashed cottages, back to back terraces and big houses. It was an unbelievable tragedy and one which influences Irish politics a hundred years later.

While the 36th Division suffered disproportionately at the Somme, other Irish regiments including the regulars of the 29th Division also took heavy losses that first day. In the August and September battles it was the turn of the volunteers from Connacht, Munster and Leinster in the 16th Division to suffer enormous casualties. Slaughter continued along the river until the rain and mud of November brought the Allied offensive to an end. The lethal reality of modern warfare was brought home to every corner of Ireland. The police were under pressure to promote recruitment. While the urban poor continued to enlist, the farming community was just not interested. But very few in Ireland advocated conscription.

One of those killed in September was Tom Kettle a former Nationalist MP and Irish Volunteer organiser, seen by many as the noblest Roman of them all. The polymath Kettle – friend of Joyce, Gogarty and Sheehy-Skeffington – had been in Europe on an arms-buying expedition for the Volunteers when the Germans invaded Belgium. He became a war correspondent and witnessed the excesses of Prussian militarism. Kettle understood the conflict as between barbarism and civilisation and saw Ireland's place as defending civilised Europe. Unwilling to ask others to do what he didn't do himself, he'd enlisted in the Dublin Fusiliers and badgered his way to the front line despite weak health. When word of the Rising reached him he was furious with the rebels, believing they'd done Ireland a great disservice, but agonised over the fate of the leaders especially his dear friend Thomas McDonagh. At the same time he was astute enough to know that all had changed, saying of the rebels that they would go down in history as heroes and martyrs while he would go down, if at all, "as a bloody British officer".

The Home Front 1916

On 1st August Sir Joseph Byrne became the first Roman Catholic Inspector General of the RIC. The appointment appears to have been widely welcomed, especially among his co-religionist rank and file members, and may have been seen as an augury of a brighter future under a Home Rule government. There were certainly hopes that the new broom would introduce structural reforms. After his predecessor's resignation, the *Gazette* commented on Sir Neville Chamberlain as "a refined and courtly gentleman" but "extremely conservative in the matter of reform". But Brig. Gen Byrne was resented and distrusted by a Unionist clique at Dublin Castle and was to suffer intrigue and lack of support in critical times. Also, it is apparent from his reports that he was a soldier, not a policeman, and he tended to think in military terms.

One of the new IG's circulars dealt with the Police duty of apprehending deserters from the Military. He asked his men to be understanding. The Army was not a compassionate employer. Soldiers who had been sick or wounded were granted a maximum of ten days leave after leaving hospital. New soldiers were given four or five days on completion of training. Normally there were no other grounds for furlough.

It would be easy for even a dutiful soldier, in the comfort of his family or perhaps dealing with a family crisis, to overstay his entitlement. Gen. Byrne directed that the Constabulary should keep an eye on soldiers at home and "act in as tactful and kindly manner as indicated" to help the soldier and also serve the interests of the State.

Another wartime duty was taking charge of a soldier's rifle when he was on leave if there was no military post nearby. Sugar rationing had to be enforced and from November permits had to be issued for travel between Ireland and Britain.

In the autumn of 1916 it was recorded that although agriculture in general was satisfactory, the potato crop was 40% below average and the prices of food and provisions were a problem. In December the IG reported that "farmers and shopkeepers did well this month" but that the poor had problems with "exorbitant prices" of food and necessities. It seems that the Gombeen Man of Famine times had been resurrected, once again gouging the pennies out of the poor.

There was other good news for the police that August. The long-requested War Bonus was at last granted at the less than munificent rate of three shillings and sixpence per week for all ranks from Constable to Head Constable. It was retrospective for only one month and would apply only for the duration of the war. For a Constable like John Hennigan with his service in the band 6 months to 4 years, his pre-war salary of 21 shillings had risen to 23/= per week; with the bonus it was henceforth 26 shillings and sixpence p.w. A Head Constable over four years in the rank would receive 49/6 p.w. DMP constables with 4 - 8 years service now received 32/= per week.

It's worth comparing John's weekly income of 1 pound 6 shillings (£1/6/0) with that of railway workers (before taking into account their own war bonus). A signalman got £2/9/0, a passenger guard £2/3/7 and a lowly porter £1/8/0, two shillings more than John. And, initially at least, the War Bonus was not paid to the families of RIC members who'd gone into the Army.

Contemporary advertisements tell us that a packet of 10 Golden Spangle cigarettes cost fourpence and the Alpha trouser press cost only five shillings. False teeth were available for 15/= a set, with a 10 year guarantee. Barton Smith, cutler of Sligo, offered razor repairs at only eightpence halfpenny, or 1 shilling and threepence for two.

Welcome as any increase in pay was, the enduring Police grievances regarding promotion continued to fester. Despite calls for its abolition, the rank of Acting Sergeant was still in place, giving the ambitious policeman the responsibilities of a Sergeant while remaining on a Constable's pay. Before the war he had to spend two years in the rank before getting the third chevron, now it was effectively three.

Some policemen found it difficult to cope with the increasing pressures on them and official support for the troubled was non-existent. In August Constable Spellman shot himself in the police station at Rosses Point, Co. Sligo; That September, Con. John Corcoran in Cork put a rifle to his head.

There was practical sympathy from other policemen. Members of the London Metropolitan force subscribed £100 at 1/= per head to a fund for the dependants of RIC members killed in the Easter Rising.

Wartime austerity measures took many forms. In October policemen were told that the period of wear for uniform items before replacement was being extended. Helmets were now expected to last for ten years instead of seven, greatcoats and capes would not now be replaced for six years instead of four and no new tunics would be issued except to Head Constables. In the spirit of generosity which didn't require expenditure, the authorities allowed policemen to retain one old greatcoat and cape for use in exceptionally foul weather.

Some news was good. In November the Chief Secretary announced to the House of Commons and the world that the RIC was being granted a pensionable pay rise of three shillings a week, retrospective for six months.

With something approaching a living wage at last achieved, ordinary policemen could consider their other grievances. Apart from the structurally embedded promotion problem, dissatisfaction was generated by a litany of petty, idiotic and frustrating regulations. With the Constabulary Code in his hand, a Bog Kaiser Sergeant or power-propelled DI could make a Constable's life a misery. These "constant petty tyrannies" of which police letter-writers complained included:

- No privacy when living communally in barracks. Even Sergeants' married quarters were not sacrosanct as officers carrying out their inspection duties were required to inspect everywhere.
- Having no right to go for a walk or ride his bicycle without getting permission and stating his destination.
- Having to be indoors at 10pm for roll-call, even when off-duty on a summer evening or sitting with friends in their home.
- Never, or hardly ever, being able to take off the government's uniform and relax in plain clothes off-duty.
- Being unable to marry until seven years had been served, and even then having to apply for permission.
- Being unable to live within a County's length of a relative.
- Being unable to live within a County's length of a wife's relative.

- Prohibited from selling a chicken or an egg, i.e. forbidden to earn any money outside the job.
- Prohibited from keeping a goat, cow, pig or lodger – with rare exceptions.

And the question was asked: is all this necessary "for the good of the service"?

The *Gazette* and its correspondents predicted an exodus to the Dominions once wartime restrictions had been lifted.

On the 1st October 1916 daylight-saving time ended and clocks were put back for the winter months. In Ireland, however, the clocks went back only 35 minutes. By resolution of Parliament in London, Dublin Mean Time was abolished and Ireland brought into the zone of Greenwich Mean Time. Up to then Dublin had been officially 25 minutes and 21 seconds behind GMT , and Dublin Time had been generally accepted around Ireland since the coming of the railways. Chambers of Commerce had campaigned for the change but there were many, especially advanced nationalists, who opposed this new extension of English hegemony. Edward Carson was in favour; Constance Marcievicz against.

The press reported in November that five DMP constables had been brought up before the Chief Commissioner on charges related to agitation of a wage increase. Also in the press, Sir Francis Vane, pressured to resign his Army commission, explained how he had attempted to arrest Capt. Bowen Colthurst for the murders of Francis Sheehy Skeffington and two other civilians during the Easter Rising. In Sligo, the monument to P.A. McHugh was unveiled by John Redmond to "deafening cheers". However, one journalist remarked that Sligo's sanitation was not the best and that "there are some miserable hovels in the place". The McHugh statue is remarkable in itself, the figure's attitude resembling nothing so much as a man standing at a bar with a pint in his hand.

In December the police had a new duty: the observation of returning internees to see how they behaved themselves. The IG believed it unsafe to allow released rebels to reside in maritime areas. As a former soldier, he would have been acutely aware that the Easter insurgents had identified the Central Powers as their "Gallant Allies in Europe". With increasing German U-boat activity killing ships around Ireland it was a legitimate concern.

Sir John Maxwell was promoted and transferred to Britain. He was replaced by Sir Bryan Mahon, a Galway man and the former commander of the 10th (Irish) Division. Of greater concern to most people was the rise in the cost of foodstuffs due to profiteering. In Britain, Lloyd George's new government had slapped a limit of one shilling on the price of a stone (6kg) of potatoes. In Ireland they had reached three shillings.

1917: Feelings Intensify

In 1917, Germany would resume Unlimited Submarine Warfare, sinking all and any shipping without warning. In the "War Zone" a quarter of merchant shipping was sunk and the loss of life among defenceless civilian seamen was appalling. The entry of the United States into the war in March was followed by the arrival of a US destroyer flotilla at Queenstown (Cobh) in Cork harbour, making it the main base for defending the Western Approaches from U-boats. Catholic Churchmen worried about the effect on the moral welfare of Cork's young women and there were street brawls between American sailors and local men. One Corkman was killed and the sailors were confined to Queenstown. In April, the Donegal DI noted that three vessels had been sunk off the NW coast and a minesweeper blown up. A British submarine base was established in Lough Swilly.

The one-act plays of Eugene O'Neill later gave expression to the experiences of the quietly heroic merchant seamen who earned a precarious living on those waters.

In January, the police management reported that farming was "very remunerative" but that, while farmers were well-off, the cottiers were desperate. The export of potatoes was stopped and a tillage campaign introduced. Fortunately shoals of herring appeared off the coast. In February the IG noted further rises in the price of food and that potatoes were being held back by farmers as there was a graduated price arrangement in place. Political unrest continued to spread beneath the surface. The IG himself believed that younger Nationalists were moving towards Sinn Fein, in the conviction that constitutional agitation had failed. There were occasional prosecutions for singing Rebel songs, most notably. "Who fears to speak of Easter Week?"

A simple demographic fact is of considerable importance: Ireland had a higher proportion of unemployed, healthy young men than any of the other belligerent nations where conscription was the norm. Only neutral countries such as Spain and Portugal could have had as many undamaged young men free to follow their own pursuits, and with small prospect of finding a job they had little incentive to do as their elders told them. Joining a Sinn Fein Club and participating in its activities was a great antidote to boredom. Many young women would have had exactly the same motivation and enjoyed their new freedom to consort with young men. And if the older generation didn't approve of this youthful rebelliousness, so much the better: they were too old and settled to understand anyway.

Policemen, whether their personal politics were Unionist or Home Rule, had to be on the side of stability and the preservation of order. Nationalists would be seen as stolidly acquiescing in the status quo while hoping for the promised constitutional change. They were about to face people who felt the exhilaration of revolutionary fervour and "All that delirium of the brave". For the young, it was an intensely romantic impulse.

When Willie Redmond M.P. spoke to the House of Commons in April before leaving to join his regiment in France, he restated the views of Tom Kettle and others who saw the war against German aggression as an opportunity for Britain and Ireland –

North and South: "… is it not possible from this war to make a new start; whether it is not possible on your side, and on ours as well, to let the dead past bury its dead, and to commence a brighter and a newer and a friendlier era between the countries?" It was his final speech and the cause of reconciliation for which he died would soon also be dead. When in June 1917 the men of the the 16th Irish and the 36th Ulster Divisions fought and died side by side the dream was as close to the actual as it would ever be.

In February, Tom Kettle had produced "Paddy", a wry parody of Kipling's "Tommy".

Yes, sneerin' round at Irishmen and Irish Speech and ways
Is cheaper much than snatchin' guns from battle's red amaze
And when the damned Death's Head Dragoons roll up the ruddy tide
The Times won't spare a Smith to tell how Dan O'Connell died.
For it's Paddy this and Paddy that, and
"The Fifth'll prate and prance"
But it's "Corks and Inniskillings – Front!" when hell is loose in France,
When Clare and Kerry take the call that crowns the shrapnel dance.
Oh, it's "Find the Dublin Fusiliers" when hell is loose in France.

In February too, the RIC Cycling Club held its Annual Ball at the Literary Institute in Ballyshannon. The proceeds went to the Comfort Fund of the Irish Guards.

All through the spring of 1917, the IG's reports refer to the "exhorbitant (sic.) cost of the necessities of life" and that while farmers were enjoying great prosperity, labourers' wages were still inadequate. Sir Joseph Byrne also repeatedly observed that while circumstances such as the apparent failure of a Home Rule settlement and the fear of conscription were promoting sympathy with SF, the movement did not attract "people with a stake in the country". This rather naïve view that a revolutionary movement needs "people of influence" for leadership was a product of its times and occurs in the reports of many County Inspectors. A more pragmatic police officer, DI John M. Regan, was under no such illusion. "Even a farm labourer, if possessed of sufficient determination and intelligence, could be a person of very considerable importance indeed in a revolutionary organisation."

In February a Roscommon by-election resulted in the success of Count Plunkett, father of the executed Joseph Mary Plunkett. While this event is often seen as the first victory of a Sinn Fein electoral strategy, Plunkett was not a SF candidate but stood as an Independent supported by SF and there was a strong sympathy vote. There were many disparate groups involved during a disorganised election campaign fought in three weeks of blinding snowstorms; the SF organisation had not yet committed to the electoral process. Only after his election did Plunkett reveal his intention not to take his seat in Parliament. He did become a SF Vice President in 1918 but never sat easily within the organisation.

In an April editorial the Nationalist *Sligo Champion* drew a clear distinction between the honourable personality of Count Plunkett and the Sinn Fein party "the rag, tag and bobtail of Irish politics".

In the first half of 1917, Sinn Fein won a series of by-elections, perhaps indicating as much a growing rejection of the Irish Parliamentary Party as expressing clear support for Sinn Fein. The IPP had failed to deliver Home Rule and its credibility had evaporated. SF opposition to the threat of conscription was popular. By July, the RIC were under some pressure in the more volatile areas. A station at Ballybunion was attacked by a mob. Returning fire, the police killed one man. At Nenagh, Joseph McDonagh was reported as saying "whenever the police are going to baton you, baton them. Whenever the police are going to shoot you, shoot them. They are responsible for 90% of the crime in Ireland." The IG reported that in some parts, Sinn Feiners "will hardly speak to a policeman". Donegal, however, remained peaceful. While SF clubs were being established, the movement there had no "substantial leaders" and it seems the Catholic Bishop of Raphoe opposed SF. Certainly, Cardinal Logue and most of the Hierarchy were strongly against it.

At Ballyshannon Petty Sessions on 23rd March there were a few cases of drunkenness. In the Children's Court a "young lad" was charged with the larceny of a vest and coat. DI Tyndall made application to have the boy removed from "his present circumstances" and committed to Industrial School "in the interests of the boy". The order was made and the Court rose.

From the 1st April new restrictions on the wine and spirit trade were introduced across the United Kingdom. Clearances from bonded warehouses were to be limited to 50% of the previous year's transactions. Also, a duty increase was expected in the coming Budget. There would be a number of consequences. As stocks were already depleted, many small Irish pubs faced closure. In official circles this was regarded as a good thing as Ireland was seen to have too many pubs. It was expected that thousands of licences would be extinguished, the costs to be borne by surviving licences. And a concern to the police was the inevitable increase in illicit distilling.

In mid-April, "a long-felt want has been supplied" by Mr Andrew Brennan with his opening of a daily charabanc service between Sligo and Ballyshannon. At five shillings for the return trip, it wasn't cheap nor, at an average speed of about 10 mph, was it particularly quick but it would have suited commercial people.

Sgt Green was conspicuous in the potato market, taking the names of traders charging as much as two shillings per stone of potatoes, twice the approved price.

The anniversary of the Easter Rising brought increased tension. Republican flags appeared overnight on public buildings and the police were given the onerous and sometimes dangerous task of removing them. Overall morale still appeared good. A poem by "Justin" appeared in the *Gazette*:

They bear the good old Irish names
Of common stock, these stalwart men.
They carry well their supple frames,
In sombre garb in street and glen,
And they have human hearts within
Where kindness gushes at its source,
And gleams out in a genial grin,
For that's the custom of the force.

Through early 1917 there was action against profiteers. At the market in Athlone, farmers tried to force up the price of potatoes to £1 a hundredweight (c. 50Kg) by holding back stocks. They declared the opening price to be 15 shillings as had been reached in the previous week, and the buyers reacted angrily. The police intervened: the official price allowed was 8/=. When the farmers tried to withdraw with their potatoes they were blocked by the angry crowd and forced to sell at the official price. The police then took similar action on eggs and milk. Their intervention was appreciated by the purchasers.

At the potato market in Cookstown, police warned vendors

not to charge more than eight shillings a hundredweight. If a higher price had already been paid, a refund was ordered.

At Clones market Police again enforced the legal limit of 8 shillings. The story was repeated in Dungannon but there the farmers held back: only six loads were sold compared to seventy at similar markets the previous year. However, the Police were aware that potatoes were being illegally sold at £11 per ton, or £1. 2 shillings per hundredweight, contrary to the Potato Main Crop Regulations.

At Ballyshannon Petty Sessions in June, Sgt Greer prosecuted a number of farmers. The fines imposed ranged from 2s 6d to ten shillings.

At the same court Patrick Sandford was prosecuted for setting fire to furze within sight of the sea. It was the first such prosecution under DORA so Sandford was fined only two shillings and sixpence and a general warning was given. DI Tyndall pointed out that notices were posted at all police stations.

There were humorous moments. A policeman who went to Mrs McIlhatton's door in Dungannon to see why a man was knocking on it scared the man away but received a bottle of rum through the letterbox. The whole story emerged at the Petty Sessions.

Alongside the campaign against sheebeens the time-honoured efforts to combat illicit distillation continued – at least officially. In February while the RIC party on Revenue duty was leaving Inishmurray Island, boatman McCourt slipped and fell into the sea as he loosed the mooring cable. There was a strong tide running and McCourt was in danger of drowning. Con. Barry from Cliffoney immediately jumped into the sea, boots, greatcoat and all, and assisted him. They managed to scramble onto the rocks and were rescued. The coastline of North Sligo in mid-winter is no place for total immersion and it must have taken a severe application of poteen to thaw out the two bathers. A couple of months later Con. Barry received the Bronze Medal of the Royal Humane Society for his action.

In an editorial comment entitled "Looking Ahead" the *Gazette* speculated about the future of the RIC in the post-war world. Implicitly evoking Turner's much-loved painting "The Fighting Temeraire" the piece used an image of an unreformed RIC being scrapped like one of the Navy's "wooden walls" in a fleet of modern battleships, a "picturesque anachronism". Reforms were needed for survival, among them issues such as promotion and a more civilised way of keeping married and single policemen in accommodation.

Daily life continued. A Dungannon Constable, fed up with comrades borrowing his helmet, inscribed inside it "Drop it. It's not yours".

June brought some good news for policemen as some of their grievances were addressed. Roll Call – effectively a curfew for those off-duty, was put back till 11pm. The leave period was extended from 7 to 10 days. The War Bonus was increased so that a married Constable with one child now received an extra four shillings and sixpence per week, with another shilling for each extra child. The unmarried were granted two shillings per week extra.The DMP received the same increases. In an editorial the *Gazette* said: "General Byrne is a soldier, and a soldier is usually a man of few words, and since the appointment of Gen. Byrne to the command of the RIC they have received more practical and substantial benefit than in all the years of his predecessors".

As well as the abiding grievance regarding promotion prospects, the duty of Barrack Orderly was a burden to many. In three-man stations, which had become more numerous, this irksome duty was shared between the two Constables which meant bearing the 24 hour responsibility on alternate days. One solution would have entailed the Sergeant taking a turn but another option was a return to 5 or 6 man stations. That would have reduced the number of Sergeants needed and reduced promotion prospects even further.

On 27th July Constable J.H. of Bundoran appeared at the Ballyshannon Petty Sessions, prosecuting James M for "being drunk on the public street". Mullen was fined 3/6 (three shillings and sixpence) plus 1/6 costs, with 7 days imprisonment in lieu.

At the same court, Sgt Farnon prosecuted Constantine Maguire with offering for sale "six ounces of Epsom salts containing 50 parts Arsenic per million, the amount allowed being 5 parts". The case was adjourned. One wonders about the consequences of such a concentration for Maguire's customers.

The police were not very effective in dealing with the illegal but popular pastime of cock-fighting. It seems to have been most prevalent in Ulster counties and the enthusiasts were more mobile and adaptable than the minions of the law. When policemen were in pursuit, they were adept at shifting location and often changed road signs around to confuse their pursuers. When one cockfight was scheduled for an island in Lough Neagh the bird fanciers simply commandeered all the boats along 20 miles of shoreline. Twelve main fights were held as the beached policemen stood helpless. Later, the frustrated Peelers intercepted some returning enthusiasts but could do no more than take names. All the boats were duly returned to their owners.

July brought D.W. Griffith's monumental film "Birth of a Nation" to the Opera House. In scathing comment on the failure of Britain's air defences – commanded by Sir John French – against German Zeppelin attacks, the *Vindicator* said: "Again, and once again, the failure of the war, must go. Removed from France, his feelings were spared by being appointed to the air command. Here again he is found to be incompetent. French must go." The editor could not have imagined that when Field Marshal French finally went, it was to Ireland he would go.

In the sort of despotic heavy-handed action which alienated moderate Nationalists, the Military seized the offices of the *Kilkenny People* and put the plant out of action.

Attitudes were hardening and signs were ominous. When Countess Marcievicz was granted the Freedom of Sligo Borough in July, she signed the roll as 'Constance de Marcievicz, I.R.A.'

That autumn farmers were still making money. The potato crop was abundant. Herrings fetched a good price. Alcohol being scarce and expensive, the police noted that drunkenness was below average but a rise in illicit distilling would soon become evident. As German U-boats savaged merchant shipping offshore, many in Donegal found a new income in salvage especially of rubber and oil.

A *Sligo Champion* report on wreckage washed up at Tirearagh illustrates the ferocity of the conflict at sea. Portions of a ship, two lifeboats, life buoys, logs, planks, fruit, meat, tobacco, five or six dead horses, and some cans of petrol were thrown up after a storm. Whether flotsam or jetsam, it could be someone else's bounty and we may wonder how much had disappeared from the beach before the police got there.

In early August a new order was promulgated by the Military Authorities prohibiting the "use or wearing in any public place of uniforms of a military character by persons other than the naval, military or police forces of the Crown". A further order prohibited the "carrying of any weapons of an offensive character". This meant that hurleys could be carried only when being used for sporting purposes. A couple of weeks later the National Volunteer HQ on Dublin's Parnell Square was raided by military, police and G Men who seized 100 rifles, blank ammunition and documents. The Newry Independent Club was raided and rifles of the National Volunteers were seized. These had last been aired in Easter 1916 when NVs and Ulster Volunteers turned out to guard the Post Office and railway station. Other raids across Ulster seized more NV rifles.

In Letterkenny the Catholic Parochial Hall was raided and two doors broken down. According to the Parish Priest "They found no arms but of course will have their success in turning the people from constitutional guidance". The priest was more clear-sighted in his assessment than the heavy-handed authorities.

In early August Ballyshannon's first Sinn Fein club was established, with Rev CC Tierney in the chair. A letter from Fr Flanagan was read: "The spirit of Sinn Fein is to do what we think is right and to respect the opinions of all honest men who differ from us. We do not wish to force our opinions upon anyone else." Fr Tierney elucidated: "There was nothing revolutionary about SF, the movement was a constitutional one... whatever should be done should be done by orderly methods, and that they should respect the opinions of their opponents, whether Parliamentarians, Nationalists or Unionists".

By September Thomas Ashe was dying on hunger strike and Eamon De Valera, at Ennis, reproached the RIC for "doing the dirty work of the enemy". On 25th September, Ashe died in Mountjoy Jail and on the 29th a Commemoration was held in Bundoran. That must have been a tense day for John Hennigan and his colleagues. Demonstrating how Government policy exacerbated the situation and was radicalising moderate nationalist opinion, the *Vindicator* stated that its editorial comment was restrained only because of the pressure of censorship. "Feeling in Ireland was never so much on the rack and who can say what the madness of the moment may bring forth."

Remembering the death of Capt Noel Chevasse, the army doctor who'd won the Victoria Cross twice and given his life in trying to save others, the paper said "The British Government sent his brother to jail for giving his name in Irish in Co. Donegal". One might suspect a leg-pull, given that Chevasse was English-born and it's a name not easily Gaelicised without humour. Ó Capaill, perhaps

While IG Byrne believed rebellion was improbable without German help, he reported in October that the "position of the RIC distributed in small parties, throughout a hostile population, is becoming more difficult and dangerous". He suggested that future offenders should be interned under DORA regulations or sent to English prisons. Otherwise hunger-strikes would open the prison doors.

There were tensions within Sinn Fein too. Liam de Róiste complained "The military side of the movement is now actively and aggressively working to dominate the civil side". Members of SF who were not also Volunteers were being pushed out of responsible positions. A very significant event in that process occurred at the Sinn Fein Árd Fhéis, or general assembly, in October when Arthur Griffith withdrew as a candidate for the Presidency of the party in favour of Eamon De Valera. That effectively shifted the party's ostensible objective to the achievement of a republic rather than any lesser form of self-government, though it's debatable how many delegates were aware of that.

In Donegal the Inspector General on his grand tour inspected the men of Raphoe under the command of DI Moore, lately transferred from Sligo. In Leitrim more NV rifles were seized. In no case was any live ammunition found.

In October the *Constabulary Gazette* suggested some reforms:

- Maximum pay attainable in 10 years
- Promotion to Sergeant attainable after 12 -15 years and the rank of Acting Sergeant abolished
- Marriage to be not only permitted but encouraged after 2-3 years

- Rural stations to be made comfortable with relaxing room and private cubicles for sleep.

These suggestions, alongside disarmament, would remain no more than aspirations.

One widely-welcomed innovation was the appointment of two women constables to the DMP. After training in London, they were given official badges but not a uniform. They had no power of arrest but could hand over miscreants to a policeman.

A joke circulating among policemen at the time told of a publican being ribbed for making his money out of gin, brandy etc. "I didn't make money out of them. I lost it. I made money out of the water." Perhaps there was a message there for the Weights and Measures Sergeant.

In November the *Gazette* again suggested "Good Service Pay" as a recompense for extra civil duties such as administering the Census. As things stood there was no reward for the Constable who tackled his given tasks enthusiastically and diligently above what was given to a colleague who was a slacker. Even the Sergeants who were Weights and Measures Inspectors, doing a job which in Britain was undertaken by well-paid civilians, received no extra remuneration beyond what came to them as a share in penalties imposed on convicted offenders. If they were too successful in their efforts, the fines would dry up.

It is interesting that throughout the history of the RIC accusations of corruption were never heard. Even in the most bitter days of "The Troubles", charges of bribery were not voiced by Republican propagandists. Opportunities for "shopping with the helmet" there must have been but availing himself of them would not just put a man's job at risk; it would earn him the contempt of his colleagues. As veteran John McKenna put it: "Esprit de Corps…was characteristic of the RIC. The members were never known to accept a bribe or money for services rendered to individuals". And again, "Accepting free drinks from civilians was regarded as mean and men in the habit of doing so were regarded as being unworthy of the Force in this respect".

The "County System" of promotion, where opportunities were linked to vacancies arising within a particular county, entailed great disparity in a policeman's prospects. Of course the underlying and abiding problem with promotion lay in the Cadet System; abolition was the only answer.

A meeting of the District force, held with permission of the IG, put forward a list of predictable suggestions for reform. However, equally predictably, the authorities declined to give further increases in pay. A Constabulary petition, carrying 11,000 signatures had asked for an increase of £2-3 per month.

Arising from the fact that some DIs insisted that a sanctioned absence after midnight had to be counted as another day's leave, there was a comment which reveals something of social life in rural areas. "A dance, as everyone knows, commences at 9 or 10 o'clock and ceases at 6 or 7 a.m".

It was also reported in November that Private T. Moore, serving with the Canadian contingent, had been severely wounded by shellfire in France. He was the eldest son of DI Moore in Raphoe and had enlisted from his job with the Canadian Bank of Commerce. In Ballyshannon, John Hennigan was under the command of DI Tyndall.

John Francis Tyndall was a southerner who'd risen through the ranks, a "P man". He'd been educated at the venerable Bishop Foy's School in Waterford. The "Blue School" was a sort of Protestant vocational school which took in working class boys. Tyndall became the school's Head Boy and after entering the Police service his promotion was rapid. He was already a Sergeant when he married in 1897 and was a Head Constable by 1910. He arrived in Ballyshannon as a DI in 1916. He'd previously been awarded a medal with clasp by the Royal Society for saving a child from drowning and had won high praise for apprehending a murderer. Tyndall was no sectarian bigot: while stationed in Clonmel he'd sent his son to a "high level Christian Brothers school to the consternation of the Rector". That son, Charles, who became a Church of Ireland clergyman, later wrote "I was never so well taught in my life".

There's a nice correspondence here with Sgt Shea, a bilingual Kerryman, who was transferred to Clones in 1920. He and his wife decided it was time for their sons to go to secondary school. As there was no Catholic secondary school in Clones, the boys were enrolled in the local Protestant school. Sgt Shea had a blistering interview with his local parish priest but stuck to his decision.

It is clear that Tyndall was an ambitious and capable officer. The reforming Inspector General Sir Andrew Reid had, between 1890 and 1900, embraced "the idea of enticing Secondary School types into the ranks with quick promotion through exams". But, as Tyndall's son Charles pointed out, "The P men were not loved by the general run of RIC men, being regarded as Toffy or superior gents!".

At Ballyshannon Petty Sessions in November, policemen as much as the general population must have been intrigued by an action between Michael Rogan, complainant, vs James Magee. It was alleged that the defendant, Magee, "did knowingly bury the corpse of one Catherine Magee in the burying place and private grave of, and used by the complainant's family without the consent in writing of any immediate relative of the late Catherine Rogan, the complainant's mother and the last member of the family interred in the same private grave, the said Catherine Magee not having been a member of the complainant's family" contrary to the Public Health (Ireland) Act 1878, 41-42 Victoria Cap 52 Section 170.

The case was adjourned. In December 1917 it was Dismissed on Merit meaning that the case had no legal merit and could not be re-entered. The complainant had to pay the defendant ten shillings and sixpence costs. At this remove, one can only speculate about the nature of the relationships which led to this rather squalid legal dispute. Love, lust and land seem likely factors.

The Christmas edition of the *Gazette* saw the difficulties of Ireland and its policemen in a wider context. "It is wholly impossible to be neutral in a war in which a nation is engaged. The war must still be prosecuted to a finish and every man who impedes the forces that are fighting Germany, even by raising his voice, is helping the enemy." To remind readers of the reality of Teutonic aggression it quotes Bismarck advising Germans how to deal with their enemies: "Leave them nothing but eyes to weep with".

Despite Ireland's peripheral position, the war was an external but constant pressure. Sugar rationing cards were being introduced, and numbers in a household were being registered as a preliminary step. SF was actively opposed to any government initiative and some citizens saw the register as a first step to conscription. At Christmas time Shaw and Sons of Limerick advertised their pork products, Beamish & Crawford, (established 1792), promoted their stout and Edwards of Belfast offered desiccated soups. Such delicacies were beyond the reach of many. At the end of the year, 600 bags of flour weighing 7 stone (c.50 kg) each were shipped from Sligo to Belmullet for the relief of people who'd been living on potatoes alone for weeks. Seventy years after the Great Famine, the Erris peninsula was still one of the poorest corners of Europe. In the struggle to distribute the flour the Constabulary had step in to maintain order.

Some time in late 1917 or early 1918, the Depot received a visit from the great Irish dramatist and contrarian G.Bernard Shaw. (He hated the name George.) In 1914, Shaw had annoyed the Authorities by publicising the scandalous shortage of shells on the Western Front but by doing so had saved British soldiers' lives. Shaw loudly advocated Home Rule and was a supporter of the War but had irked the authorities again with his play "O'Flaherty VC". He must have annoyed them even more by defending the right of the 1916 Rebels to take up arms and his efforts to spare Roger Casement from the gallows. Nonetheless, at the Depot he was given a formal reception and recruits in training were paraded in his honour.

A New Iconography

After the Easter Rising, new images began to appear in many Irish houses. The most accessible and affordable were probably the many cards and posters which depicted the executed leaders. The most enduring depiction of the scene inside the GPO has to be Walter Paget's *Birth of the Irish Republic* which did not appear until 1918. With idealised fighters at their posts in the background, the wounded James Connolly is the focus of the painting. It has been much reproduced, and copied but not improved upon in the years since.

The events of 1914 & 1915 had already given Ireland two iconic paintings from apparently opposing viewpoints. Matania's depiction of the Last Absolution being given to the Munster Fusiliers by Fr Gleeson was an emotional evocation of imminent death for many of the Irish soldiers as they moved up to the front line. Prints of this picture were on the walls of many Irish home decades later. In contrast, *Bachelors' Walk In Memory* by Jack B. Yeats is a powerfully emotional commemoration of the shooting dead of three civilians by Scottish troops in Dublin. The image of the flower girl dropping her rose in tribute is a haunting figure.

Sean Keating's *Men of the West* was begun in 1915 but not

exhibited until 1917. Were it not for the Irish tricolour in the background, it could be celebrating cowboys in the American Wild West. His *Men of the South,* however, was painted during the Truce period in 1921 and the models were real IRA men with their own weapons. They are figures in heroic mode.

In *"High Treason, the Court of Criminal Appeal"*, a monumental work some 2m x 3m, Sir John Lavery conjures up the courage and pathos of a noble individual facing the terrible majesty of The Law. Unfinished until after Casement's execution, the scope of the work matches its size. Lavery was present in the courtroom at the invitation of the judge. Because it wasn't on public view until recently, it cannot be seen as contemporary iconography of the revolutionary period but it has great significance for us today. There are many individual portraits within it – the judges in their panoply, the defence team offering their arguments, spectators anguished and curious – but the indisputable focus of the work is the diminutive figure of Roger Casement, doomed but unrepentant in his righteousness. Established power is about to crush naive rebellion but can it snuff out the faint flame of a revolutionary ideal? There are no villains, just the humans who embody two differing views of the world. Lavery, the knighted war artist and Irish nationalist, understood this very well. The painting wasn't completed until the 1930s and his presenting of it to the National Portrait Gallery in London was to endow them with an embarrassment. The public couldn't be trusted to see it for many decades afterwards.

Compared to revolutionary episodes in other countries, there is a remarkable dearth of striking images in contemporary Irish posters. Sinn Fein inspired nothing like the popular images produced by Diego Rivera, for example,. It should be remembered that Ireland, unlike Mexico or Russia, was from the late 19th Century a highly literate society, and revolutionary appeals could be textual and sophisticated. The Irish love their words and poets and polemicists did the job most skilfully. "Stories that live longest are sung above the glass" and ballad-makers told the stories that caught, and wrought, popular opinion.

1918: Little Cheer for the Police

In January 1918, a number of rifles having been stolen from soldiers on leave, the Army decided to no longer allow soldiers to bring their weapons home. A branch of the radical Transport Workers Union was formed at Ballyshannon. There was no serious crime in Donegal and drunkenness was down. A magistrate, Patrick McLaughlin JP, was fined five shillings on 11th January for having in his possession a ram infected with sheep scabies and failing to inform police. On the 13th, after a Sinn Fein meeting in Bundoran, supporters returning to Ballyshannon were attacked with stones by soldiers as they passed Finner Camp. According to the Police, "it was an unwarranted and unprovoked attack". The soldiers were from the 36th Ulster Division and shouts of "Up Sinn Fein" were exchanged with insults against the Pope. Thirteen SF members were injured as were two soldiers. Some revolver shots were fired by SFs but nobody was hit.

Around the country there were frequent raids on farmhouses for guns. Generally shotguns were surrendered peacefully if not willingly but one elderly former soldier tackled intruders who had mistreated his wife. Grappling with one of them he was shot three times but the wounds were not immediately fatal.

Although Donegal was peaceful, agrarian agitation continued in other parts of rural Ireland. In Galway and Clare, the Land War had been constantly bubbling since the 1880s. In those counties, 182 people were under police protection which for the policemen often meant manning 'protection huts' – Board of Works structures, cold, inhospitable and vulnerable.

The New Year brought some good news for the Roberts. An increase in the War Bonus was granted and back-dated to 1st December. This meant an extra £1 or so next payday. A report from London and the Home Counties was a reminder that one's neighbours could be worse off. Each adult there was allowed four coupons per week for meat. Sausages could be made of horse, butcher's meat or offal. The weekly allowance amounted to one shilling and threepence worth of butcher's meat plus other meats equivalent to 5 ounces of butcher's meat. The other meats could be bird, bacon, hare, rabbit, venison or horse. Back home, 25 tons of Donegal herrings were offered for sale; these were cured fish in barrels.

A public meeting of the Women's Patrols in Dublin revealed that from January 1916 to January 1917 they'd brought 34 cases and secured 33 convictions in the courts. Those involved were 21 men and 13 women and the charges were "immorality and indecency in the streets".

The Chief Secretary dampened spirits in February by announcing that there would be no change in the system of promotion. Ambitious rankers were again deprived of incentives and left to consider their many real grievances. In many police stations the Sergeant's wife and family had no real privacy as they had to share much of their living space with unmarried policemen. Constables were being put in charge of some small posts without remuneration or any distinguishing insignia.

"He has to exercise authority without such authority being recognised." Even if rewarded by promotion to Acting Sergeant, he received two stripes but not a penny extra. Head Constables were also in a very difficult position. Senior HCs were being denied further promotion because of the age restrictions. For every DI post which became available, 100 or more experienced HCs had to be passed over solely on age grounds. As 48 was the cut-off age for a HC's promotion, only the younger and less experienced were eligible for the District Inspector rank.

In a speech at Dundalk Eoin McNeill offered some interesting opinions: "No doubt the police had received instructions from their officers not to protect order but to protect disorder. At the same time he believed that no one could cherish a republic more than the police themselves. Many of them would be delighted to hear the words IRC instead of RIC".

IG Joseph Byrne earned more respect and gratitude from his men when it was announced that the rank of Acting Sergeant was to be abolished forthwith and all those with two stripes were to be given the third immediately. However, there was still no allowance given to Sergeants performing the duties of Weights and Measures Inspectors. A humane but belated concession was the extension of the War Bonus to those who had "married without permission".

On the other hand, Sir Joseph's tolerance did not extend to those who opposed the political status quo. On the eve of St Patrick's Day his office issued an order that, in the event of police having to deal with unlawful assembly accompanied by bands, the Constabulary were authorised to seize the instruments and break them up on the spot. To smash an Irish musician's instruments, whatever his politics, seems an extremely insensitive and provocative act. The directive may or may not have been implemented.

Some policemen were becoming more outspoken in their

expression of grievances. In Britain some of the police had succeeded in re-establishing the National Union of Police and Prison Officers which had previously been organised and suppressed in 1913. Some members of the RIC and DMP set up an Irish Branch of the NUPPO with Sgt T.J. McElligott as its general secretary. These moves were opposed by the editor of the *Constabulary Gazette* but supported by the *Irish Independent.*

There was a spate of cattle drives, often turning violent. A special promotion to Sergeant was given to Con. John Egan of Clare who, when his two companions were floored and disarmed by a hostile mob on a cattle drive, stood his ground, fired his weapon and allowed all three opportunity to retrieve the stolen carbines and safely withdraw. There is no indication that anyone apart from the two policemen was injured.

Cattle drives, the forcible removal of cattle from disputed farmland, continued to be a major occasion of conflict between agrarian activists and the authorities. Whatever local policemen may have thought, the attitude from on high was uncompromising. In a circular at the end of May, the IG's instructions to the Police were clear: "It is essential that such parties should be roughly handled and compelled to accompany and drive back the cattle to the place whence they took them". It's easy to see how agrarian grievances in western counties became entangled with constitutional issues and how government reaction only provoked further animosity. And telling policemen to "roughly handle" those who broke the law wasn't calculated to improve relations between Constabulary and community. It must have been seen as the police taking the side of the "ranchers", i.e. graziers, against the small farmers – the stock most policemen themselves came from. Were it not for the bother it caused them, many Peelers might have approved of the slogan: "The land for the people and the road for the bullocks".

Between the 7th and the 9th March 1918, regimental colours of the Connaught Rangers which had been laid up in the little Catholic garrison church at Renmore, Galway were stolen. The *Connacht Tribune* reported it as "Daring Sacrilege at Renmore Church". Acccording to the report: "The police have made diligent enquiries but have failed to find any clues. It is supposed that the perpetrators of this daring outrage removed the colours by gaining entry to the church with a skeleton key." The editorial in the *Galway Observer* said "the larceny of the colours of the Connaught Rangers – sacrilege rather – from the chapel at Renmore was no doubt a considerable capture by the Sinn Fein soldiers". The pro-Sinn Fein *Galway Express* used its report of the theft to poke fun at the Rangers and at Nationalist civic dignitaries.

There was a reminder of the U-Boat menace in a new order from Admiral Bayly, Commander in Chief of the naval forces in Ireland, restricting the use of lights for five miles inland. From sunset to sunrise windows had to be blacked out and blinds had to be used on trains and other conveyances. Enforcing the blackout was yet another responsibility for policemen.

Behind the Castle Walls

Far above the discomforts and dangers of everyday policing, intrigue in the higher levels of Britain's administration in Ireland became more and more intense. John Denton Pinkstone French became a presence in Irish politics. As Chief of the Imperial General Staff in 1912, Sir John French had given an undertaking to Hubert Gough that the Army would not be used to enforce Home Rule in the North East. Appointed Commander of the BEF in 1914, he had not, it was alleged, given adequate support to his French allies as they were being slaughtered in the ferocious German advance. Replaced by Haig in 1915, French was 'parked' as Commander of Home Forces for the duration. In that role he had dispatched Gen. Maxwell to Ireland at Easter 1916 and supported Maxwell's policy of executing the rebel leaders.

Early in 1918 the Government had the notion of setting up a triumvirate of "Justices" to exercise the powers and duties normally carried out by the Chief Secretary. These three -French for military and police matters, James Campbell looking after legal matters and Lord Midleton dealing with civil affairs – would run Ireland. It was unworkable. In May, French was established as Lord Lieutenant with wide-ranging powers.

The new Viceroy saw himself as a Pro-Consul or military governor. He wanted conscription introduced and military law established in Ireland and set about displacing those who did not share his views

Lt Gen. Bryan Mahon, General Officer Commanding in Ireland (and former commander of the 10th Irish Division at Gallipoli), and Sir Joseph Byrne assessed the likely results of imposing conscription in Ireland. The report by the top soldier and top policeman was extremely negative. They concluded that conscription could be implemented but only with the greatest difficulty. "It would be bitterly opposed by the united Nationalists and Clergy". They forecast the need to divert extra troops to Ireland, military rule, mass arrests, bloodshed and disruption. And the harvest of able-bodied men would be doubtful in numbers and reliability. Byrne was even more pessimistic than Mahon. This was not what Sir John French wanted to hear.

Like many a successful man, French was a contradictory fish. Owning two Irish properties, he considered himself Irish, and a Home Ruler, and made clear his intention to remain in Ireland once a settlement had been reached. In the microcosm of Dublin Castle, he and his mistress "the beautiful Mrs Bennett" were whispered about as "Pinkie and the fairy".

He was certainly a politician. Gen. Bryan Mahon was dropped as Commander in Chief in Ireland and French worked to marginalise and get rid of IG Byrne.

1918: The Conscription threat returns

Lower ranking policemen could have had no notion of the goings-on at Cabinet level and in the higher echelons of the Irish administration. Higher-ranking Police officers may have had intimations and suspicions but this was wartime and speculation was dangerous. On the other hand, everybody knew that the Germans, with their opponents on the Eastern Front out of the war, were trying to defeat the Western Allies before the Americans arrived in force. And they were very close to doing it. France was bled dry and Britain's manpower reserves were exhausted – except for Ireland.

Irish public frustration and anger erupted in springtime. The Constitutional Convention reported on its utter failure to come close to an agreed settlement of the Home Rule issue. Then in April the IG reported to the government: "Early in the month the country became ablaze with furious resentment" at the passage of the Military Service Bill, allowing for conscription to be imposed on Ireland. It was clear that if the government decided to go ahead, the onus would fall on the unfortunate RIC to implement it; in the absence of a Register of Males, the authorities would have to rely on their local knowledge. One Constable later stated: "After the Rising had died down there was nothing of note that took place till the Conscription Act for Ireland was passed. As far as I can remember the police resented this to a man and I believe that had any attempt been made to enforce it, the police would not have done it."

Sir Joseph Byrne pointed out that "for the first time the RIC has been assailed through their consciences by the Church. Some priests are saying enforcement of conscription would be a mortal sin – tantamount to murder". In Donegal as elsewhere, conscription overshadowed every other issue. It was probably a key factor in alienating people from the RIC. De Valera was telling SF that Conscription would suit their policy; they should shoot the recruiting agents. Boycotts of police had already begun in 1917.

In May, a "German plot" was wondrously discovered by the government and facilitated the internment of 51 people including De Valera. Other SF leaders headed warnings and went into hiding. The *Gazette* rather fatuously referred to the exercise as "a brilliant piece of police work, admirably conceived and ably executed", thus demonstrating that myopia wasn't just the monopoly of the politicians. What the government had done was lock up many people who would be considered moderates.

Government decisions and indecisions, actions and inactions in the first half of 1918 were very ill-judged and unhelpful to moderates. By pushing through legislation permitting conscription in Ireland it had united in opposition Catholic clergy of all levels, Nationalists and Sinn Fein. But when conscription was not enforced, it was Sinn Fein that got the credit.

A policeman's letter, captioned "Petticoat government causes transfers", referred to one of the perils of those barracks which constables shared with their sergeant's family. It alleged that during the Sergeant's absence from his County Derry station his wife listened and took notes of conversations in the day room. When the Sergeant returned, she talked and he believed and reported upwards. The result was the immediate transfer of two policemen.

For the next couple of months Donegal remained prosperous and peaceful. Instances of wartime restrictions were five shilling fines imposed for selling food without a licence and the prosecution of Helen Lockhart of Scotland and Rev. Fullerton C.C, of Belfast for visiting Tory Island without a permit.

June 1918 brought more ominous signs. In Kerry an attempt was made to murder two policemen, leaving Sgt Fallon wounded. Worse, some hundred bystanders helped the gunmen to escape. Arthur Griffith was elected as MP for East Cavan and Sligo Corporation gave the Freedom of the Borough to Fr Flanagan, the SF Vice-President (and formerly the Curate at Cliffoney, between Sligo and Bundoran). In Buncrana there was unrest after a travelling cinematograph showed a film of Thomas Ashe's funeral. A few months later, a cinema film "Rory O'More" was taken off by police in Buncrana as being "of a nature detrimental to recuiting". During a service at a church in Co. Longford, three policemen left and told the priest that they'd been annoyed by a section of the congregation. Fr Keville condemned those responsible, saying that if the police were replaced by military people would be worse off.

In a heavy-handed response to the growth of separatism, on 5th July Lord French proscribed Sinn Fein, SF Clubs, Irish Volunteers, Cumann na mBan, and the Gaelic League. The consequent raids and dispersal of meetings did not win the RIC any friends. Lord French, did not, however, order the detention of his radical sister, SF member Charlotte Despard – an omission which would be regretted by the new Free State Government in 1922.

A 50% rise in rail fares affected policemen as much as any section of the population inasmuch as they were not given concessionary rates. The *Gazette* complained: "It is disgraceful that the RIC War Bonus should be so substantially lower than that awarded to every other class in the community" and suggested that the cause was that the disenfranchised policemen, unlike other interests and their British colleagues, could not put their case directly to politicians. It also noted that "It is notorious that the spirit of lawlessness in Ireland is so prevalent that in many districts the lives of the Constabulary are unsafe". Perhaps it was that spirit which led to the government admission that "Colonial" troops were not being allowed to spend their leave in Ireland and its hedging the question in Parliament by saying it was a matter for the national contingent concerned.

There was a whiff of alcohol in the air. A report of the seizure of a still and wash in Belfast, referring to the tenacity of one policeman, said that the saying "'It takes a Connaughtman to smell poteen' is a truism". A Professor Daly of Harvard University advanced the theory that German barbarism was due to the lifelong drinking of beer. "Those crimes have been ordered by men who for decades have been poisoned by beer". The unintended consequences of the Volstead Act which brought Prohibition to the USA must surely have led to some modification of Prof. Daly's theory.

Yet the normal patterns of life seemed to continue in South Donegal. On 26th July, Denis Maguire was brought before Ballyshannon Petty Sessions by Constable John H. on a charge of drunkenness. He was fined 3 shillings and sixpence (3/6) plus 1 shilling costs, the alternative being seven days in jail.

Mr Balfour asserted in the Commons that the Germans were advocating polygamy as an answer to the demographic imbalance caused by the astounding loss of their young men in battle. Frederick the Great of Prussia was said to have recommended the practice after one of his more sanguinary campaigns. This led the *Gazette* to sourly contrast that approach with the ban on RIC members marrying during their most biologically productive years. But while few RIC were dying in battle on the Continent, another killer was abroad. Even among policemen, probably the healthiest and fittest males in the Irish population, deaths from influenza were being constantly noted.

In early August, the *Gazette* put forward the suggestion that the new Lord Lieutenant, Field Marshall French, be invited "as an Irishman" to see for himself the conditions under which the Constabulary had to live and work. In an editorial it fulminated "The maintenance of a DI or HC taking charge between them of a half dozen rural stations is a monstrous waste of money. Both one and other of them are inadequately paid: both are dissatisfied: the bill is excessive and the result demoralising". In a following editorial the editor hit his stride: "The RIC machine corresponds exactly with a wooden velocipede – a marvellous invention fifty years ago. No man has ever had the courage to throw it on the scrap heap and construct a new one". "We believe that the RIC like the Dublin slums, needs an earthquake or something thereto akin to make it habitable."

It is incontestable that the pay and conditions for Irish policemen were well behind those of their British colleagues. At this distance one is tempted to think that, for the ruling class and officialdom, the Irish police forces were just another segment of the "mere Irish".

On 17th August, Constable J.H. brought up Peter Kangley on a vagrancy charge, "wandering abroad without visible means". If the unfortunate Peter was really destitute he might have welcomed the month in jail awarded by the Bench, had it not been accompanied by hard labour.

In August, the IG's report again said , while farmers were doing well, workers were suffering from the "enormous rise in the cost of living", Although Donegal was generally quiet, on the 15th a deserter was arrested and taken to the barracks at Middletown. A mob attacked the barracks and Police fired revolver shots from upper windows to disperse them. The deserter was handed over to the military the next day. In the words of the County Inspector "They are a rough uncivilised people in this locality but I doubt if they will ever face determined armed police".

The following month, it was the same old story: "farmers continued to reap substantial profits ... inflated price of agricultural produce". In Donegal the misery of the poor was exacerbated by abnormally bad weather. The fishing was bad and the grain crop was still in stooks late in September. Most of the rank and file police coming from farming stock, they must have been acutely aware of the implications for the coming winter. The news from mainland Europe was better: the Hindenburg Line had been breached and the tide of war had clearly turned against Germany and its allies. The conscription threat also receded but it was obvious that there was still "a dangerous state of disaffection in the country". During searches, police found shotgun cartridges whose birdshot had been replaced by lead slugs.

There were "signs of incipient trouble" in Ballyshannon. A number of SF activists were arrested. A local barber called Murray was a leader. DI Tyndall with three other policemen had the duty of bringing him to Dublin for trial. Hearing that a hundred of Murray's supporters were coming from Bundoran to attend at his departure, Tyndall had the brainwave of bringing him to Beleek to board the train but the SFs got wind of this and remained on the train until it reached Beleek. Confronted by them as he stood on the platform with his prisoner, Tyndall was forced to draw his revolver. Although the confrontation was resolved peacefully, the DI became extremely unpopular locally and his son noticed that he went about constantly armed.

Transferred to Portadown in 1918, John Tyndall's health began to decline. Demobilised in 1922 on the verge of promotion to CI, he suffered from nervous debility in his retirement and died in 1928 aged 59.

Rev. Charles Tyndall reflected long afterwards: "the greater number of the 40-50 year group seemed to have died rather young".

The Conscription Crisis had given an impetus not only to Sinn Féin but to the efforts to establish a police union. In September 1918 after a one-day strike by some British policemen the National Union of Police and Prison Officers received official recognition in Britain. Lloyd George himself met the strikers and all their demands were conceded. The Commissioner of the London Met was quietly let go (with a baronetcy as compensation) and was replaced by Neville Macready, son of the famous actor. From his previous job at the War Office Gen. Macready brought with him the reputation of a bureaucrat without adaptability. The Irish Police and Prison Officers Union then applied, through its general secretary T.J. McElligott, for recognition as an affiliate of the British union. There would be no official response until the following February.

The *Gazette* counselled caution. "Many men think they see their souls' salvation in a Police Union. But even a Union is not always an unmixed blessing. Police authorities regard a Union with a feeling not far removed from horror." Referring to the Belfast police strike of 1907 as an "emute" (an uprising or rebellion), it suggested that strike was a tragedy which arose out of very little. The editorial line was that there was need for an alternative structure, a representative board in which policemen could debate and present their grievances.

On 26th September, John Coyle was prosecuted by Con. J.H. with Con. Hunt as a witness. The charge was Drunk and Disorderly. The fine imposed was 21/= (£1, 1s), plus 1/6 costs, with a prison sentence of one month in lieu.

In rough seas on the morning of 10th October 1918, there occurred the third of Ireland's great maritime disasters of the 20th Century. Unlike the sinking of the Titanic in 1912 and that of the Lusitania in 1915, the loss of the RMS Leinster was soon forgotten and remained so for many years. Bound for Holyhead, about 16 miles out from Kingstown (now Dun Laoghaire) the Mail Boat was torpedoed twice, with cold efficiency, by U-Boat 123. Authoritative sources put the loss of life at 529 souls out of the 771 aboard. The ship was owned by the City of Dublin Steam Packet Company and most of its crew under Dubliner Captain Birch were from either Holyhead or the Dublin area as were the twenty-two Post Office sorters working in the mail room where one of the torpedoes struck. Among the dead was the Royal Navy's first "Wren" to die by enemy action; she was Josephine Carr from Cork. Why then was the disaster deleted from popular memory? It was simply because most of the dead were soldiers, Irishmen in the British Army returning from leave and about to rejoin the fight against the Kaiser and his allies. (It didn't help that the military censors concealed the number of military dead.) In independent Ireland, references to Irish participation in the Great War were not encouraged. Even those leaders of the new Irish state who must have squirmed at the notion of endorsing such actions by "gallant allies" probably thought it prudent not to awaken old atavism. And so the mists of Celtic amnesia fell across the land and the poor, drowned dead were forgotten.

The sinking almost scuppered secret overtures towards peace. On 6th October Germany had sent a message to U.S. President Wilson asking him to initiate talks towards a ceasefire. On the 14th Woodrow Wilson replied saying, amongst other things, that no peace was possible until attacks on passenger ships ceased. On the 21st October U-Boats were forbidden to attack merchant ships and all were recalled to their bases. It was too late for Captain Robert Ramm and his crew; on the 18th October U-Boat 123 had struck a mine in the North Sea and all aboard were lost.

When news of the Armistice came on 11th November, it brought a sense of relief to Ireland but "no universal enthusiasm". As Sir Joseph Byrne pointed out: "The people had not suffered any serious privations consequent on the war".

J.R.W. Goulden was a witness to changes in the political atmosphere:

> Yet from the end of the war in 1918, there was a different feeling abroad. The younger men were not really hostile but were to some extent openly defiant, as though unsure how far they could go. They did not seem very clear as to what form this new attitude should take or as to where it should lead them. For the most part, they expressed themselves in more or less friendly discussions with my father about the day which was coming when he and his like would have to leave. In the meantime, 'outrages' as they were called, were taking place in other parts of the country. In our part, everything was still fairly normal on the surface.

UVF rifles were being surrendered, but only to the Military and not the distrusted Police. The RIC received no information on the number of weapons handed in.

All sides now prepared for the coming General Election. Their cause now spent, many Irish Party MPs did not seek re-election thus leaving 25 SF candidates unopposed on Nomination Day. The Inspector General was dismissive of the SF candidates: "a few doctors, solicitors, farmers, shopkeepers, together with clerks, ex PO clerks, students, teachers, commercial travellers, a labourer and other persons of insignificance".

Ernie O'Malley later described the impatience of the younger and more energetic members of SF and the derision which they heaped on established politicians:

> We're leaders of this mighty Irish nation
> Though some folk say our leading days are done
> But don't forget whate'er may be our station
> The Constitutional movement must go on.
> And on and on and on for ever more…
>
> We've Home Rule now the Statute Book adorning
> It's there to be seen by every mother's son
> We brush the cobwebs off it every morning
> For the Constitutional movement must go on.
> And on and on and on for ever more…
>
> Five hundred pounds a year is very handy
> It helps the party now to carry on
> In London boys, we all can act the dandy
> For the jobbery and corruption must go on.
> And on and on and on for ever more…

The December election was a resounding victory for SF – under the "first past the post" system. In January 1919 Proportional Representation (PR – the single transferable vote) was tried out for the first time in Sligo's municipal elections. It was a proven success in breaking a long-standing political deadlock and hailed as such by both Nationalist and Unionist opinion. The *Freeman's Journal* said: "the first elections, on the principle of proportional representation by the single transferable vote, have resulted in the fair representation of all parties" and the *Irish Independent* similarly endorsed the new system. The Unionist *Irish Times* declared that the Sligo election "has established beyond dispute two big things in favour of proportional representation. The first is that it is a thoroughly workable system … the other big thing – and it is really big – is the proof that in proportional representation we have the Magna Carta of political and municipal minorities". The difficulties faced by minorities would increase in all corners of the emerging Ireland but it would take more than PR to alleviate them.

Had PR been used in the general election, SF's winning less than 48% of the votes cast would have given them far fewer seats. In fact, the result represented as much an abdication by the Irish Parliamentary Party as a SF victory given that 25 of the seats were uncontested by the IPP. The Labour Party also chose to abstain from contesting the election in the national interest, a decision which arguably set back the Left in Ireland for a generation. Sir Joseph Byrne claimed that "a very bitter feeling towards RIC" existed among the youth and was being inflamed by Catholic clergy. He again warned that "a strong military force is absolutely necessary" especially when the wartime security measures had been lifted. While it's easy to see the old soldier in Byrne, it must be acknowledged that he didn't see it as the job of his policemen to apply the physical force which might be needed to maintain public order in the developing situation.

In a November editorial the *Gazette* had looked at the recent changes in British police affairs, essentially the acceptance of the Union of Police and Prison Officers and the establishment of Police Representative Boards in the Metropolitan Police. It approved of the stance taken by Gen. Macready, newly appointed Commissioner of the Met, that while there was no bar on policemen joining the Union, he would not countenance any being pressured into doing so. Following hard on the resignation of his predecessor, Macready's address seems very measured and even-handed. The editorial opined that "it was the outside Union, that of the UPPO, which organised the

London Police strike, and any Union which can take so drastic a step must be regarded by those responsible for efficiency and discipline as menacing and dangerous". The editorial called for the right to meet and discuss their situation and for the immediate establishment of Representative Boards.

In another editorial entitled "The End of the War" the *Gazette* said "The Chief Secretary has expressed the opinion that it is not desirable that the Irish Police should join a labour union, and with this view, in the abstract, we fully agree, and so, we are convinced, will the great mass of the RIC." But it stressed that policemen needed the right to articulate their concerns and grievances. "Reconstruction and reform are in the air. In Ireland these should find a beginning in the house of the Royal Irish Constabulary. It is an old-fashioned edifice built in early Victorian days and entirely out of touch with modern ideas and progress of human freedom and civilisation."

The *Gazette* listed the continuing grievances, pointing out that the RIC was the only United Kingdom police force

- Where there were artificial barriers to a Constable's advancement
- In which policemen were forbidden to marry for seven years.
- Where Constables had to wait, on average, 20 years for promotion.
- Where policemen had to pay rent for a 'home' that wasn't a home.
- In which policemen had no vote in parliamentary elections.

The end of November, however, brought some overdue good news for Irish policemen. New pay rates were announced. John, as a Constable with between 5 and 7 years' service, would now receive 39 shillings, almost £2, per week. When he'd served seven years his pay would go to 2 pounds, 1 shilling. With the increase backdated to 1st September, on the next payday everyone would be handed at least £7, probably more money than they'd ever before had at their disposal. The *Gazette* welcomed the change as "the first real increase in over fifty years". It lauded the IG as "an officer who has regard for the welfare of his men" and said "since Sir Joseph Byrne took charge of the RIC the progress of the Constable has been unparalleled in our time".

A SF public meeting organised for Bundoran was banned. After a lot of clever strategems and the use of decoy speakers, SF managed to hold a short meeting before they dispersed. There was no confrontation with Crown forces so no injuries resulted.

A November newspaper advertisement claimed that many deaths from Spanish Influenza had been averted by the use of Veno's Cough Medicine, available at 11½ pence per bottle. Perhaps a more practical precaution was the use of carbolic acid to fumigate dwelling spaces. The procedure was to place one live coal on a shovel, pour an egg-cupful of carbolic acid over it, close doors and windows and leave the room forthwith. The menace was very real as deaths from influenza were reported daily in the press. The disease had taken hold in a war-exhausted Europe and was probably spread by soldiers returning to their homelands. Newspapers in neutral Spain were the first to report the pandemic and so it earned its popular name. Before it came to an end it killed some 100,000 people in Ireland. Estimates of worldwide fatalities range from 30 to 100 million people.

Reaction in the belligerent countries was slow, perhaps because wartime censorship concealed the extent of the problem. It was noticed that the fatality rate was greatest among young adults. It is believed now that over-reaction of the immune system, strongest in that age group, ravaged the body. Once infected, victims could die within a day. The infection was spread in crowded places; thousands of fresh U.S. soldiers, healthy farmboys for the most part, died aboard troopships before they ever reached the battlefields of Europe. And in Ireland, crowded places included military barracks and police stations.

An end of year advertisement for Raleigh bicycles struck a more cheerful note. Mr S. Rowland of Cheetham, Manchester had ridden a total of 108,000 miles on his Raleigh "all-steel bicycle" without mishap. At one and a half pence (1½d) per mile, the railway rate, this represented a saving of £675. "It would buy you a house and garden."

On the same note of Post-War optimism, the *Gazette* welcomed "the most promising Christmas season that the present generation of Irish policemen have experienced".

The General Election held on 14th December was without precedent. The Representation of the People Act, of February 1918, had extended the franchise to all males over 21 and married females over 30 who met a property qualification. The electorate had been trebled and most electors had never voted before.

Sinn Fein candidates gathered enough votes to win in North, West, and South Donegal. In East Donegal, however, where the Irish Party's E.J.Kelly got 7,596 votes and the Unionist Major Moore got 4,797, the SF man received only 40 votes.

The 1918 election has suffered no shortage of analysis. It does seem fair to say, though, that there could have been many who voted SF who had no clear idea of what Sinn Fein stood for. Self-determination and self-government, yes, but precisely what did these terms mean? Up to this point at least, it's reasonable to see the SF movement as a sort of community with no defined ideology. Its aims were sufficiently vague to allow it to encompass many diverse views. Fr O'Flanagan, SF Vice-President, is alleged to have said "The people have voted Sinn Fein. Now we have to explain to them what Sinn Fein is".

One can also see the nominations as a power struggle between the moderate and extreme wings of Sinn Fein. Arthur Griffith had started the movement with a proposal for a dual monarchy, along the lines of that then existing in Austro-Hungary but that model had been swept away by the Great War. Even some who understood what a Republic entailed might have seen their demand as a bargaining position: if you're selling a bullock you don't start at your final price. And, in any case, three years of warfare and terror wasn't one of anybody's election promises.

Behind the public facade, however, a more chilling scenario was being revealed to initiates. The 4th edition of the IV journal *An tÓglach* in late 1918 carried this message:

> We must recognise that anyone, civilian or soldier, who assists directly or by connivance in this crime against us, merits no more consideration and should be killed without mercy or hesitation as opportunity offers.

How many General Election voters were aware of this injunction? For that matter, how many Volunteers who'd read it took it seriously? Did the rank and file policemen know about it? No doubt the gentlemen in the Castle were aware of it but did they simply dismiss it as the effusion of yet another group of Irish malcontents?

1919: Radical Changes and Widespread Violence

Among the influential books published in 1919, alongside the English translation of "The Four Horsemen of the Apocalypse" by Ibáñez, and John Reed's "Ten Days that Shook the World", was H.G. Wells's "Outline of History".[vi]

For the police the year began quietly enough. The Dublin Advance Company of Belfast offered loans to RIC members on their own personal security. Loans from £2 to £100 were available at an interest rate of one shilling in the pound. (If per annum, that was a rate of only 5%.) The *Gazette* pointed out to its advertisers the value of policemen as consumers of boots, bicycles, watches, civilian clothes, shaving requisites, pipes and tobacco. Editorially, it called for the establishment of Police Representative Boards like that of the London Met. When a letter writer complained about the lack of public respect for the RIC "I think one of the main reasons is the part some of our brave fellows played in fearlessly helping to suppress the 1916 Rising… the people who were sentenced are nearly all MPs now and Ireland has mostly all turned Sinn Fein" the editor's response was unsympathetic. "You are a pessimist, friend! …

The cool attitude of the public is only skin deep. This temporary attitude is not permanent."

New Year 1919 was the first without total war since 1914 but it was a fragmented and troubled peace as four old empires crumbled into history. In Ireland there was much labour unrest and some persons of influence believed that the new scheme of unemployment relief was demoralising the workforce, causing many to quit work in order to claim benefits which would then "largely be spent on drink". The Versailles Peace Conference, at which SF hoped to get a hearing, opened on 18th January. In Dublin on the 21st, those SF MPs not detained in prison met to declare themselves an independent assembly, a parliament for Ireland.

On that same day at Soloheadbeg in Tipperary, two country policemen, Con. James McDonnell and Con. Patrick O'Connell, were gunned down as they escorted a horse and cart carrying dynamite to the County Council quarry. It was an action carried out by local men who were determined to start their own war by killing as many policemen as possible and it clearly shocked and embarrassed many members of the new SF *Dáil*. It also put the leadership of the Irish Volunteers in an awkward position: who was setting the strategy and dictating tactics on the military side of the movement? Over the next four years, Volunteer GHQ struggled to impose control over local activists but never fully achieved it.

In this context it may be worth reading the words of Joe Good, of Irish parentage but London born and bred, who'd arrived in Dublin just before the Easter Rising and remained an active participant in violence until the end of the Civil War.

> Historians will no doubt in years to come try to show the period of 1915 to 1921 as a period when there was a

> definite insurgent army and nation with campaigns and battles. It will be a damned lie.
>
> ...(Post 1916) The first action occurred in Cork and Tipperary. The Volunteer HQ in Dublin tried to restrain this. It was a case of the tail wagging the dog: most likely the fact that Collins was a County Cork man made it possible for him to guide, restrain, and give them final absolution.
>
> What happened in early 1920 in southern Ireland, and the audacious attacks on the RIC and their barracks was received with amazement in Dublin. "Little Apples" had grown again but they were not the same fruit expected by those who had made that epic stand in 1916.

Joe Good went on to become part of the Active Service Unit of the IRA's Dublin Brigade – in his own mock-Shakespearean words, "this happy few – this band of killers".

According to the testimony of Dan Breen who survived it all to become a serially elected Fianna Fail TD, he and his comrades Robinson and Tracy were impatient with Sinn Fein doing too much talking and not enough doing. He says that Tracy and himself had determined to kill the escort but hadn't confided their intention to Robinson, ostensibly their superior. In his own words: "Our only regret was that the escort had consisted of only two Peelers instead of six. If there had to be dead Peelers at all, six would have created a better impression than two". In a sort of back-handed compliment to the Peelers he says "In answer to our challenge they raised their rifles, and with military precision held them at the ready. They were Irishmen too, and would die rather than surrender". So that's all right then.

Given the acknowledged significance of Soloheadbeg, it's worth comparing the accounts of the confrontation as given in Dan Breen's *My Fight for Irish Freedom* in the original 1924 edition and in the edition which appeared forty years later. In the earlier version, the two policemen approached with rifles in hand which rather stretches credulity. Who, trudging for over four miles along a country road with no reason to expect trouble, would carry a 4kg carbine in his hands? As the old Gaelic proverb has it: even a hen gets heavy by the end of a long road. Any sensible fellow would sling it from his shoulder. And the writer suggests that the policemen had recently had training in bomb-throwing. It was winter: they were probably wearing greatcoats rather than bomb pouches .

"Our hour of trial was at hand; we were to face the enemy with life or death in the balance." Dan Breen paints the picture of nine men summoning their courage at the approach of these grenade-familiar highly trained policemen with rifles ready at the port. What those fit young men in hiding really faced was Con. O'Connell a thirty-six year old single man from Cork and Con. Mc Donnell, a widowed veteran with thirty-years service and looking forward to his pension. He had seven children to support.

"Again and again we called on them to put up their hands. We would have preferred that they surrender without bloodshed, but they were dogged and stubborn, and now it was our lives or theirs...Their fingers were on the triggers. Another appeal on our side would be useless – perhaps too late for ourselves. Quick and sure our volleys rang out. The aim was true. The two policemen were dead."

The 1964 version of the confrontation offered a cold rationale for taking the initiative in killing policemen:

> "We had resolved not merely to capture the gelignite but also to shoot down the escort. This action of ours would proclaim to the world that there still lived Irishmen who had made up their minds not to allow free passage to an armed enemy."

Of course by 1964 the author was Mr Dan Breen TD, by then part of the establishment in the new state he had once opposed in arms. The style is altogether more polished and the attempt at justification more considered. Perhaps there was a different pen at work?

"The moral aspect of such action was vigorously criticised after the event. Many people even former friends branded us as murderers. We had thoroughly discussed the pros and cons and arrived at the conclusion that it was our duty to fight for the Irish Republic that had been established on Easter Monday 1916." After that we have the infamous wish that more Peelers had been shot down. And then the man of action scorns those who would discuss and negotiate: "Our former friends shunned us. They preferred the drawing room as a battleground; the political resolution rather than the gun as their offensive weapon."

Espousing the supremacy of the gun means the abnegation of democracy, the abandonment of rational discussion. It is embracing the creed that might is right. At the time of the killings, at least one local clergyman did not share Breen's views: "The men responsible should go to their graves with the brand of Cain on their foreheads".

The IG's report for January 1919 notes the deaths of two policemen but doesn't give their names Whatever about the IG and his senior officers, the Government probably wasn't interested in the identities of murdered Constables or whether they left orphaned children. There would be many more to come anyway. They were mourned by their families and their comrades:

Two Irish homes are full of gloom
Two hearths are sad today,
Two gallant men have met their doom
In murderous affray.

Outside old Tipperary town
Without one warning word
By felons' hands those men shot down
Lay welt'ring in their blood.

More reflective comments later came from Sgt Jack O'Mahoney who had served in South Tipperary from 1913 to 1919 and knew Constables McDonnell and O'Connell well:

> That affair was vehemently condemned in the press and from the pulpit. It created a feeling of horror. It is said that when Arthur Griffith heard of it he said 'if this thing goes on we will wind up by shooting one another'. He never realised how terribly true his words came to be.
>
> At the time of the Soloheadbeg ambush and as late as April 1919 it wasn't Dail Eireann policy to kill police. The Dail then would go no further than pass a resolution moved by De Valera to ostracise politically and socially members of the police forces.... Except among the more active Volunteers and other ardent workers of the nationalist movement the RIC were not unpopular...
>
> Many there are who would be hard to convince that the old RIC were a popular and god-fearing body of men respected by all. I served in Wexford, Tipperary, Kilkenny and Dublin and at social functions like dances and I was always invited and made welcome.

The *Donegal Vindicator* reported the deaths in a 3 inch, single column report. Editorially, the newspaper was far more concerned about the Bolshevism it perceived in the Belfast and other strikes then occurring, the work of "revolutionary anarchists". It reported that the Red Flag had been hoisted over Monaghan Asylum but resisted any urge to make facetious comments.

In February the *Vindicator* returned to the theme with an editorial attack on Peter (Peadar) O'Donnell, a labour organiser.

"The O'Donnell phenomenon is not new. Long ago we met it. The genus comes across some books on Socialism, Theosophy, Origin of Species, and it devours every line from cover to cover, then it knows all there is to know about the subject." Then the writer mentions atheism and the bloody significance of the Red Flag. "The red terror has to be met and fought and beaten or the Ireland of the future will become the France of before the war... We warn Labour to take heed when this Irish Bolshevist leads."

Yeats couldn't have bettered the apocalyptic tone of a further editorial which warned the Peace Conference at Versailles to get on with its job. "Red Flagism or Bolshevism is rampant and the agnostic fanatics who were kept under by fear and force are now raising their heads and staring with bloodshot eyes at civilization."

Another threat to the social order arose from the wartime restrictions on whiskey distillation, imposed as grain was needed as food. During 1917-1918, the Jameson distillery in Dublin was closed completely under the cold eye of Customs and Excise.

Donegal had been generally quiet since the election. The shortage of whiskey had restarted illicit distillation especially in the Inishowen Peninsula. Molasses which was stocked for feeding cattle was being used rather than sugar, the sale of which was restricted. The demand for *Poitín* was futher promoted by the great Spanish Influenza epidemic which was sweeping across Europe. For many people, traditional medicines such as Carrageen seaweed porridge liberally laced with poitin were all they had access to. Despite the best efforts of the police and Bishop O'Donnell the authorities could not eradicate the trade.

Soda water bottles partially filled with water and containing tightly rolled packets of carbide were left on barracks windows in Letterkenny. The devices didn't explode. In the words of the

CI, they were "no doubt concocted by some of the SF corner-boys of Letterkenny".

At St Columb's Hall in Derry, the CYMS amateur actors offered a programme of six short Irish plays. One of them was *The Rising of the Moon*, a piece by Lady Gregory in which a mature RIC Sergeant is persuaded, by an appeal to his dormant nationalism, to let a fugitive slip away. He relinquishes a big reward but regains something of his youthful idealism. It seems inconceivable that the production would have been allowed under wartime DORA restrictions. Peacetime Ireland was never subject to the system of licensing of theatrical performances that obtained in England where the Lord Chamberlain could effectively ban any production deemed offensive (and did so until 1968).

On 1st February the *Gazette* welcomed a circular from the IG which declared that compulsory retirement awaited "inefficient" members of the force, whatever their rank or period of service but it stressed the desirability of merit pay to reward the diligent and the need for overall pay increases to cope with the continuing rise in the cost of living. Gen. Byrne instructed his CIs to identify those who had given good service but who had become tired and inefficient, distinguishing them from those whose aim was to do as little as possible until they collected their pensions. Well-intentioned it may have been but, according to W.J.V. Comerford, the ruling was deeply resented by some who felt they'd been treated unfairly in being compulsorily retired.

The Authorities also announced that those Constables who had served in the Army during the late war and been commissioned – Lieutenants, Captains and Majors – would, at the first opportunity be promoted to Sergeant. While there was no statutory obligation to do so, it was the Inspector General's wish. The catch was that there were few vacant posts at Sergeant level and the returning ex-officers would have to be content with returning as Constables pending a vacancy for the three stripes, with increased remuneration then being retrospective. The advice of the *Gazette* to returning policemen was the same as that of *Punch* to the man about to get married: DON'T.

Nonetheless, the several dozen people involved were, by their existence, making an important point: the ranks of the RIC contained men of proven leadership and management ability. The principles which maintained the Cadet system were exposed as what they really were: caste and sectarian prejudices. In that realisation, the indignation of a letter-writer puts the matter in forcefully down-to-earth terms: "The Force expects to be treated as men and not as 'gorsoons' of an unruly type".

Far from being unruly young fellows, the bulk of the Constabulary were of mature years. In 1919 the average policeman was 35 years old and had served fifteen years. About half the Force were married men over the age of 41 and with 21 years' service. Sergeants were older still; in January 1920 almost 60% of them had enlisted before 1895 and had served more than 25 years. Young men of ambition were sorely frustrated.

Still, it's unlikely that many of them felt sympathy for two policemen who were convicted in March of robbery from an American Naval post in Cork . Cornelius Cadogan, a married man with 18 years' service, was given nine months hard labour while Michael Rogers, a single man with 3 years' service, received three months. Rare as they were, such cases reflected badly on the Force as a whole. It's probable that their detention was extremely unpleasant.

For those ambitious Constables planning to take the "P" examination route to promotion, publisher Alex Thom of Dublin offered special textbooks for the RIC: Modern Geography, English Grammar, Spelling (with Etymology and Pronunciation), Arithmetic, and General Information ("will help students to learn some of the laws of life and the working of some of the world's great wheels"). Volumes cost about a shilling each.

In February also, the embryonic Irish police union received an official response to its request for recognition: the Lord Lieutenant could not permit the RIC to join the NUPPO. A report in the *Irish Independent* of 8th February stated: "... practically all the members of the DMP had joined... including the Harbour Police. The majority of prison officials were also members, and so far about 3,500 of the RIC". Confrontation with authority was inevitable.

The circular issued from RIC headquarters over the signature of William M. Davies, Deputy IG read:

POLICE UNION

> County Inspector: Officers and men in your county should be informed that His Excellency, the Lord Lieutenant, cannot see his way to permit members of the force to join the National Union of Police and Prison Officers. Inasmuch as the RIC is a semi-military force, directly under the control of the crown, and subject, in many respects, to the same conditions of employment and discipline as the army and navy forces.

No such circular was sent to members of the DMP or the Prison Service. However, DMP men were strongly discouraged from membership of the Union.

The *Gazette* responded to the call by "Pro Patria", i.e. Sgt T.J. McElligott, for RIC and DMP members to join the union. It blamed the authorities for not allowing men to make representations regarding their grievances and concerns but it made the point that membership of a union could take away freedom of choice: they could be called upon to strike over something that didn't remotely concern them.

The same issue published a letter by Pro Patria" dealing with the question of disarmament:

> One of the most important questions in reform is the maintenance of an armed police force. If there was any justification for an armed police force it may have existed in 1822 at the time of its formation by Sir Robert Peel. . The principle, admitted good only for Ireland, was wrong from the very beginning…police officers by virtue of their calling must necessarily be on good terms with the people, and if they are used in military fashion they will be treated with "military" respect.
>
> "When arms are used by a policeman in Ireland, moreover if life is taken, the line in that locality is quickly drawn between the people and their "oppressors". The worst feature of the position is that the necessity for firing arises, in almost every instance, out of some public or political grievance. This aggravates the evil, and it has earned for the RIC the title "the enemies of their country."

The writer also pointed out that force had not been used impartially and contrasted the gun-running episodes at Larne and Howth and he cited Mr Headlam, the Treasury Remembrancer, is support of his argument that firearms were not needed by the RIC. He concluded by stating "we demand that our status as police officers alone should be recognised".

The text of this letter is substantially the same as one which appeared in the *Irish Independent* a few days later. Later in the month the *Gazette* responded: "Pro Patria continues to correspond with the *Irish Independent* concerning Police policy in Ireland. Some of his ideas are excellent and have long been advocated by ourselves. There are other matters to which he calls attention which we confess are extremely puzzling from any point of view." And, again: "This Union is allied with the Labour federation whose appeals for justice invariably take the form of a strike. Such a Union allied to a branch of the public service becomes a public tyranny, and must sooner or later bring the police and the public into conflict."

As an affiliated branch, the Irish Union was invited to attend the annual conference of the NUPPO in London at the end of March 1919. Despite official disapproval, McElligott attended as RIC delegate alongside William Hetherington for the DMP and John Brennan of Sligo representing the prison officers. McElligott set out his members' demands: improvement in financial and other conditions, reform of promotion procedures, and the disarming of the force and its emergence as a civil police service. The Irish delegation was warmly supported by their British colleagues.

However, controversy erupted at home after the publication of a report which appeared in the *Irish Independent* of 28th March. Referring to the roles of police and prison officers in dealing with political offences, it stated that "The Irish delegates expressed their repugnance in having to deal officially with men with whom they were politically in agreement".

The report was seized on by political Unionists and supporters of the status quo, and caused consternation among police trade unionists. In a letter to the *Irish Independent*, McElligott, as RIC delegate, stated they had put the case that they had more difficult and disagreeable duties to perform in Ireland in connection with the political prisoners. "Without expressing either approval or condemnation, we explained how we were affected by political crimes and political prisoners, and it is correct to say 'the delegates listened attentively'".

Attempts to discredit McElligott and the police union took

the form of letters to the *Constabulary Gazette* over his pen-name *Pro Patria* during March and April. He responded in a letter to the *Independent* on 12th May disavowing those letters as forgeries .

In Dublin on 29th and 30th April the Irish Police and Prison Officers Union held its first and last general meeting. One motion which was carried unanimously was:

> That we endorse the resolution passed by the Council of Delegates to immediately disarm the RIC, and do further urge that the rifles are responsible for all attacks on the police, raids on barracks, and loss of life; that they are not required by the DMP and that they are useless and unnecessary for the RIC, except for drill and ceremonial purposes; that men are withdrawn from practical police duties, and, like soldiers, confined to barracks, which are now being converted into magazines and stores for arms, ammunition and in some cases explosives, and that, failing immediate disarmament, means be adopted for giving effect to the resolution.

As expected, discriminatory moves against the Union's known members began immediately. Members found themselves subjected to more frequent inspections and petty harassments and peremptory transfers to "bog stations". Towards the end of May, Sgt McElligott himself was ordered on transfer from Trim in Royal Meath to Belmullet, Co. Mayo. Rustication to the wastes of impoverished Erris was not to his taste; he refused and had no option but to resign from the Constabulary.

While there was considerable support within the ranks for the establishment of a police trade union, many may have had reservations. Most of the RIC were farmers' sons and came from the innately conservative rural class which had wrung concessions from the landowners through bitter struggle. They had been transformed from tenants-at-will to peasant proprietors. Now people 'with a stake in the country', they had reason to support the established order insofar as they did not want to destroy the economic machine so much as climb into its driving seat. For those with land, the radicalism of the Land League days had been supplanted by a phase of consolidation. It was the marginal farmers and the landless who continued the land agitation in western counties especially in Clare and Galway. Respectability being desired more than revolution by the small farmer class, there was still deference to authority figures both religious and secular. And farmers had done very well out of the war. Police attitudes towards organised labour would have been affected by the labour troubles during 1913 which indeed showed neither side in a very creditable light. Even if not directly a witness to events in Dublin, John Hennigan would have been acutely aware of what had happened in Sligo when blood was shed on the docks, James Larkin was denounced as Anti-Christ from the Dominican pulpit and, as folklore has it,the elderly and scholarly Col. Woodmartin knocked to the ground and his revolver taken from him. James Connolly had participated in the 1916 insurrection in the interests of extreme nationalism rather than workers' rights and this association with violent revolution must have contaminated the cause of Labour. It certainly did nothing for the working man or woman. Although, being urban, the DMP may have been more receptive to the principle of a trade union, the Citizen Army had been directly responsible for the murder of several unarmed DMP men. There was no love lost in either direction: during the 1913 Lockout, at least one RIC man was shocked by the lack of restraint shown by the DMP in wielding their batons.

T.J. McElligott's record of "Subscribers" to the Union shows

4,308 members. Constable John Hennigan of Ballyshannon was number 2,870. In the Ballshannon Station, Sergeants Michael Green and James Furnan along with six Constables were also members.[4]

In Bundoran, Sgt Dominick Crilly and two Constables had subscribed. At Sligo No.1 Barrack, Sgts O'Hare and McLoughlin along with thirteen Constables were members. At Wine Street's No.2 Barrack, Sgt Marrinan and eight Constables had joined.

It is interesting that in a few stations subscribers felt the need to use pseudonyms e.g. Turf, Pencil, Kerry Kid. At the large Eglington Street station in Galway nine policemen were listed as "anonymous". Most likely there was a fear of being victimised by superior officers.

Later in 1919, the first all-Ireland RIC Representative Body was officially set up. DI Henry John Moore, who had accepted John Hennigan and his friend John Gilmartin into the Force, became a committee member.

By April, however, there was increasing unrest and hostility towards the police. This expressed itself in verbal attacks and increasing ostracism. The Republican women's group *Cumann na mBan* forbade its members to speak to, or sit in the same pew in church with, a policeman.

Early that April, as the RIC's war veterans were being welcomed home, Resident Magistrate J.C. Milling was shot dead through the window of his home in Westport. Having previously been a DI in the RIC, he'd been appointed Mayo RM to replace Alan Bell who'd been transferred to Portadown. The threateningly capable Mr Bell would himself become a specific

4 If the sequence of numbers is an indication, John Hennigan seems to have joined later than the others in Ballyshannon. They are numbered consecutively from 1,749. Perhaps he was initially reluctant or, perhaps, simply absent on a given day. The register does not give dates. Sgt Perry at Cliffoney was member 3,997, with his men, including Constables Laffey and Lynch, numbered consecutively from that.

target for Michael Collins quite soon after and would be taken from a tram and coldly executed on a Dublin street.

Warning of the danger from extreme Nationalists, the *Gazette* quoted Lord Shandon, Sir Ignatius O'Brien, a former Lord Chancellor, calling for "the fulfilment in some form of the statutory contract to be found in principle in the Home Rule Act."

In May, the Soloheadbeg killings were echoed at Knocklong railway station after one of the Tipperary Volunteers responsible had been arrested. On the train, under police escort, he was rescued by others of the group, killing two policemen. IG Byrne was again arguing for the retention of a strong military force in Ireland.

The *Constabulary Gazette* quoted at some length the words of Lovet Fraser in an article titled "Ireland Cannot Wait" in the *Daily Mail* "The advocates of physical force, or 'direct action', are in the ascendency. The detached and rather literary flavour which marked the inception of Sinn Fein has vanished, and it is now frankly revolutionary. It has formed an unnatural alliance with the Syndicalist movement in Ireland. The alliance is unnatural because Syndicalism is entirely remote from the true spirit of the Irish race, which on its own is inherently conservative"

Lovat Fraser offered no suggestions but demanded that the government stop doing nothing and pretending it was a policy. He saw the moderate nationalists being outflanked and thought the government needed to acknowledge that the 1914 HR Act was dead in the water and move on from that. Unfortunately, once again HM Government seemed incapable of listening.

Under a headline "Police Traditions" the *Gazette* retitled some of these as "antiquated and mischievous customs". It returned to an old grievance and called it a noxious rule: the prohibition on wearing civilian clothes when off duty. "It deprives the Constable of a certain amount of legitimate freedom which every man of his kind in Great Britain enjoys, and, in the next place, it encourages the feeling of the people in their conviction that the Police of Ireland are not a civil force."

Far off in London, the Special Service Branch at Scotland Yard was made a separate entity under Basil Thomson. It was an institution which would play its part in the Irish embroglio when the flow of information from the RIC dried up. The new intelligence service was much less effective than the Constabulary. Some of Thomson's ideas were decidedly fanciful and when in 1921 he fell out with Lloyd George he was asked to resign. However, he may have been one of those British officials who thought a settlement could be brought about despite the politicians. He seems to have used the American journalist Carl W. Ackerman as a conduit to the SF leadership.[5]

Also in London the Union backed down from a threatened strike by the Metropolitan Police. The Union was becoming more clearly identified with organised labour and many policemen were unhappy with "Bolshevist claptrap". A circular from the Irish branch of the Union called on policemen not to support the Gazette: "The *Constabulary Gazette* is opposed to our Union…quoting and copying the untruthful articles in the Capitalist Press, the *Irish Times* and the *Daily Mail*". In response, the *Gazette* offered to pay £100 into Union funds if they produced any evidence that it was inspired by or supported by the authorities.

By June the atmosphere in Ireland was becoming more threatening. In Roscommon, at Boyle's RC church, notices were posted: "Shoot the Peelers, Shoot as many blackguards as you can. Remember we are at war." A Sergeant was warned by his Parish Priest: "No policeman's life is safe at present". In Thurles,

5 In 1925 he was charged with public indecency in Hyde Park along with Thelma de Lava, "actress" and was fined £5. His defence that he was researching a book on London's vice trade was not accepted by the court.

DI Harte was murdered after the Races. In the middle of a crowd, he was shot twice in the back at very close range and the bystanders facilitated his murderers' escape.

There were happier moments. On the 15th, the Marconi station at Clifden sent dramatic news: airmen Alcock and Brown had crash-landed in a nearby bog after an arduous first-ever flight across the Atlantic. Neither was hurt and their Vickers Vimy aircraft was damaged but repairable. Ireland, and Europe, was now linked to North America in a way that few could have imagined twenty years before. The British Empire and the world had two new heroes.

Donegal remained peaceful and prosperous, although poitin-making continued in full swing. Throughout the summer of 1919, Constable John appeared in Court several times but the cases were far from political. At Ballyshannon Petty Sessions on 26thJuly Michael Tunney of Tullymore had to answer the charge that he "did allow a horse your property to wander on the public road". Mr Tunney was fined sixpence plus an additional shilling for costs with 7 days in gaol if he chose not to pay. Petty Sessions must have been rather intimidating for the ordinary policeman as well as the defendant. Major H.C. Owen, Resident Magistrate, who normally acted as Chairman, was supported by eight part-time Magistrates. Among the other policemen stationed at Ballyshannon were DI Hicks, Sgt Walsh, and Constables Kilfedder, Bruen and Scanlan.

In July, the ideological conflict between the *Gazette* and the Union with McElligott as its personification was aired again. Under the headline "The Police and the Red Flag", the *Gazette* reported on the mass meeting of police in London where Union leader ex-Constable Marston declared "Now is the time to show them (the authorities) who are the masters". The *Gazette* responded "If Messrs Marston and McElligott (of the RIC) are to be the masters then the British Empire may sing its swan song". McElligot had asserted that "the Irish Police were ready to strike to a man", a claim which was entirely fanciful. In any case, the Government faced the Union down, strike action did not materialise and many London policemen lost their jobs. Even the well-known Socialist and Irishman Bernard Shaw declared that the Police Union had overestimated its strength and failed utterly. The *Gazette* held to the view that Representative Boards were the avenue towards the rectification of injustice and improvement in pay, conditions and pensions. The Desborough report resulted in immediate improvements in pay and conditions for British policemen but the RIC and DMP were again bitterly disappointed that they would have to wait until Parliament resumed its sittings in October before finding out what was being offered to them.

In the meantime the realities of everyday policing in Ireland continued to assert themselves. In early August Constable Murphy, aged 20 and fresh from the Depot, was shot dead and his Sergeant John Riordan mortally wounded on foot of a long-running agrarian dispute in Clare where they manned a protection hut.

On 25th August, Con. J.H. prosecuted Andrew Harrison, a farmer, for being "drunk on the public street". Harrison was fined a shilling with sixpence costs. On the same day Francis Gallagher answered a charge by the Constable that he "did allow a horse to wander on the public road". He escaped with a caution. A month later, Con. J.H. brought Daniel Kerrigan before the Bench for being "drunk on the public street"; he was fined 5/= , plus 1/= costs. Whatever post John was attached to around Bundoran, it seems to have been an oasis of tranquillity with drunks and horses wandering the streets.

The picture elsewhere in Ireland was not so tranquil. In July, IG Byrne complained that "inveterate political unrest now is a serious menace to the public peace". Indeed the country seems to have been in political ferment. There were reports of dissension in the Labour movement between leaders who held "communistic and revolutionary principles" and more moderate rank and file. There were rumours of threatened resignations within Sinn Fein by such as Griffith and Fr Flanagan over support for murders. Carson was threatening to reactivate the UVF. Ordinary policemen must have felt confused and threatened. How much information was fed back to them about the overall situation? The IG continued to stress to the government the need for a strong military presence. That summer, Donegal seems to have remained relatively untroubled. American liners called at Moville and poitin continued to pour out of Inishowen. Police suspicions about the illegal use of sugar led to prosecutions under the Sugar Control Act of 1917. And a house raid by police in Moville yielded up an old sword.

But arbitrary death was beginning to stalk those who wore the Constabulary uniform. In early September Sgt Philip Brady was walking with two Constables at Lorrha when they came under fire from behind a hedge. One of the two Constables was seriously wounded, the other unscathed. The Sergeant died on the spot.

Sgt Brady left a bereaved widow and nine children. At Sunday Mass the Parish Priest Rev. J. Gleeson was unequivocal in his denunciation: "Each morning when I look out from my window I shall see the place… We cannot restore life to the dead, nor remove from the clay of the parish the stain of blood. But we have a duty to perform. We must denounce this murder and we pray for the soul of him who was murdered and for his afflicted wife and orphans. The cause which is founded on murder and cemented by human blood is cursed by God and doomed to vengeance. May the curse of Cain, the curse of the widow and orphans, the curse of the priest and the curse of God fall on those who are guilty of this murder and may God have mercy on their souls."

Fire-fighting practice at the Depot c.1900.

Firefighting, First Aid and Artificial Respiration were seen as essential skills for policemen.

Courtesy of the Garda Museum

Artificial Respiration practice

Courtesy of the Garda Museum

A Sergeant with revolver.

This photograph was probably taken at the Depot in Phoenix Park.

Courtesy of the Garda Museum

Unknown Constable c.1912

Ready to step out of the Depot, this smartly turned out policeman carries a swagger stick. The bayonet is decorative.

Courtesy of the Garda Museum

Sergeant with Carbine

His sleeve badge identifies him as a musketry instructor.

Courtesy of the Garda Museum

The former RIC barrack, Drumquin, Co. Tyrone.

A typical small-town police station with out-buildings at rear.

Courtesy of Fairywater Credit Union

Police tender at the Depot c.1920

This Ford Model T vehicle bears the RIC badge on its side. The rain hood was detachable. Registration IK refers to Dublin County – not Dublin City.

Courtesy of the Garda Museum

Cahirciveen RIC barrack, Co. Kerry

At the other end of the scale, this structure is built to impress and, perhaps intimidate.

Courtesy of the Garda Museum

Police with Crossleys at Sligo No.1 barrack (now Garda Station)
The numbers indicate that these vehicles were registered in Manchester. There is no record of their ever returning to Britain.

Courtesy of the late Bobby Brown, Scarden

Group at Sligo No.1Bk, c.1920

An interesting group: the two men on the left may be regular RIC members. The trio on right look like Black and Tans. The old RIC took pride in the uniform. Soft caps were often worn by drivers. Removing the wire stiffener would not have been tolerated in the RIC proper.

Courtesy of the late Bobby Brown, Scarden

Crossley chassis outside Sligo No.1 Bk
The three-storey building beside the Courthouse in the background was the premises of Messrs Williams, coachbuilders and motor garage.
Courtesy of the late Bobby Brown, Scarden

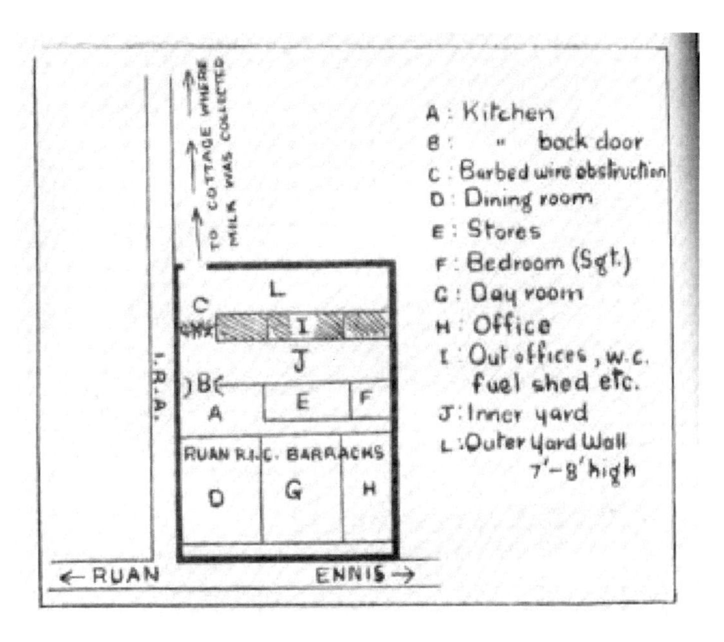

Map of RIC barrack at Ruan, Co. Clare

The plan appears to have been prepared for IRA use. Note the references to barbed wire and milk collection.

Courtesy of the Garda Museum

Ben Bulben, Sligo's storied mountain, seen from the south.

Photograph by John the Map Callanan

Dublin Opinion cartoon 1922

Handley Page type 0/400

This is J2259 at Baldonnel (now Casement) aerodrome, home of 100 Squadron. A former bomber, it seems to have been adapted to carry passengers.

Courtesy of the Royal Air Force Museum

John Hennigan in later years.

It became clear during the summer that British Government policy was to replace the British Police Union with a Police Federation, an internal organisation. In Ireland permission was given for RIC men in each county to appoint a representative to a conference in Dublin to consider the recommendations of the Desborough committee which looked at police conditions in Britain. It was to be an opportunity for policemen to express their grievances and opinions in a controlled environment.

Despite his resignation from the Police, T.J. McElligott had continued his efforts on behalf of the Police Union and sought support from public figures such as Tim Healy. He was a prolific writer of letters to the press but pressure was being applied. In September he received a letter from T.R. Harrington, editor of the supportive *Irish Independent*:

> My experience for several weeks past that the Press Censor invariably prohibited the publication of your letters, the reason being, I believe, that they apprehended there was much more underneath what you wrote than what appeared on the surface. The same reason applies to the enclosed communication.
>
> Since the Press Censorship ceased we have been definitely and specifically cautioned and warned that we incurred risk to our publications if we publish any of your letters, and under the circumstances I regret I am unable to publish enclosed.

At the same time British policemen who had gone on strike and been dismissed found the authorities to be adamant in rejecting appeals against dismissal. Concessions were granted, policemen were to be allowed representative bodies to air their grievances, but affiliation to organised labour was a step too far. This was the era of post-war labour unrest which in Britain led to the General

Strike of 1926 and the government simply could not allow the Police, any more than the Military, to assert divided loyalties.

In editorial comment on 20th September, the *Gazette* may have sounded patronising but was probably accurate. "Mr McElligott was a manly, straightforward, and able policeman. He had convictions and he had the courage of his convictions." In the view of the *Gazette* he lacked sound judgement and was led astray.

In a letter submitted to the *Irish Independent* before September 1919 but unpublished until March 1920, McElligott wrote: "By immediately disarming the RIC, raids on barracks will be prevented and all police stations in Ireland will be safe from attack as the DMP are at present. In the outskirts of the city there are two police stations within 100 yards of each other – one RIC and one DMP. The former is locked, barred and bolted and the men confined within a fortress of sandbags and wire, armed with rifles, bombs and rockets. The latter is even more open than Bishopsgate in London and less likely to be raided."

In mid-October a *Gazette* editorial entitled "Police Discontent" looked at the temptation for policemen to emigrate. "The Irish Constable would vastly prefer to remain at home if his life were a pleasure. The fact remains that it is almost void of pleasure. The authorities cannot prevent the attitude of the public. This, however, we believe to be a passing phase. With a change in the political wind the hostility which is now at its worst will disappear. The Police are Irishmen, and men of honour. Their fidelity to duty will never count against them. On the contrary it will redound to their credit."

A letter in that same issue put forward the suggestion that army surplus bicycles and motor cycles be offered to policemen at a discount. It was too radical a suggestion to win bureaucratic approval.

Towards the end of the month Constable Downing of the DMP was shot down as he walked his beat unarmed in High Street. Such arbitrary bloodlust was to become increasingly common. A twenty-nine year old Corkman, Michael Downing died of his wounds in Mercer's Hospital where a colleague Con. Neary donated blood in an effort to save him, an unusual procedure at the time. Neary later received an award from the British Red Cross.

On the first of November there was good news as a new Parliamentary Bill for the first time gave Irish policemen pay parity with their British colleagues. Showing business acumen, Star Furnishing Company of Camden Street, Dublin, continued to provide discounts and special terms to members of the DMP and RIC. To those policemen determined on advancement, Hughes's Academy of Belfast offered "P" exam candidates tuition at three levels: Beginners, Intermediate and Advanced, serviced by a team of six tutors.

But despite progress in wages and salaries, reform was still needed. As it railed against the existing rank structure the *Gazette* declared that the Cadet system should become the "Cast-out System". Although the war had demonstrated the stupidity of the old way, Constables who'd risen to military NCO or Officer rank now rejoined the RIC as Sergeants while demobilised officers with no police experience could apply for Cadetships.

The job was getting more difficult. Crime rates were up and detection rates down as ordinary criminals took advantage of the reduced effectiveness of the police. Violence against the RIC, though still sporadic, was becoming more common. On 31st October there were simultaneous raids on two barracks in Co.Meath. Con. Agar, doing duty as Barrack Orderly at Ballivor, was shot dead as he answered the door. The three other policemen were taken prisoner. At Dillon's Bridge they didn't open the door.

As the winter of 1919 drew in, the authorities started to close down smaller isolated police barracks, presenting as a positive step what was obviously a retreat. IG Byrne reiterated his call for a "strong military garrison". In Donegal, however, things remained relatively peaceful. Two police bicycles were destroyed in Glencolumcille and poitin-making resumed there. There were 38 prosecutions for unauthorised sales of sugar. It seems molasses, while readily available, was less suitable for the production of the spirit.

Post-war commerce was lively, at least in agriculturally prosperous Ireland if not in the exhausted and devastated nations of Continental Europe. Heather's of Arran Quay in Dublin offered for its Autumn Show gentlemen's tweed suits at a cost of 50 to 70 shillings (£2.50 to £3.50). Boots, with or without toe-caps, were on offer from 21/= to 29 shillings (roughly £1.10 to £1.50).

One might wonder though at the number of advertisments, aimed at policemen, which offered confidential loans. R. Cantwell of Wicklow Street, Dublin specialised in "Cash lent Privately by Post in any part of Ireland".

In a letter to the *Gazette* on the subject of the RIC's prohibition on a Constable's marriage before he'd served seven years, a correspondent who signed himself *Au Revoir* offered opinions which could upset modern sensitivities: "Better for the State to have the help of physical (sic.) and strong healthy children by letting good men marry than to have a population of our country built on dwarfs and illegitimates".

Even as the going gets rough, humour helps to ease the tensions and lift the stress. The versifier who styled himself Justin clearly owed a debt to Gilbert and Sullivan:

I'm an Irish policeman
On a very careful plan,
    I am made my various duties to perform.
Trained in many Crafts and Arts
I'm a man of Many Parts
    Adapted well for Terror or for Charm.

I'm a Gauger, I'm a Proctor
I'm a first-class First Aid Doctor
    I'm a Keeper of the Fishes and the Game
I'm a Veterinary Inspector
And a Company Director
    If that Company is any way to blame.

I'm a Bailiff (more's the pity),
I'm a Watchman in the City
    During all the long and lonely hours of night,
I'm a Rate and Rent Collector
I'm a Sanitary Inspector
    With the Public Health forever in my sight.

I'm a Technical Inspector
In the realms of Agriculture
    I'm a Local Food Controller since the war,
I'm an expert in explosives
And in Poisonous Corrosives
    And I supervise the Salon and the Bar.

I keep the Nation's Food
Very pure and fresh and good
    I test the Nation's Spirits, Milk and Beer
I prevent Adulteration
And Illicit Distillation
    And I keep the Streets and Highways ever clear.

But my powers have limitations
And my heart has aspirations
    That are ever doomed by fate to fade or fall,
And my manifold professions
Have not brought me great possessions
    Sure, my Income Tax as yet is rather small.

And so on for another few verses. Brevity wasn't always regarded as the soul of wit.

That nervous equanimity did not last the year. The outstanding outrage was the attempted assassination of the Lord Lieutenant, Sir John French. But Donegal suddenly became all too lively. On 6th December, three policemen attempting to sort out a drunken row were set upon and badly beaten. Sgt Mulvey received death threats on the 8th for any policemen who interfered with the distribution of Dáil Loan leaflets. On the 12th, DI Wallace and three other policemen were ambushed near Dungloe. All were wounded. On the 25th, shots were fired into the lodgings of Con. Cashlin at Ballybofey.

Perhaps putting a brave face on it for his superiors, the County Inspector emphasised that Donegal was still "in most part peaceable", pointing to the absence of agrarian crime (presumably such as continually plagued Clare and Galway). Possibly the fact that December was an exceptionally wet month – the wettest in 48 years – dampened enthusiasm for outdoor violence.

Increased drunkenness he attributed to ex-soldiers and the fact that drink was now more plentiful.

The greatest shock for the ordinary policeman must, however, have been the report in the *Gazette* of 27th December under the heading "Amazing Rumour". It referred to a rumour that Sir Joseph Byrne was about to be superseded as Inspector General. Acknowledging the huge regard in which Gen. Byrne was held as the Champion of the ordinary policemen, "the RIC loves their Inspector General", the *Gazette* offered its opinion: "Our view of the rumour is that we earnestly hope it is one of those stories that finds its origin in gossip, and that many new years may find Sir Joseph occupying the Chief Command of the Royal Irish Constabulary".

Bringing the year to a melancholy conclusion was a small paragraph in *The Derry Journal* under the headline "Ulster Family Tragedy". It told how the children of the Ringland family of Crossgar, Co. Down succumbed to influenza. On the 21st December, the first victim was a youth of sixteen. The following day, his six year-old sister died. Then on Christmas Day, their big brother of 19 followed. As his funeral was leaving the house on St Stephen's Day, his baby brother James, aged 3, died. And on the 29th, their sister Jenny, a young woman of 19, passed away. Was Mr Ringland, a garden labourer, able to afford medical help for his children? And, given the virulence of the Spanish Flu, would it have made any difference?

The Municipal Elections were held in January 1920 and the results are worth considering. Of the 1,815 members of municipal bodies elected, 559 were SF, 394 Labour, 355 Unionist, 238 Nationalist, 161 Independents and 108 Ratepayers. Nonetheless, outside of Belfast and Derry all the Mayors elected by municipal authorities were SF; the party now controlled 172 out of 206 urban and borough councils.

Having achieved constitutional union in 1801, the British Government did more to keep Ireland separate from Britain than did any other agency. Throughout the 19th Century it enacted an extraordinary amount of legislation specifically for Ireland, most but not all of it to do with Coercion. Its handling of the Great Famine in the 1840s was disastrously inept. Britain's failure to stop food exports from Ireland, the inadequate and degrading relief measures and, above all, the culpable ignorance and indifference shown by those in power would be long remembered by the survivors. It fostered a bitter hatred towards Britain, especially among the Irish in the U.S.A. There were some people still alive in 1920 who had lived through the 1940s Famine as small children.

Under the Union, rather than direct rule from Westminster, a subordinate government was put in place, centred in Dublin Castle and with a Lord Lieutenant as representative of the Crown. The Chief Secretary was a Minister at Westminster and there was never clarity as to which office was subordinate. The Castle became a byword for jobbery and intrigue as the old Protestant Ascendancy sought to cling to its privilege and power. The very first Inspector General of the Irish Constabulary resigned after two years because of political interference in promotions. Remaining unchanged until 1921, the Government of Ireland with its many Departments and Boards was inefficient, and unaccountable to the people of Ireland. The Under-Secretary, or chief civil servant, was normally the most powerful man in the system. Some Under-Secs contributed to the welfare of ordinary Irish people; most were nonentities. We should ever raise a glass to Charles Drummond: "Property has its duties as well as its rights; to the neglect of those duties in times past is mainly to be ascribed that diseased state of society in which… crimes take their rise…". But Drummond was exceptional.

The cultural problem was rooted in the ethnic and religious prejudices shown by so many of the rulers towards the bulk of the population. Churchill wrote to his wife Clemmie about the Irish: "I expect it is that treacherous, assassinating, conspiring trait which has done them in in the bygone ages of history and prevented them from being a great responsible nation with stability and prosperity". There was nothing new in that view. At the height of the Great Famine, Charles Trevelyan who was responsible for relief to the starving gave it as his opinion that the famine was a judgement of God on the Catholic Irish for their wicked ways. Although a friend of Allingham, the poet Tennyson expressed the opinion: "I heartily wish it was in the middle of the Atlantic, a thousand miles away from England. I like the Irish, but they're a fearful nuisance". In 1919 General Macready wrote "I loathe the country you are going to and its people with a depth deeper than the sea and more violent than that I feel against the Boche". Could it really have come as a surprise that there were many on John Bull's Other Island who reciprocated such views?

1920: A Year of Horrors

1920 was to prove a year of appalling savagery. The January Constabulary report to the Government stated that the RIC could not patrol in strength and could do little more than defend their barracks. The IG's call for a strong military force was repeated. The government continued to maintain the pretence that the situation was one of domestic civil unrest rather than the guerrilla war it was fast becoming. Consequently they chose to militarise the police rather than commit more troops; it seemed to them more politically digestible. In the later words of a Black and Tan, they "persisted in treating this armed and widespread rebellion as though it were an exceptional crime wave". That perpetual intriguer Henry Wilson, Chief of the Imperial General Staff, wrote in his diary on 13th January: "Spies and murderers everywhere, the Cabinet absolutely apathetic. I urge with all my force the necessity for doubling the police and not employing the military". Sir Henry was quite willing to sacrifice the Irish Constabulary rather than sully his British Army.

The strain under which policemen operated was intruding into their domestic lives. In Tubbercurry Co. Sligo, Sgt McGovern was remanded in custody, charged with shooting his wife with intent to do her grievous bodily harm. Con. Gallagher testified that Mrs McGovern was bleeding from a wound in her shin. The Sergeant claimed it was an accident. In Ballybofey, Co. Donegal, a bullet fired through the window of a Constable's lodgings hit the bed on which his infant daughter was lying.

On the 2nd January, the *Observer* of London accused the Government of using unrest, especially conspicuous outrages, as a pretext for shelving reform. "Everywhere stupid reaction and the militarist instinct try to conjure away the storm by smashing the barometer." The piece continued: "With every day the extremists become more numerous and more violent, and the moderates fewer and more helpless". It referred to the suppression of an edition of the *Freeman's Journal* as "an act of futile madness".

In January the first temporary constables, better known as Black and Tans, were recruited and took up duty in March. Not trained as policemen but soldiers, they were nonetheless subject only to police discipline rather than the more rigid military discipline which the situation required. For example, police barracks contained no guardrooms in which to detain errant members; in desperation, some senior officers established unofficial ones in larger stations.

The Temporary Constables' nickname came from their rather bizarre clothing. Lacking sufficient police uniforms, they were issued with a mixture of tunics and trousers combining Military khaki with the Constabulary's near-black dark green. To maintain some cleanliness two complete outfits were required. When issued with one police uniform together with a military one, the new arrivals, with the pragmatism of old soldiers, paired the tunic of one with the trousers of the other and thus achieved a uniformity of sorts.

Both top-and-bottom colour combinations were used. In May an approach was made to the Admiralty for surplus Royal

Marines jackets and trousers. Nothing seems to have come of that so they were never clad in blue; Black and Tan they remained. The nickname persisted even when the new fellows were fully kitted out in Police green; maybe it seemed appropriate to the Irish psyche to call those men after a pack of dogs, albeit foxhounds. It would have suited the regular Constabulary to have the public draw a clear distinction between them and the newcomers. It was a distinction they themselves made. But to confuse the issue, the RIC was now drawing recruits from Britain as the number of Irish-born applicants to the Depot had diminished.

Despite the general public and the regular police marking the newcomers as different, it's important to remember that they never had a separate structure nor did they operate as a separate entity. They, and the new recruits of Irish and British birth were there as reinforcements for the regular police and they worked alongside the "old RIC". The new Irish recruits included men who would not have met the stringent standards in physique and education of earlier years. But once issued with police uniforms, the Temporary Constables were indistinguishable from the regular Irish policemen except perhaps by their often shorter stature and wartime medal ribbons. Former soldiers also often chose to wear pistols in military fashion on the left hand side of the belt. Much of the time when people spoke of the Black and Tans they were actually referring to Auxiliaries. Confusion still persists.

The *Constabulary Gazette* referred to this initiative as "an ill-conceived experiment" and said that the new temporary constables were "hopeless candidates for the police service of their own country".

Recruitment procedures for Temporary Constables could indeed be perfunctory. Shortly before taking his final vows, former monk Douglas Duff had left his English Catholic monastery on a Friday morning. On Tuesday he presented himself at the recruiting office at Scotland Yard, and on Thursday returned with his birth certificate and other relevant papers. Once seen by the doctor, he'd had his arm marked with a rubber stamp and was told to report to Euston Station to catch the Irish Mail that evening. On Friday morning he sailed into Dublin's North Wall where he and the rest of his group were issued with rifles for protection on the short drive to the Depot.

On the 24th January, Percy French died at Glasgow. The amiable Ireland he had depicted in much-loved songs like *Come Back, Paddy Reilly* was being supplanted by a far more ugly reality. Barbarism lurked behind the mask of patriotism. In Killorglin on 10th January, ten armed men raided the home of T.Mangan and cut off half of each of his ears. They twisted Mrs Mangan's arms and cut off her hair. His aged father was knocked down and kicked. Why? Mangan had instituted proceedings for trespass. Ten arrests were made.

On the previous day, the Tralee home of Mr Slattery, a solicitor, was raided by armed men. Shots were fired at his guest Serjeant Sullivan, King's Counsel, the man who had defended Roger Casement. Motive enough would have been Sullivan's outspoken opposition to Sinn Fein and the proponents of political violence. Only a couple of weeks before, he had written to Dr Walsh, Catholic Archbishop of Dublin, protesting that the Church was failing to condemn secret societies who "publicly represented murder as a sort of religious function". Sullivan remonstrated: "The silence of the pulpit is diligently misrepresented as the approval of the Church". Of course, to the revolutionary generation Sullivan was a Castle Catholic with a fat income.

Serjeants at Law were an elite order of barristers dating back to the 14th Century and having preferential status in eligibility for judgeships. Sullivan was the last Serjeant in Britain or Ireland. Incidentally, while Sullivan was often criticised for his handling of Casement's defence, given the evidence of Sir Roger's activities in Germany there really was no answer to the charge of High Treason. Certainly, Casement would have been appalled by this murderous attack. He was a gentleman who wrote from The Tower to his RIC captors in Kerry thanking them for their kindness while he was in their custody.

Fifty years later, looking back on the period, former policeman Pat Mahon wrote: "While one can concede the romantic and chivalrous aspects of 1916 we can only envisage the successors of the poets and idealists as hard-faced men planning the most sordid type of guerrilla warfare with assassination as its main feature".

In the Ballyshannon Municipal elections on 16th January, two Unionists were returned alongside ten SF members. On the 23rd, the *Donegal Vindicator* said in its editorial: "The killing of Irish policemen by Irish non-policemen is such a villainous act of folly that we cannot grasp the frame of mind which inspires it... Should it be decided by the wise-heads of Ireland that shooting is essential for the freedom of this country, why shoot policemen? They are mostly very decent chaps who took the job because there was no other handy".

On the 30th the same paper approvingly quotes remarks made by Mr Henderson of the British Labour Party while visiting Ireland: "The crowning disaster in the long history between the Irish people and Great Britain came in the suspension of the Home Rule Act of 1914, and the subsequent policy of the Government by enacting the Conscription Act then refusing to put it into operation".

There were severe gales at the end of the month with 100 mph being recorded at Quilty, Co. Clare on the 27th. Trees were uprooted and much structural damage was reported. Probably severe weather was welcomed by policemen as it curtailed their patrolling and made things difficult for the revolutionaries.

In February 1920 more outlying barracks were shut down although "this facilitates the criminal classes". During the month eight barracks were attacked and one policeman died. Donegal, at least according to the CI, was fairly peaceful. An elderly man called Curran was tied up by intruders who stole £272 from him; four persons were arrested. But distillation and drunkenness continued to increase.

On the 25th February, the counties of Longford, Louth, Sligo, Westmeath and Wicklow were added to the eleven cities and counties already on the list of Proclaimed districts. The security situation was getting demonstrably worse.

Having been increasingly marginalised by Lord Lieutenant French, and the Unionist clique in Dublin Castle, Sir Joseph Byrne was finally removed from the post of Inspector General. As a Catholic and a moderate he seems to have been always mistrusted by them.

Whatever his shortcomings, Byrne was popular within the Force; there were unprecedented protests from the rank and file during his prolonged going. As early as January the *Gazette* had printed a large photo of Sir Joseph and called his dismissal "deplorable". Later, in September, a letter-writer referred to the whispers against Byrne – that "he was a good soldier but a bad policeman", and said his dismissal had been deplored by the rank and file because he showed practical sympathy with them".

No official reason was ever offered for Gen. Byrne's removal. No doubt he was seen as insufficiently ruthless in stamping out the supposed Bolshevism represented by the police union, and in suppressing Nationalist sentiments among policemen. He also favoured a negotiated settlement rather than all-out coercion. IG Byrne had also stated in his annual report for 1919: "If we had no rifles we should be quite safe… we do not need rifles for the discharge of our ordinary duties". Next, he was complaining the new Temporary Constables were not adhering to the RIC Code of Practice.

According to then County Inspector Vere Gregory, the proximate cause of Byrne's dismissal was his opposition to the policy advocated by Field Marshal French of closing small police stations. Byrne saw this as abandoning huge swathes of the countryside to the IRA and lawlessness; he advocated bringing in soldiers to protect the policemen. His mistake was to voice this opinion in the Kildare Street Club where it was overheard and carried to French. The result was a curt note on Byrne's desk ordering him to take immediate leave – indefinitely.

In the House of Commons on 21st February, Mr Macpherson said that "Sir Joseph Byrne had been granted three months leave pending a reply to a request that he should avail himself of an opportunity to send in his resignation… The Government came to the conclusion… that he was unequal to that active discharge of all the essential duties of Inspector General… for which in the circumstances now prevailing in Ireland, the Government were compelled to look."

A Resolution from the new Representative Body for Head Constables, Sergeants and Constables regretting the dismissal of General Byrne was not accepted by the authorities.

Sir Joseph, now with the King's Police Medal among his decorations, went on to have a distinguished career in the Colonial Service as Governor in turn of the Seychelles, Sierra Leone and Kenya.

As already stated, Byrne had opposed the new policy of closing the smaller barracks and concentrating the RIC in the larger, more defensible barracks. Rather than militarising the police, he had favoured disarmament and civil policing. The policy disagreement was fundamental. Donal O'Sullivan puts it clearly: "As a result of the policies embarked on by Lord French, the force virtually became a military force, confined to the larger barracks, which were heavily fortified and sand-bagged, and preoccupied with its fear of attack rather than taking a pro-active policing role".

Of course, conditions varied widely across the country, a contrast which would grow more pronounced. At the end of February, Dublin was subject to a midnight curfew. Street lights, apart from tramway lights, were turned off at 11.30 and soldiers patrolled the streets. In Derry city, moving pictures enthralled the public: 'King Solomon's Mines' and Charlie Chaplin in 'Charlie in the Park' were on offer. Chaplin's 'The Pawnshop' was a coming attraction.

In March, Sir Thomas J. Smith was officially named as new Inspector General. He was a Protestant of Orange sympathies with a reputation for toughness and efficiency and presumably the Government thought him more amenable to their policy. His tenure would last for only nine months. For the moment, both he and General Byrne drew salaries as IG of the Royal Irish Constabulary: taxpayers' money.

On 23rd March 1920 Gen. Nevil Macready, late Commissioner of the London Met, accepted the job of General Officer Commanding the Military forces in Ireland. Before taking up his new position he spoke with Sir Henry Wilson, Chief of the Imperial General Staff, the same Sir Henry who had intrigued to subvert his government's plans for Home Rule before the Great War. "Before I crossed to Dublin we had several long talks on the general situation from which it was clear that he firmly held to a policy of stamping out rebellion with a strong hand, a policy with which I was in absolute agreement on the understanding that the government would provide the necessary means, a vital condition on which I was by no means sanguine, even then".

Along with Martial Law, French was an enthusiastic advocate of the use of air power and Macready agreed. He argued that there were "undoubtedly cases where fire from aeroplanes would materially assist the forces on the ground, with little or no danger to harmless individuals". French's idea was to establish fortified "air camps", one to each province, from which aircraft could "play about with either bombs or machine guns". His gleeful opinion that air power "ought to put the fear of God into these playful young Sinn Feiners" was echoed by Macready who thought "a few rounds fired from the air would have a great moral effect, even if no casualties were inflicted". Churchill was enthusiastic at Cabinet. One might catch a faint echo here of putting manners on faraway colonials. However, Sir Hugh Trenchard, in command of the RAF, pointed out the difficulty for an airman in distinguishing hostile groundlings from the innocent. He called it the "reckless use of a powerful arm" and rejected the proposal as "ineffective and highly dangerous".

In Ireland ordinary policemen would have been blissfully unaware of what these military minds were considering. As the conflict intensified, the RAF did provide useful spotting abilities to military and police parties on the ground even if impeded by lack of radio communication. Dropping a message from the air could result in its being delivered into IRA hands. The RAF never fired its guns in anger in Ireland; the first use of air to ground fire was by the new National Air Service against irregular forces in 1922.

Still less could the population at large have imagined such acts of war in their own fields. In March 1920, the Ballyshannon Amateur Dramatic Society diverted the public with "The Pope in Killybeck" and another short comedy "A Minute's Wait", set at a rural railway station. Those with country skills and a need for cash might respond to the advertisment placed in the *Vindicator* by an English wholesaler: "Rabbits! Rabbits! Any number fresh killed or trapped wanted". The same newspaper gave as its opinion: "Martial law reigns and fools pot policemen at short range, Holy Ireland a nation of assassins is a new feature". As adroit with the gossip as any society rag, the *Vindicator* quoted the official bulletin: "Lord French left for England on Saturday. He motored from Dublin, having a strong bodyguard of military and an armoured car". Then, "Was 'the lady' with him?"

Major Gen. Sir Henry Hugh Tudor was appointed in February as Police Advisor to the Viceroy, his friend Lord French. In May, he was given the new title of Chief of Police. During the first six months of 1920 there was an effective purge of the upper ranks of the RIC. The rank and file, learning of these changes, must have realised that their world had become even more inhospitable.

When, on the resignation of IG Smith in December, Gen. Tudor was put in charge of both the RIC and DMP, the ordinary Peeler, forced to become a soldier, must have felt abandoned.

In April Sir Hamar Greenwood was appointed Chief Secretary for Ireland and was to be the last holder of that Cabinet post.

> Said Lloyd George to Macpherson 'I'll give you the sack,
> For to govern Ireland you have not the knack.
> I'll send over Greenwood, a much stronger man
> And he'll do my work with the bold Black and Tan'.

The *Freeman's Journal* of 21st May, under the headlines "A Tudor in Charge" and "Militarisation of Irish Police" criticised the Authorities for suppressing news of the RIC pleas for disarmament. "The government are using the RIC as a unit of their army of occupation and repression. All the trouble in which the force has been involved has arisen from that fact. Officers and men of the force, indeed, have actively made representations to the government on the matter". The paper claimed that during the War the Defence of the Realm Act had been used to censor news of the policemen's requests. Since the end of the world conflict, the Castle had prevented newspapers from publishing "their suggestions for their own security. The most serious of these suggestions was that they should be disarmed of military weapons. The possession of these weapons was, the police themselves said, only a source of danger to them and an invitation to attack. If there were no weapons in the police barracks, they declared, there would be no raids by the IRA." In many parts of the country, conditions seemed to support the contention that unarmed police could function normally. Around the end of May 1920, soon after the abandoned Tourmakeady barracks had been burned, young James Goulden was taken for a spin:

> I went out with my father in the Crossley to Tourmakeady the day the steel shutters were sent to Derrypark. There was no escort except my father, who carried a revolver, and I sat between him and the driver, Baker, who was unarmed. Baker had a curious way of tapping his left arm with his right hand as he drove. I stayed poking around in the ruins of my former home until they picked me up on the way back. I quote this as an example of what little danger was anticipated at that time.

That same month, the Lord Mayor of Cork, Thomas McCurtin – an IRA officer – was murdered in his home by masked men widely believed to be police. In the opinion of Patrick Shea, "this deed was the beginning of anarchy, the end of a great police force". The police officer who was suspected by the IRA to have led the raiding party, DI Swanzy, was subsequently murdered with McCurtin's own pistol as he emerged from church in Lisburn, a killing which in turn incited Unionist mobs there to attack local Catholics.

At the end of March the Donegal Republican leadership issued a proclamation.

> Whereas the spies and traitors known as the Royal Irish Constabulary are holding this country for the enemy and whereas said spies and bloodhounds are conspiring with the enemy to bomb and bayonet and otherwise outrage a peaceful, law-abiding and liberty-loving Irish people.
>
> Whereas we do hereby proclaim and suppress said spies and traitors and do hereby solemnly warn prospective recruits that they join the RIC at their own peril. All nations are agreed as to the fate of traitors. It has the sanction of God and man.
>
> By order of GOC
> Irish Republican Army

Around the same time the military authorities endeavoured to force railway men to end their ban on carrying military personnel and material. The IRA response was to infiltrate the maintenance sheds at Bundoran and remove essential parts from two locomotives. The railway company responded by closing Bundoran station for some time.

A Dáil resolution of 10th April 1920 gave formal expression to the boycott of policemen. The women of Cumann na mBan threw vitriol worthy of the Old Testament:

> For money their hands are dipped in the blood of their people… They are the eyes and ears of the enemy. Let those eyes and ears know no friendship
>
> Let them be outcasts in their own land. The blood of the martyrs shall be upon them and their children's children and they shall curse the mothers who brought them forth.

Peter Gallagher, a Constable stationed at Tubbercurry, Co. Sligo, later recalled: "I was respected when I joined but after a while I wasn't. People were friendly until the troubles, then you wouldn't have one to talk to you." In a revealing reference to Protestants, he said "They'd have less to do with us than some of the Republicans, because they'd be afraid to be accused of giving us news, so they kept away from us altogether to keep safe." It was a common enough prejudice that Protestants, even if not actively Unionist, were less Irish than Catholics.

An IRA leader, Flor O'Donoghue, later explained how British policy-makers had historically needed intelligence on the national pulse: "...they had been well and faithfully served by the RIC since the establishment of the force. From its country-wide network of stations, manned by a body of men generally conscientious and intelligent in the discharge of their duties, having an unrivalled knowledge of the inhabitants and a shrewd understanding of Irish character, a constant flow of information reached Dublin Castle through the filter of RIC organisation". Of course policemen understood the character of the people; under the uniform they were themselves of the people. Had their political masters paid attention to their observations and framed policies for the benefit of the people, much bloodshed and grief might have been avoided.

Policemen were not spies; there was no need for espionage. They passed on information that was common knowledge. Statements by such as Dorothy Macardle that they spied on the people are assertions. RIC veteran Thomas Fennell wrote that Macardle was simply wrong. Intelligence gathering, in any case, was the responsibility of Sergeants and District Inspectors. Ordinary Constables would be guided by what the Manual had made clear: "The men should make it their business to know if possible every person in their sub-districts. They should have a friendly intercourse with all the respectable inhabitants, and a *useful* one with all the bad characters".

The boycotted Police had to commandeer food and other necessities. Sympathetic but intimidated shopkeepers would stand back while policemen helped themselves from the shelves then left the money on the counter.

On 25th May 1920, Kerryman Sgt Cornelius Crean was gunned down in the street at Ballinspittal, Co. Cork. The murdered Sergeant was a brother of Tom Crean, who'd participated in three voyages to the Polar wastes alongside Sir Ernest Shackleton – arguably a greater explorer than Scott in that he never lost a man. Now, almost a century later, when Tom is properly celebrated as an Antarctic explorer, Cornelius has been forgotten.[vii]

On the 3rd of May 1920, the Government of Ireland Act came into force, setting up Home Rule parliaments in Belfast and Dublin. Institutionalising partition, this provided the structure for the Northern Irish state and many of the police serving in that area would be absorbed into the new Royal Ulster Constabulary but it wasn't an automatic transfer. Ireland's own Orange State would demand different loyalties from its police, loyalties which many RIC members could neither subscribe to nor stomach. When the Southern Irish parliament convened, only four Unionist MPs attended and it was adjourned *sine die.*

May also brought a long-overdue increase in police salaries. A Constable with nine years' service could now earn 88 shillings per week or a total of £273 per annum but John Hennigan wasn't quite at that point..

Official duty for Constable John seems to have continued much as before. On the 25th March he brought John Ward of Erne Street before the Court on a charge of being "drunk on a public street" Mr Ward was fined a Half Crown – two shillings and sixpence – plus one shilling and sixpence costs. A month later Patrick McCawley found himself in court on the same charge but his fine was only one shilling plus costs.

By June 1920 the situation had deteriorated. The new–style IG reports, organised by county, said Donegal was not in a satisfactory condition. On 1st June there was an attempt to burn down the Ballyshannon Courthouse. It may have resulted from an excess of Republican zeal, given that the County Council had already passed a resolution giving SF Courts the use of the courthouse. SF had now a majority in the County Council and most of Donegal's District Councils. A new pro-SF weekly newspaper "*An Dail*" had appeared in Ballyshannon. It was put out by Miss McAdam, daughter of the proprietor of the "*Donegal Vindicator*" which expressed Constitutional Nationalist views.

By July 1920 the situation in Donegal had worsened. Indictable offences rose to 70, up from 40, and almost all due to the SF boycott of police. Rail travel was suspended due to the Railway Unions refusing to carry soldiers or police. There were a number of attacks on police in remote areas. Men wearing IRP armbands (Irish Republican Police) appeared on the streets of Ballyshannon on the 19th. On the 28th, a car was stolen and dumped in the river. It emerged that it belonged to a commercial traveller for a Belfast firm. This was a reflection of the hostility being expressed towards Unionist traders in Ballyshannon as a consequence of the Belfast sectarian disturbances.

It was a bad month for the RIC with 15 policemen murdered; four Army and two Naval personnel also died. The IG's report stated: "In many parts of the country…the police lived under conditions so irksome, depressing and hazardous as to impose strain which very few bodies of men, however highly disciplined, could be expected to bear".

It has been pointed out by analysts such as Robert Kee that in the early stages of the campaign, at least, the police generally refrained from acts of retaliation. When they were reinforced by the new Temporary Constables from Britain, that would change. The Black and Tans had no links with, or understanding of, the community. All civilians must have seemed equally suspicious to them; they could trust nobody and commonly took refuge in alcohol. One of the "Old RIC" recalled them as "all English and Scotch people… very rough, f-ing and blinding and boozing and all. They'd have shot their mother, oh desperate altogether". Members of the Protestant and Unionist communities disliked the new arrivals as much as did those of the Catholic and Nationalist persuasions. They "did not know a Unionist from a Republican and hardly bothered to make the distinction".

Training for the new recruits was minimal at best. Former Naval Midshipman Douglas Duff's group had been sent on to Gormanstown Camp where kit was issued. Those who'd been infantrymen, or pretended to have been, were given three days' training. This consisted of bomb instruction, ten rounds of aimed rifle fire, and revolver practice with six shots fired from each hand. An hour's "lecture on the Game Laws or something" was their introduction to police duties and off the new "Constables" went to reinforce the proud RIC. Those without infantry backgrounds spent three or four weeks in training.

Patrick Mahon had been sent to London in August 1920 to assist in recruitment. He loved it. He pointed out that only men who had received a "Good" character from the Army were accepted; a "Fair" character meant rejection. They also needed a certificate from their local police station.

Mahon was assigned to assist the Medical Officer, Lt Col. Brown, by keeping notes. On one occasion Brown was examining a heavy, florid man for appointment to a "B" post – cooks, orderlies etc. The former regular soldier told Brown that he'd only one testicle as a result of a gunshot wound. The Colonel said "One is quite adequate in the place you're going to, Connemara probably".

In Connemara, in the Clifden area, Constable "Ducksie" Cronin earned his nickname by his habitual response when he encountered young women who showed hostility to the uniform. Beaming his widest smile, he'd say "Hello, Ducksie". Transferred from Galway to the Curragh, Ducksie was put in charge of a hut full of Black and Tans undergoing their perfunctory training. He couldn't handle them and, when his request for transfer was refused, he resigned. Returning to his native Kerry, he found himself subject to the suspicion that his resignation was a ruse. Rejected in his home place, he reapplied to the Force and was accepted but died within a few months. A colleague suggested it was a "psycho-somatic malady".

Against the backdrop of all this political and military activity, Constable John Hennigan continued to bring inebriated citizens before the Petty Sessions. On 27th July it was the turn of Alexander McGanley, "drunk on the public street". Alexander's case was adjourned for three months "to see how defendant behaves himself". The case was subsequently Dismissed on Merit. Perhaps it was the absurd normality of these proceedings which gave some psychological comfort to policemen in the increasingly febrile atmosphere of mayhem and murder.

In July also the first Auxiliaries began to arrive. The idea for such a force seems to have originated with Churchill in May. Churchill had lots of bright ideas, many of which seemed to involve bloodshed. Ostensibly the Auxiliary Division of the RIC with the title of Police Cadets, they were organised into hundred-strong Companies under the direct command of Brig. Gen. Crozier, a former UVF organiser and Great War veteran. With no attempt to bring them under real police or military control, they acted just as independently as their command structure allowed. Some police officers of military background or experience may have welcomed them as reinforcements but many ordinary policemen wanted nothing to do with them. As former military officers, the Auxies didn't have much regard for the Constabulary either.

It is undeniable that they were probably the most highly decorated military force in the world with two VCs, and lots of DSOs, MCs, Croix de Guerre, and other medals among them. It says a lot about the land fit for heroes that they'd been promised at war's end that these World War veterans ended up in Ireland. Many were still very young men and they were not simply the thugs portrayed in Irish folklore.

Crozier asserted that he found the RIC demoralised and abusing and killing the innocent because they couldn't catch the guilty but that the Military were well behaved. This is a view that was embraced by Republic propagandists. Thomas Fennell later said that actually the reverse was true. It does seem clear that unofficial reprisals carried out by policemen were selective whereas those made by the soldiery were indiscriminate – as at Fermoy.

Frank Crozier may not be the most reliable witness. He was regarded with deep suspicion by some on his own side. Sturgis referred to him as "this beauty Crozier" and said he was "a perfectly worthless fellow" who was "more truly responsible for indiscipline in the Auxiliaries whom he commands than anybody else". CI John M. Regan thought him "a chancer" and said he was "libellous and untruthful", inducing a "feeling of nausea".

Reflecting their independent status, separate from the Military and Police, the Auxiliaries wore a distinctive outfit, military in colour and cut but with flourishes to identify them as an elite unit. Later a blue uniform was issued. Headgear was the Tam O'Shanter, a bobbled bonnet, and breeches were favoured. Pistols were commonly slung low on the hip in Wild West gunslinger style. Heavy gauge shotguns and grenades completed the tough image and bandoliers across the chest evoked fashionable cavalry regiments. Temporary Constables acted as servants in the Mess. But behind the façade, all was not as elite as it seemed. Many of these officers had been commissioned from the ranks in the later stages of the Great War and lacked extensive military training and experience. Lack of scruple was perhaps their most distinctive characteristic.

The Auxies' organisational deficiencies were recalled by Con. Gallagher. "They took over our house in the Barrack. They weren't there more than a week till everything was topsy-turvy, there was nothing right about it. So the RIC had to supply them with a Head Constable and a constable for office work; there wasn't one of them Auxiliary officers who was a first-class scholar. All of them high ranks in the army and no education. The RIC had to do the whole paperwork."

Auxiliaries wore a shoulder flash with the letters TC, ostensibly 'Temporary Cadet' but by their own definition it stood for 'tough cunts' . It's not hard to see how the untravelled farmers' sons who made up the ranks of the RIC must have been disconcerted by contact with these hardened soldiers, allies or not. Contemporary comments include: "Never was a relieving force so dissimilar to those to whose aid they came" and "They brought help but they frightened even those they had come to help". Their own preferred name for themselves was "Tudor's Toughs".

"Rough" is an adjective that recurs. "They were rough chaps indeed." "They were rough, no doubt about that. They just got somebody that were doing something wrong, they would lift him and throw him in this van and take him away with them". "In Clare… fairly rough, they done their work in a very rough way…The Auxiliaries were in kind of world of their own. They raided rough". Interestingly, these roughness comments are the recollections of late recruits to the RIC – including some Black and Tans.

Ordinary policemen had little contact with Auxiliaries. "The Auxiliaries didn't mix with the police at all." Con. McIvor said "We had no truck with the Auxiliaries at all". "I did meet the Auxiliaries but we never mixed with them" said Con. Sullivan. "The Auxiliaries kept to themselves" recalled another veteran.

What did the "Old RIC" think of the Black and Tans? One view was that of Republican Piarais Beaslai who wrote extensively on the period. "The Old RIC who were left in the Force viewed with disgust their compelled association with those off-scourings of rascaldom, who stole one another's money and belongings, who had no code of honour, no scruple, and very little discipline. But they were the right men for Sir Hamar Greenwood's job."

One former policeman, ten years later, inelegantly expressed very trenchant views:

> For us who prided in such fame and worth
> 'Twas bitter mead of vinegar and gall,
> That from across the sea should sally forth
> To queer our pitch at Britain's beck and call,
> The rabble spawn of workhouses and jails,
> - The moral perverts of the under class –
> The jumble-scrub of dosshouse head and tails
> From John O'Groats, away down to Penzance,
> May vengance dire its blackest wrath pour down
> On those who engineered pollution's trade,
> And set themselves to mate without a frown
> Our men with cut-throat scum a hateful blend,
> For better to be wiped out to a man
> Than seek support from brutish Black and Tan.

Relations between RIC and Tans were rather more complex than that. Like it or not, when a Police barrack was reinforced by a few Tans, they had to coexist. "Some of the Black and Tans were alright, some of them were decent fellows, and some of them were a real damned nuisance, you know. Drink; they were a bit rough, especially when they got drink taken, but you know, there were some fine fellows among them."

Con. Bratton at Navan, Co. Meath, later recalled the Black and Tans who joined his station. One he remembered as "a decent man", another was "all right". "As for the rest, they were "a low-down lot of scoundrels, and it was believed that they were mostly jail-birds and men of bad repute." The allegation of criminal records was promoted by the very able Republican propaganda machine but now appears to have had no basis in fact. There was no shortage of unemployed ex-soldiers in Britain to recruit from. Con. Sterrett remembered "we had two, they were two gentlemen and they wouldn't associate with the others. They always kept to themselves, they were reading books and all this...There was a couple of Scotch fellows there and they were a bit rough, but these two Englishmen, they were terrible nice fellows."

They have divided opinion then and since. Rev. Charles Tyndall referred to "the degrading effects on the regular force of being in contact with the auxiliary police. Many became alcoholic addicts and morale declined rapidly". He was probably quoting his father, the Ballyshannon District Inspector.

Con. Crawford gave his view: "The regular force didn't have much contact with them at all, we didn't really know them, they were stationed along with us in different huts but they were never popular with the regular force. We just didn't approve of their methods of work and you can understand why. I don't think it was the proper way of dealing with it, an emergency like that. You make a lot of enemies and turn people against the police force in general because they put them all down as the one force."

The confusion and contradictions in British thinking

were made explicit at a meeting between British Government ministers and officers of the Irish Administration in late July. Ulster Unionist James Craig was invited in. Judge Wylie offered his opinion that the failure to deliver Home Rule had caused the increase in support for Sinn Féin and suggested an immediate offer of Dominion Home Rule. Wylie predicted that "within two months, the Irish Police Force, as a Police Force, would cease to exist…. fifty per cent would have resigned through terrorism, and the remainder would have to go about in considerable force, committing counter-outrages". Wylie suggested that the "Irish policeman either saw white or saw red; if he saw white he resigned from the force through terrorism, and if he saw red he committed a counter outrage".

His view was supported by Sir John Anderson, Andy Cope and Generals McMahon and Macready. Anderson's opinion was that the government "had either to give way or to go very much further in repression". He was opposed to introducing Martial Law. Tudor advocated a hard line and was supported by Churchill and Birkenhead. Churchill accused Wylie, who was Law Advisor to The Castle, of condoning murder; he himself favoured "summary justice". There was no unity of command: Macready showed contempt for the Police and had a poor relationship with Tudor. Field Marshal Henry Wilson thought all politicians were "frocks" anyway. As Tudor advocated "drastic measures to crush the present campaign of outrage", Lloyd George backed away from any accommodation with Sinn Féin and started to adopt a more hawkish attitude.

In early August the Restoration of Order in Ireland Act was introduced. Essentially it was bits of the wartime Defence of the Realm Act with new powers. The jurisdiction of Courts Martial was extended to cover civil matters and they had the power to impose capital sentences. Coroner's courts were replaced by Military Courts of Enquiry, averting the embarrassment of juries returning verdicts of murder by Crown forces. Civil law was being subverted by the government, the judiciary sidelined and the police reduced to expendable infantrymen. They, as much as the mass of the people, were pawns in a brutal struggle being waged between the forces of reaction and of revolution.

At the end of August, policemen in Ballinasloe wrote to Sir John Anderson calling for the RIC's disbandment. Their major complaint was the inability to perform civic police duties: "we consider it almost an impossibility to carry out our functions as a civil police force under the pressure of present circumstances. The strain on the force is so great… we are now useless as a civil police force. We as a body of men are not able to restore law and order". Of course the "old RIC" was an aging force, long suffering from the thrombosis of a stultifying promotion system. Trying to turn it into an army was a gross abuse of its members.

Reporting from Cork West Riding in July 1920, the County Inspector painted a grim picture:

> The loss of life inflicted on Government forces cannot but have a disastrous effect on the morale of the men.
>
> The RIC hitherto have been indomitable and have carried on with fearlessness, courage and initiative, but recent events point to the breaking point being reached.
>
> This is evidenced by the numerous applications to resign made by men who, having no means of livelihood outside the force after resignation, have to face the world again to win bread for themselves and their families.
>
> So far as the RIC is concerned in this Riding, they may be considered to have ceased to function. The most they can do is to try and defend themselves and their barracks.
>
> It would seem that the time has arrived for the military to supersede the RIC in this Riding.

> If action is not speedily taken the RIC will exist only in name.
>
> Further resignations may be expected daily.
>
> The men consider that they are merely pawns in a political game.

Another aspect of the redefinition of the RIC's role was the appointment of Divisional Commissioners, intermediate between County Inspectors and Police HQ. Initially there were five, one per province plus one for Dublin, but this was increased to seven. Henry John Moore, promoted to CI in June 1920, was appointed Div. Comm. at Clonmel. He served until pensioned off on 22nd July 1922.

In July 1920 Bundoran and Cliffony IRA members met to plan the burning of Classibawn Castle at Mullaghmore. A raid by British military disrupted the meeting but all except one escaped. It was decided to burn the Mullaghmore Coastguard station instead of the castle. This was done without casualties on either side.

Doing duty as Barrack Orderly became more dangerous. Previously, when it was a policeman's turn to take charge of his station the role was onerous mainly in the sense of being confined to the barrack for a 24 hour period, dealing with members of the public as required and attending to the minutae of everyday routine. Now, at least in the most troubled areas, the BO had to be armed with a revolver at all times and wear a steel breastplate when unchaining the reinforced door for bona fide customers. He never opened the door alone but had to be backed up by another man. They were almost siege conditions.

There was news from John Hennigan's former station in neat little Drumquin. Constable Munnelly was Barrack Orderly when the terraced house that served as a barrack was attacked on 26th August, a fair day. When IRA men knocked on the door, Munnelly answered it and was shot in the forehead. As the raiders burst in, Sgt Bradley, at the top of the stairs, was wounded but managed to throw down a grenade. There are conflicting accounts regarding the number of weapons taken by the IRA but James Munnelly, aged 30, was indisputably dead.

At Collooney Co. Sligo, Sgt King was offered many suggestions that he should resign, but steadfastly refused. As his son put it, he preferred to risk being shot rather than reduce his family to penury and be branded a coward. The Collooney station was reinforced by five Temporary Constables. The King family with its eight children lived in a nearby house. Auxiliaries from Sligo rampaged about the countryside. One day, three drunken Auxies arrived at the wrong house to carry out a search and proceeded to ransack it. It was the King family home. When the Sergeant returned he drew his revolver and ordered them out. They were arrested.

In the insane symmetry of the time young Cecil King was one of a number of teenagers ordered by armed men to dig a trench across a road. In the morning when Police and Tans arrived to investigate they were ambushed. Sgt King was unscathed but had a tunic button shot off. Later in the day Cecil was again one of a group forced by Auxiliaries to fill in the trench. After the British withdrawal, in the spring of 1922 when the town was occupied by anti-Treaty IRA, young King would be among the teenagers ordered to commandeer provisions on their behalf.

On Wed. 4th August Constable Brennan was interviewed by Assnt Under Sec. Andy Cope, Acting Assnt Under Sec. Mark Sturgis, and Inspector General Smith. Brennan was the representative of the Leinster RIC men. They had issued 2,000 leaflets saying Dominion Home Rule was the only way to save their lives. Leinster was actually the quietest part of the country. Sturgis noted in his delightfully indiscreet diary "A bonny job to start Coercion by having to coerce the RIC". Around the same time, the *Irish Times* published a leader supporting Dominion HR.

The 7th August edition of the *Constabulary Gazette*, commented on reports that Auxiliaries with the nominal rank of Sergeant would have priority of promotion to DI posts thus causing "very resentful feeling" within the RIC. The journal called for the adoption of the system used in Great Britain making all ranks up to County Inspector open to ambitious Constables. County Inspector was the equivalent of an English Chief Constable of the time and in Britain the post might be expected to be filled by a retired senior military officer.

A further grievance concerned the wearing of mufti, that is civilian clothes. Although free to wear their own clothes when on leave, policemen when off-duty had to remain in uniform. It's incredible that this regulation persisted at a time when the police were at daily risk of assassination by an enemy who never wore a uniform.

During August the situation in Donegal deteriorated further. "Outrages" increased from 69 to 82, of which only two were classed as agrarian. At the end of the month, four barracks in the Ballyshannon area were attacked simultaneously but the attacks were repulsed. Four vacated barracks were burnt down. Major Johnstone, aged 70, was murdered by Republicans. As no juror dared to attend, the inquest fell through.

The attacks on the Ballyshannon and Bundoran barracks were essentially diversionary and intended to draw the Military from Finner Camp while the major action was to take place in Fermanagh. At Bundoran the IRA opened fire from front and rear and the Constabulary replied in kind. It was 30th August and the town was full of holiday-makers. It rapidly emptied and the IRA's action did not endear it to those whose livelihood depended on the brief summer trade. Simultaneously in Ballyshannon shots were fired into the barrack.

Rail operations were an IRA target, particularly in the Ulster counties. Republican sympathisers on the footplate were willing to comply with the IRA embargo on the carriage of police or troops, but drivers who tried to avoid politics and do their jobs as normal could be subjected to IRA intimidation. If they refused to carry Crown forces, they were liable to dismissal by their employers. The situation was exacerbated by the Belfast Boycott, a Republican embargo on goods originating from areas where sectarian violence was worst. In August 1920, following a series of incidents including kidnapping of railwaymen, the Great Northern Railway shut down the Bundoran branch line. This was a very severe blow to the economic life of the area. Amongst those affected were pilgrims to "St Patrick's Purgatory" on Lough Derg and visitors to the railway company's own Great Northern Hotel at Bundoran.

Reprisals by Crown forces were increasing. The infamous "Sack of Balbriggan" occurred on the night of 20th September. This small town in North County Dublin was hardly a rebel heartland and had contributed many of its men to the Colours in the World War. There are conflicting accounts of how trouble began that evening but what is indisputable is that IRA men entered the pub where Head Constable Peter Burke was having a drink with his brother Sgt William Burke and opened fire on them. HC Burke died instantly and William was wounded but eventually recovered. To celebrate Peter's recent promotion the brothers had gone in for a drink together as the new HC was passing through Balbriggan on his way to Gormanstown Camp where he served as an instructor.

Soon afterwards, truckloads of Black & Tans from nearby Gormanstown together with Auxiliaries descended on the town. Houses belonging to Republican sympathisers were torched. Two Republicans were brought to the Police barracks for interrogation and did not leave it alive. A hosiery factory giving employment to hundreds was burnt out and the town's second hosiery factory only escaped a similar fate through the intervention of a local policeman.

The following day the smoking ruins of several dozen houses were visible to the local and international press and the terrorised residents told their stories. It was a propaganda disaster for the British Government although not all in authority immediately perceived it as such.

On the other side of the country, 22nd September was a particularly black day for the RIC. According to Richard Abbott, a single-vehicle RIC patrol ran into a well-prepared IRA ambush at Rinneen, halfway between Miltown Malbay and Lahinch, Co. Clare. Four policemen – Constables Kelly, McGuire, Hardman and Hodnett – apparently died in the initial fusillade of rifle and shotgun fire. Sgt Michael Hynes died of his wounds two days later. On the 23rd, the body of Con. Michael Harte was discovered some distance away.

Michael Harte had been a classmate of John Hennigan in the recruit intake of 24th January 1912. A Catholic, he was seven months younger than Hennigan. Being also from County Sligo, it seems probable that he and John would have spent a lot of time in conversation, in those exploratory dialogues beloved of rural Irish people when they meet beyond their own parish. On leaving the Depot he was sent first to Co. Westmeath and transferred to Co. Clare in 1917. That autumn day in The Banner County he was shown no mercy.

An official enquiry in October reached several interesting conclusions. One was that the wounded Con. Harte had managed to crawl 400 yards away from the ambush scene but was hunted down and killed. Another was that while the IRA ambush party lay in wait in their straw-strewn positions they were clearly visible from the railway line. Although several trains had passed, neither their crews nor passengers reported the presence of a large body of armed men. Another finding was that "dum-dum" bullets had been used by the IRA.

This allegation about the use of expanding bullets by the IRA was a recurrent one. In the Great War, prisoners found in possession of such ammunition by either side were liable to be summarily executed. In the IRA context it seems likely that their secret weapons workshops were incapable of producing jacketed bullets. A soft lead bullet fitted to a refilled cartridge would obviously expand on impact with devastating effect. However, the repeated reports of horrific wounds inflicted by dum-dum bullets, including those on civilians caught in crossfire, suggest that ammunition was indeed being tampered with to cause maximum damage to human flesh and bone. Some captured IRA ammunition had been scored across the point of the bullet.

On 22nd September, the same day as the Rineen ambush, County Clare also saw the murder of Capt. Alan Ledrum, MC & Bar, Resident Magistrate at Lahinch. One version of his killing is that he was buried up to his neck on the beach to await the incoming tide, and this appalling story has persisted down the decades and rewritten as fact and in fiction. However, the official enquiry concluded that the cause of his death was shooting by a person or persons unknown. As Ledrum's body wasn't recovered until 1st October and had been under sea water in the interim, it must have shown the signs of immersion. The burial on the beach story seems to have first surfaced in Blackwood's Magazine and the anonymous *Tales of the RIC* published in 1920. It seems likely that it originated with Basil Clarke's propaganda department at Dublin Castle. If Capt. Lendrum's widow and his relatives were not appraised of the true facts it was a vile cruelty.

The fate of the RM remained unknown for some time and he was presumed to have been either kidnapped or killed. But the police deaths at Rineen provoked immediate and fierce reprisals. Troops had come on the scene immediately after the ambush and there was an exchange of fire which led to the death of a RASC driver. Over the next couple of days, soldiers, policemen and Auxiliaries burned houses and businesses in Lahinch, Miltown Malbay and Ennistymon and four men were shot dead.

By October the situation in Donegal had reached a point where the government's writ no longer ran over much of the county. The Army chose to withdraw from the western part which led to the unprotected Police having to withdraw from Dungloe and concentrate their Ardara personnel at Glenties and Killybegs. All West Donegal and the coastline had been handed over to the "lawless element".

There were some indications that realism and a willingness to adjust attitudes might yet end the nightmare even if such realism wasn't apparent at the Cabinet table. At the end of September, General Sir Hubert Gough, one of the instigators of the Curragh Mutiny of 1914, wrote in a newspaper article:

> Far from self-government for Ireland in the form of Dominion Home Rule or any other, breaking up the Empire it will establish it more firmly than ever. To deny her this right, on the contrary, is to endanger the Empire and create the first fissures in its foundations. The Empire can only hope to survive indefinitely if she has the wisdom to make her subjects love her and not hate her.

Of course General Gough was now writing after Partition had been established and Loyalists of the North East had got a statelet of their own. But Major General Sir F. Maurice expressed his view that the only hope was to withdraw troops to the ports and declare an armistice for negotiations.

On the other side of the house, not everyone was happy with the excesses of Republican violence. Father O'Flanagan publicly deplored acts of "selfish terrorism" carried out in the name of Sinn Fein and Dail Eireann. He said men were going out at night with guns and firing into the windows of houses with women and children. He stressed that was not Sinn Fein, not Dail Eireann, not Republicanism. "It was, pure and simple, blackguardism". Speaking in Co. Leitrim, O'Flanagan said that violence doesn't make things better; it makes them worse. It was probably closer to a Christian message than the Republican leadership was comfortable with.

For policemen all over the country, some satisfaction must have come from the death of Sean Tracy in a Dublin gun-battle. With Dan Breen and Seamus Robinson in Tipperary, he had initiated the whole campaign of violence by the killing of Constables O'Connell and O'Donnell in January 1919. Welcome though the news was to them, it seems likely that RIC members would have preferred to see Tracy hanged as a criminal rather than die by gunshot. The well-worn shoes that Tracy was wearing that day in Talbot Street were on display at the Cistercian College in Roscrea in 1960. That item of rather necrophiliac appeal was one exhibit in a small military museum containing mostly IRA weapons: strange relics for a contemplative order, even in Tipperary.

Perhaps it may seem less strange when we remember that in 1921, RIC DI Gilbert Potter was brought to Mt Mellary monastery by his IRA captors. What did that Christian community imagine would be Potter's fate? There's no evidence that the priests and brothers even questioned his presence, much less protested. While most of the Hierarchy of the Catholic Church denounced the violence, many younger priests were active supporters of Sinn Fein and some encouraged the bloodshed. The silent acquiescence of many clergymen in the face of murder was in itself an abject failure of moral authority.

The October 16th edition of the *Constabulary Gazette*

referred to talk of Dominion Home Rule. The editorial urges RIC members to hold fast to their traditions: "it will be the maximum of folly if they permit the temporary trials through which they are passing to keep them from regarding their occupation as their career".

Close to Home: Moneygold, October 1920

On 25th October, the war came close to home for John Hennigan. On visits to his parents he had to pass through the village of Cliffoney which then had the only police barrack between Ballyshannon and Sligo. Grange had been abandoned the previous November. Cliffoney had never been attacked, probably because it seemed impregnable due to its commanding position and good defences. That Monday, a bicycle patrol of nine men set out from Cliffoney and cycled southwards towards Grange, their carbines slung across their backs. Cycling some distance ahead but careful not to outpace them was a young IRB member who lived within sight of the Cliffoney station. His name was Patrick McCannon, a student at Sligo Vocational School, and his task was to give warning of the policemen's approach to an IRA ambush party lying in wait. This group, about thirty strong and armed with shotguns and a few rifles, was commanded by Sligo Brigade leader Billy Pilkington and included Eugene Gilbride, Seamus Devins, Martin McGowan and most of the Grange Company. Many of them would have been personally known to John Hennigan even if some were only children when he went off to the Depot. Eugene Gilbride, however, was less than a year younger than John.

As they approached Grange, at Moneygold, the cyclists had to put weight on their pedals as they faced a rise in the road. Ahamlish Church was close ahead on the right and the Hennigan homestead only a couple of miles away. As they leaned on the handlebars and pushed up the hill, the policemen were ambushed. Rifles cracked and shotguns roared. Relatively harmless at long range, a shotgun at close quarters did appalling damage to a soft-skinned animal, tearing flesh and sinew to shreds. Often Volunteers substituted larger pieces of scrap metal for birdshot. Sometimes they poured molten candle wax into cartridges to form slugs of terrifying dimensions. Within seconds several policemen were dead. On the open road amid the tangled bicycles the unwounded policemen attempted to return fire at the hidden enemy as the dead and wounded lay about them. When they surrendered, the IRA men emerged and seized their weapons and ammunition, then stripped the dead and wounded of theirs. As midday was approaching the IRA party disappeared. One of them rushed to do his duty of ringing the Angelus bell at Grange Church. All Catholics themselves, the slain policemen did not hear the call to prayer. The dead included Sgt Patrick Perry from Co. Meath. Aged 51, he left a widow and 11 children. The others who died on the road were Constables Patrick Keown, 25, from Fermanagh and Patrick Laffy from Galway, aged 41. Cavanman Con. Patrick Lynch, aged 33, died of his wounds within hours. His wife, who lived nearby, was soon at the scene and tried to comfort her dying husband. He did not respond. Two other men were wounded. Father Brian Crehan, a Republican sympathiser who attended the casualties on the roadway, said that the sight was so horrible that he would never forget it. A local man told the

Sligo Champion what he'd seen: "The scene was terrible. There was nothing but pools of blood and caps and bicycles thrown around." Later, a military lorry carrying some of the dead and their relatives passed through Sligo town. A banner across it read "Sinn Fein Victory – 3 widows, 19 orphans".

Sgt Perry was a close friend of Sgt King. Perry, "who had a wonderful sense of humour", had volunteered to take over Cliffoney when King had wanted to transfer to Colooney.

John Hennigan must have known the four Patricks well. The Cliffoney barrack was the nearest to the family farm, within the same parish of Ahamlish, and close to his own police station. Those policemen would have known the family. Probably John had dropped in to say hello on occasions while cycling homewards. Perry, Lynch and Laffey had signed up to the Police Union at the same time as John. That bleak and windswept stretch of road must afterwards have been a place of painful significance for all the Hennigan family. Today, the topography has changed, the hill having been reduced to facilitate the new road. A cyclist no longer has to rise from the saddle.

There were reprisals by Crown forces. The temperance hall adjoining the RC church in Cliffoney village was badly damaged by fire but the sign saying "Ireland Sober Is Ireland Free" was still valiantly visible. The hall had been used for SF meetings. A new slogan was painted on the wall by Crown forces: "The Vacated Home of the Murder Gang". The house of County Councillor Devins was burnt as were other houses in Tullaghan and Cliffoney, and the creamery at Ballintrillick at the backside of Ben Bulben was severely damaged.

E Company of the Auxiliaries, based at Coolavin Co. Sligo, was reported as conducting a two-day search in the Grange area. It was as much a punitive expedition as a search. Did John Hennigan, or others of the regular police, participate is these reprisals? It would be understandable if they did, especially if targeting known Republicans. On the other hand, it's impossible to see him willingly involved in the collective punishment of his neighbours such as the burning of a creamery.

How did Fr Michael O'Flanagan, SF Vice-President and Chaplain to the Dail, respond to this? Grange and Cliffony had been his parish in 1914-1915, when he had led the local agitation on turbary rights and land redistribution. In his position he must have had close relations with the civil power as represented by those local policemen in both villages. During the campaign against conscription he had mocked them in speeches and the Peelers themselves had to laugh at his wit. What had he now to say about their slaughter? I have found no record but in view of the comments he had recently made about violence it seems probable that his conscience was sorely in conflict.

A report in the *Donegal Vindicator* gave some details of the injuries. "Con. Lynch is not expected to recover. He has a bullet wound in the head, several wounds in the body, and a fractured knee… Con Clarke has a broken arm, a wound in the wrist, two wounds in the head, and a wound in the leg… Con. O'Rorke is wounded in the legs and arms." The paper goes on to say that the Coronor had been instructed not to hold an inquest but that there would probably be a military enquiry. "Police and military searched the entire district on Monday evening, but in the houses there was no one to be found except children and old people. Everyone appeared to have fled and Grange and Cliffony were deserted villages." It also reported that, fearing reprisals, many people had left Sligo. "Hitherto, friendly feelings prevailed between the people and police."

The newspaper's Peripatetic Pressman column the following week contained this item: "Talking about Reprisals… Three policemen were shot at Cliffoney Co. Sligo, a fourth good chap – may God see him safe in heaven is my prayer – died afterwards". Then followed a list of the houses burnt by Crown forces.

A few days after the Moneygold ambush, soldiers stopped a car travelling southwards beside Lough Gill. It was driven by Linda Kearns, a nurse who was an active Republican sympathiser though not a member of Cumann na mBan. Rifles were found in the car along with related equipment which was identified as some of that taken at Moneygold. Kearns, Eugene Gilbride, Jim Devins and Andy Conway were arrested although there must have been some temptation to shoot them out of hand. The three men were later put on trial in Belfast. According to Eugene Gilbride's later testimony, a Constable Joyce who knew him could have revealed his true identity but declined to make a positive identification "though pressed very hard". On the last day of the trial Joyce spoke to him during a lunch break: "I could identify you if I liked but I'm a damn sight better Irishman than you".

Liam Pilkington went on to become Commander of the energetic anti-Treaty IRA in North Connacht during the anarchic mayhem of the Civil War of 1922-'23. He subsequently became a priest in the Redemptorist Order which was renowned for hellfire and brimstone sermons especially in relation to sins of the flesh. However, Fr William Pilkington spent most of his ministry in South Africa but spent his final years in Liverpool. Seamus Devins died on Ben Bulben in 1922, one of "the Noble Six". Eugene Gilbride "the silent man from the west" as *Dublin Opinion* had it, served as a Fianna Fail TD from1948 to 1969 and as a County Councillor for almost fifty years.

The composition and character of the RIC was changing. In the week ending 19th September 1920 there were 10 police deaths, 29 retirements, 36 had put in their resignations, 8 members were discharged or dismissed: the total wastage was 88. Among the 229 recruits that week only 7 were from Ireland, the rest from Britain. Added to that 222 were another 40 'B' men, drivers, cooks and such. The total Constabulary strength was now 10,002.

In the tumult of a countryside with no clearly accepted moral and legal order, revolutionary politics were frequently the cloak for sectarian and agrarian attacks. On the 19th September, Roscommon farmer W. Glover was raided by a dozen or so armed and masked men. He was told he would have to surrender his farm of 140 acres. He refused. He also refused to submit the dispute to arbitration. The wife of Sgt Lambert who was living in the farm's gate lodge was give 48 hours to clear out. Con. O Rahilly's wife, living in an out building was also given an eviction notice.

November was to be the worst month of a very bad year. On the 1st, medical student Kevin Barry was hanged and would prove more valuable to the IRA as a martyr than as a combatant. His execution provoked horrific violence in some areas. There were unsubstantiated reports that abducted Constable Ernest Bright and another missing policeman had been disposed of in the furnace of Tralee Gas Works, possibly whilst still alive. The 4th November saw the resignation of the RIC Inspector General Smith. Sir Thomas Smith, Gen. Byrnes's replacement as IG, was relieved of his duties and Gen. Tudor became chief of both the RIC and DMP. Smith was the last Inspector General. The Administration in Dublin Castle continued to flounder in its lack of clear direction, purpose or policy. Insider Mark Sturgis conveyed something of the fevered atmosphere: "Here one is up to the neck in intrigue, plot and counterplot, with a small spice of danger all mixed up with the life of something like a big country house in the old days". Outside the Castle enclave, lives continued to be led and were sometimes brutally terminated. The unarmed beat Constables of the DMP, going about their everyday business with the tacit permission of the IRA, arrested miscreants, dealt with unlighted vehicles, enforced the licensing laws and frequently took into custody drunken Black and Tans who were a danger to all elements of society. When Sturgis heard that Countess Markievicz and three men had been arrested in a car for not having a tail light, he commented: "I believe she's a thorn in the flesh to SF so it may be a pity to take her away from them". But there was menace in the streets. Assassinations occurred in crowded places and occasionally gun battles broke out. Tactically it was a different war from that in rural parts, fought here with pistols rather than rifles. Although the danger to bystanders inhibited the use of bombs, grenades were a sufficient menace to convince the Crown forces that their lorries should be protected by wire-netting cages overhead. Some ingenious revolutionaries tried festooning their bombs with fish hooks but they still bounced off. Narrow streets offered opportunity for ambush and troops nicknamed Camden Street "the Dardanelles". Under cover of curfew, Auxiliaries and Military raided houses, smashing in doors and often terrorising the innocent. Sporadic gunfire reverberated around empty thoroughfares, disturbing the dreams of just and unjust alike.

Donegal continued to be relatively calm although on the 5th November the *Vindicator* carried the headline: "Killybegs up all night. A night of terror" over a story about uniformed men on a rampage after a shooting. The next panel held an advertisement for the Gibson Hotel group in Ulster "patronised by royalty" which included among their amenities golf, yachting, touring, fishing – and shooting.

On the same date the Peripatetic Pressman wrote: "I hate, detest, abhor this murder of policemen campaign but, then, the men (who killed them) were sent there by the people who have accepted a policy of the kind. It is horrid, inhuman and fatal to Ireland's best aspirations. But for it we would have no tenpence-an-hour Black and Tannery swashbucklers looking for blood from helpless girls and silly boys. The policy came from hell to ruin the one clear issue in this land of saints and sinners." Then follows a list of reprisals which were clearly the work of the Auxiliaries but the writer confuses them with Black and Tans. "And all because some mad-souled Irish men see in Irish policemen men who deserve death without possibility of absolution."

In the adjoining column, the *Vindicator* editorial dealt with the execution of Kevin Barry: "… the horror of the outraged conscience of the world has struck through 'the hide-bound coalition', and there is a real fear in the atmosphere. … the boy is dead but his spirit lives, and will inspire countless thousands in every land the wide world over for centuries to come".

On the 12th, the *Vindicator* protested against reprisals against the Press; thirteen newspaper offices had been smashed up, type broken up etc. "An obit notice now is not safe, a Black and Tanpence an hour may take offence and up you go in petrol fumes."

From Rebel Cork, Carl W. Ackerman told his American readers: "As I drove or walked about the city I met the same groups of eight, ten or twelve members of the Royal Irish Constabulary, huddled together in a corner of the post-office building or at a theatre or a street corner, armed with rifles, also defiant. But their defiance was pathetic. Last night eight of these policemen, armed with rifles and revolvers, were standing in a corner of two buildings near the post office, silent and, from outward appearance, terrified, while across the street crowds of young men, women and boys passed, avoiding the police as if they were contaminated".

In mid-November the *Gazette* expressed concerns about the training of A, B and C Special Constables in the new Northern Ireland entity, seeing these forces as less than professional. An article on "The Cocaine Scourge" stated that the pre-war price had been 2½ pence per ounce; the current price was given as £500 per ounce. Regulations of 1916 under the Defence of the

Realm Act had prohibited the drug's sale and possession. Before the war cocaine had been entirely unregulated.

Striking railwaymen and the Republican ban on Crown forces' travel paralysed the rail network in Donegal. IRA activists were also cutting telegraph wires so that communications within the county were severely disrupted. Police in south Donegal moved back on Killybegs after attacks on patrols, and premises had to be commandeered to accommodate them.

Some practices continued in their own sad cycle. At the hiring fair in Letterkenny business was brisk and wages high. Youths 16 – 18 were offered farm work at £22 to £28 per half year plus board and lodging in Scotland. Ploughmen could earn £38 to £44. Girls between 16 and 18 were offered £12 to £16 while capable female servants for farmsteads could be paid £18 to £22 for their six months of servitude. Without this temporary migration, many Donegal families could not have fed, clothed and housed themselves.

Despite the horrors, hope and optimism had not yet died. The *Vindicator* of 19th November offered a remarkable vision: "Ireland, for all her virtues and her sins, is the kernel of the world. Why she should be so is the mystery but such she is, has been, and probably will be. The missionary nation of the world" (sic.).

The 20th November *Constabulary Gazette* editorial stated "The clouds are black indeed but…we will not waver in our conviction that the bright dawn of peace and reconcilement cannot be indefinitely delayed".

"Through a tangled combination of circumstances the Police and a large section of the Irish people are now estranged. Of all estrangements there is none so bad as a family quarrel; and this is a family quarrel if ever there was one."

The next day, November 21st brought grim news from Dublin. Early in the morning of what quickly became known as "Bloody

Sunday" the IRA killed twelve military officers in their lodgings in the belief that they were Intelligence agents. Some probably were; some definitely were not. Caught in their beds, some were shot in front of their wives. For one of the killers it was his first time to see a naked woman and it shocked him. That afternoon a group of Police, Auxiliaries and Black and Tans fired indiscriminately into the crowd at Croke Park, killing fourteen. That night, two arrested IRA officers and a civilian were killed after interrogation by Auxiliaries, They died while "trying to escape" from Dublin Castle. Taking into account those who subsequently died of wounds, that day's violence resulted in forty one deaths: IRA, Crown forces, and civilians including two children.

The Donegal Vindicator editorial on 3rd December referred to events in Dublin: "The men, the women, present in Croke Park had no hand or part in the murders… in face of it the world is asking questions. Is this the power that wept for Belgium? The murders were terrible, but the official order to murder on a straight line, and without chance of escape, was damnable, abominable, and we believe deliberate and by order." An unknown sub-editor neatly juxtaposed this with the advertisement for the Londonderry Picture Palace's coming attraction: "J'accuse!".

The 27th November issue of the *Gazette*, referring to "the Civil Side" asserted "gangs of desperadoes, under the masquerade of service in politics or service to the Crown are committing all sorts of robberies and burglaries both in town and country". The editorial refers to eventual peace and the need for "a highly-trained efficient and honest constabulary for the protection of the public". The journal reiterates the need to educate young constables and refers to "the lapse into soldiering" as "a passing misadventure".

Interestingly, the Editorial also extols the advantages of tropical Australia for white settlers.

On the 28th, the Auxiliaries lost their sheen of invincibility. At Kilmichael in West Cork, seventeen "Cadets", the entire patrol, were disposed of by the IRA under the command of Tom Barry who had previously served with the British Army in Mesopotamia. This may not have been the disciplined business claimed by Barry in his memoirs. Some of the IRA veterans subsequently declined to endorse Barry's account of a false surrender by the Auxies and it appears that one survivor, Cecil Guthrie, was captured and shot days later, and his body buried in a bog. Another survivor, H.F. Forde, was left for dead but was found alive the following day. He recovered from his wounds, and with £10,000 Government compensation emigrated to Southern Rhodesia, now Zimbabwe. Forde died in 1941. The subsequent enquiry heard evidence of expanding bullets and of shotguns fired into their victims post-mortem.

Col. Smith, in command of the Auxiliary Company to which the dead men belonged, resigned from the force, returned to Britain and later shot himself.

However, there was a respite in December with no attacks on Police barracks. In Donegal rail services started to resume. That lull did not last long. While there were no murders in January, Donegal recorded 54 outrages, an increase of 31 over December. Between Dungloe and Burtonport a troop train was derailed and fired upon: there were no casualties. The RIC barrack at Falcarragh was attacked, again without casualties.

At Ballyshannon in early December three SF supporters, one a grocer and another a member of the County Council, were arrested and brought to Finner Military Camp in handcuffs. The *Vindicator* speculated that Police raids on houses connected with the motor trade were connected with a raid on the Sligo to Ballyshannon mails. The postal service was vital to the Authorities and to the community at large. Even though it was a District HQ, Ballyshannon Police Station may not have been then connected to the telephone. The Sligo District HQ boasted the number Sligo 1.

In Dublin Judge Wylie, Law Advisor to The Castle, was "hiked off a tram at gunpoint" by Auxiliaries or Tans: "Come down, yer bloody Irish Barstard" as Mark Sturgis recorded it. When, under Martial Law imposed on Cork, Limerick, Tipperary and Kerry, the death penalty was decreed for possession of arms or wearing uniform (Irish or British) Mark Sturgis acidly commented: "We ought to declare war on them and shoot them for being out of uniform not in it".

The question of uniforms was not academic. After the Kilmichael ambush it was alleged by the Government that the Auxiliaries had been lured into a trap by a man wearing a British officer's uniform. Tom Barry said he'd worn a Volunteer officer's uniform which the Auxiliaries had understandably mistaken for a British one. In September the IRA mounted an attack on the RIC barrack in Beleek, Co. Fermanagh. They used an ambulance commandeered at gunpoint by two men dressed as British Army officers. The ambulance belonged to the Army and had been given for civilian use to the Ballyshannon Board of Guardians. It was the Trojan Horse which allowed the IRA to capture the barrack without a fight and was used to transport the seized weapons and other stores back to Bundoran.

When Sean MacEoin "The Blacksmith of Ballinalee" was being held in Mountjoy Jail under sentence of death, an audacious plot to free him using a captured British armoured car was led by Emmett Dalton wearing his own uniform as a former British officer decorated with the Military Cross. His accomplices were also dressed as soldiers.

The *Vindicator* of 10th December has a most interesting editorial. The dichotomy at the heart of The Movement is here revealed:

> An irresponsible body, not Sinn Fein, has been engaged in killing policemen, soldiers and others. That is not war, it is barbarism, and we are in a position to state it is not Sinn Fein policy. Far from it. These acts have led to an influx of new police and of soldiers from England in tens of thousands. Sinn Fein did not want that… The new police have run amok. They slay, burn and generally play the devil all over the country. Sane men are at a discount. Sane Sinn Feiners are in camp or in jail and the ones who should be there are absent.

The IRA planned an attack on Collooney barrack. One evening when Sgt James King came home as he regularly did for supper with his family, a small man called to the door. In a bizarre declaration he announced while brandishing a revolver that he wanted to marry the elder daughter but that he wasn't there to "ask her hand" that evening. Instead his "mission" was to tell the Sergeant that the barrack was about to be attacked and to request the surrender of the police as all they wanted was the guns and ammunition. The 14 stone, 6 foot Sergeant seized his visitor by the collar and seat of his trousers and literally slung him out the door, telling him to "expect a hot reception". When Sgt King stepped outside to return to the Station, a "friendly" IRA man stopped him and told him to stay at home. It was clear that to proceed was to invite death.

It must have been a dreadful dilemma for the Kings as they waited in the house. Figures could be seen moving about in the moonlight. With no telephone, there was no way to warn the policemen in the barrack. Pistol shots could have alerted them but what then would be the consequences for the family? At 3 a.m. a huge explosion blew in the front door followed by calls to surrender. A Black and Tan called Everett threw himself upon the rubble and, using the shattered door as a shield, held off the attackers until the rest of the Station party "took up their posts quickly without waiting to dress" according to the County Inspector. One IRA man was believed shot and the barrack did not fall to the attackers.

A subsequent enquiry exonerated Sgt King from official blame. Why was King treated with such consideration by the IRA? It seems most likely the consequence of his place in the community. His six sons and two daughters were known to all in that small place. The school his sons attended was staffed by a husband and wife team, sympathetic to the Republican cause but who never allowed the boys to be bullied. A single man in uniform might have found his life more readily forfeit. Nor of course was the case of King in any way the result of policy.

Sgt King was offered a post as District Inspector in Co. Wexford, a double promotion but probably seriously injurious to his life expectancy. He declined it and carried on until disbandment at Sligo in April 1922. In the words of his son Cecil: "As the carnage went on, discontent within the ranks of the RIC reached boiling point by the time the London discussions on a proposed cease-fire commenced". The Truce of 1921 would be greeted with a sigh of relief by policemen and their families.

But for now they just had to endure what was thrown at them. On Christmas Eve, DI Murphy of Midleton, Co. Cork, received a letter. "Prepare, your life is forfeit, so marshal your little dug-out six feet by three. Wishing you the compliments of the season."

Under Boycott

Ostracism has been used by various societies around the globe for many different purposes. We Irish didn't invent it but we embraced it and refined it and even gave the world a name for it. It was the weapon of choice during the Land War and proved highly effective. Of course the land agitation still simmered away, a low-intensity war especially along the western seaboard, and the same techniques were now being used for a manifestly political purpose. Consider the power of Parnell's words at Ennis in 1880:

> When a man takes a farm from which another has been evicted, you must show him on the roadside when you meet him, you must show him in the streets of the town, you must show him at the shop counter, you must show him in the fair and in the market-place, and even in the house of worship, by leaving him severely alone, by putting him into a moral Coventry, by isolating him from his crime as if he was a leper of old – you must show him your detestation of the crime he has committed, and you may depend on it that there will be no man so full of avarice, so lost to shame, as to dare the public opinion of

> all right-thinking men and to transgress your unwritten code of laws.

Compelling words indeed and the prospect of such comprehensive ostracism must have terrified many in Land League days. But it should be remembered that Parnell put this tactic forward explicitly as an alternative to physical violence.

Abbott suggests that the boycott was adopted generally by Sinn Fein on foot of its demonstrated local success during the 1917 Clare bye-election when used against those who refused to vote for De Valera.

In an informative and credible Witness Statement to the BMH, J.R.W.Goulden, son of Sgt Henry Goulden, describes intimations of new attitudes in a Mayo village:

> Yet, from the end of the war in 1918, there was a different feeling abroad. The younger men were not really hostile but were to some extent openly defiant, as though unsure how far they could go. They did not seem very clear about what form this new attitude should take or as to where it would lead them. For the most part, they expressed themselves in more or less friendly discussions with my father about the day which was coming when he and his like would have to leave.

After Tourmakeady barracks was closed, Sgt Goulden was transferred to Partry but his family remained in the former village.

> My father visited us every day through the winter of 1919-20. Sometimes he carried a revolver, but very often he did not bother because of the weight. He was completely confident that no local would ever interfere

> with him. Often they met him on the road and they used to remark: "Are you not afraid we would shoot you some night going home?". He always turned it aside as a joke and still called them all by their first names.
>
> I think it was Easter Week 1920, that a large number of barracks from which the police had been withdrawn were burned and the women and children who had been left behind were turned out. For a little while before this we had found difficulty in getting milk, and generally used condensed milk. However, on occasions on which any child was ill, we always managed to get supplies. There was always a sort of undercurrent to be felt, but no one was unpleasant though we were frequently asked if we were going away soon. I think the local people did not wish us to be put on the road and just wished to know that we were going.

Con. Pat Mahon recalled life in the village of Hugginstown, Co. Kilkenny. In the evenings he might have a game of cards with neighbouring couple, Matt and Judy. Children wandered about, visiting houses. He used to regularly drop in on an elderly woman living alone. Then a "boycott ukase" was enforced. One day in Thomastown he encountered two women on the footpath. They stopped, and one of the women crossed herself and said to her companion "You should always do that, Asthore, when you meet the Divil". He noted the public tolerance of soldiers outside the Courthouse and the derision directed towards policemen.

The Republican boycott of the RIC was both direct and indirect. Policemen were to be denied social intercourse and normal commercial transactions. Anybody who spoke to them, or sold them a box of matches, could be seen as breaching the boycott and thus subject to the same sanctions and occasionally vicious punishments.

Consequences could be severe for those who breached the boycott. In Donegal suppliers of milk and turf to the police were threatened. Some had the shafts and wheel spokes of their carts sawn through, thus depriving them of a livelihood. Even if there were money for repairs any wheelwright foolhardy enough to take on the job would find himself subject to boycott sanctions in turn.

People who worked for the police were in the front line. In July 1920 two armed and masked men visited Mary McSharry who worked as a servant at Cliffony police station and forced her to go on her knees and swear that she would never work there again or speak to policemen. She swore as demanded, and abandoned her work and its modest income. On 6th September 1920 Mary Brogan who was a barrack servant at Killybegs was threatened by men with scissors. She resigned. Mary was lucky compared to Ellen Gillen similarly employed at Ballyshannon. On the 7th, Ellen was taken from her lodgings by armed and masked men, gagged, taken to a field where her hair was cut off, and then she was kicked in the body. The woman was 60 years of age.

John Hennigan must have known her well. What did he and his colleagues feel about such treatment of an elderly woman?

The threatening letter was another aspect of the campaign of intimidation. Rather than risking active service with the IRA, it was a tactic very suited to anonymous bullies of either or any sex. Many a mute Milton found expression behind a pseudonym in a form inherited from the Secret Societies of the 18th Century. Sgt Thomas Staunton of Buncrana received a typical example: "Prepare for death. You are a doomed man. – Avenger".

Another such was: "Beware your time is drawing nigh an end. Prepare to meet your maker before six days. Police will not save you. – Rory of the Hill". One of the Ballyshannon policemen received "Warning Traitor and Raider. Prepare you slave."

One masterpiece of epistolatory rhetoric was a letter to Sgt Coughlan of Brosna, Co. Kerry. It's a tribute to the efficacy of the National School system and the diligence of its teachers:

> You are herewith warned to keep your nose clear of affairs in this parish for the future. I might as well inform you of the fact that you are a marked man and you can look out for squalls at the first favourable opportunity that you will get (sic). You have done your best and you were a good diligent and efficient servant for the Crown, so I think it is high time to end your gallop, and the reward we will give you for good and faithful service is about half an ounce of lead, deadweight. I now advise you not to chance a sin on your soul for even one hour for the future you are branded as a traitor and you shall most surely perish. Our governers (sic.), Sinn Fein, have decreed it.
>
> The rifle clean and sabre bright
> Can freely speak and nobly write.
>
> Someday soon – and very soon – you will feel the above in reality, and take your seat with Lord Kitchener, sitting at his right hand and the Devil at his left. Won't he have ye well matched! This is not a humbug, for fear anything would tempt you to think that it is.
>
> Signed, on behalf of the Brosna Volunteer, The Captain.
>
> It was I who attacked the Bobby at Fealebridge near Abbeyfeale and would have shot him dead only for trying to avoid little girls who were taking a walk.

Attached was a list of "Chivalrous and glorious deeds" from the previous week. According to the IG's report, "This was a chillingly precise list of Police casualties around the country".

Also attached was a drawing of a rifle and of a coffin with the Sergeant's name on the breastplate.

What had Sgt Coughlan done to inspire such malevolent loquacity and fearsome threats? Was he a notorious felon-setter? How many innocents had he sent to the gallows?

The Police explanation was "The Sergeant recently identified a large number of persons stealing timber on the Drummond estate over which there is a good deal of ill-feeling."

In Ballyshannon the police were reduced to commandeering food and other necessities of life. It is difficult to imagine the state of mind of policemen who had to do it. Most RIC rankers came from the same small-farming background and gone to the same sort of schools, played the same games and attended the same village churches as those who now violently opposed them. But now they were being cast out from that society which, for all its faults, had nurtured them. Bound by a common poverty and history of dispossession, there were traditions of *meitheal,* of cooperation in house-building and harvesting. Now they were being excluded and marked with the brand of Cain.

This wasn't the cruelty of foreigners, of Prussian troops in France or Belgium; it was the refined cruelty of internecine strife. John Hennigan was less than twenty miles from his parents' cottage by the sea.

Although possibly incited by women, attacks on women seem to have been carried out by men and were usually sadistic. Perhaps a twisted and thwarted sexuality may have played a role. On 30th May 1920, a girl had her hair sheared off at Tuam. Some of the attackers suggested cutting off her ears. Her crime? Her brother was a soldier.

A fortnight earlier, also at Tuam, Annie Devine was staying at the home of her grandfather W. Mannion when she was seized. Her hair was sheared off. She had been written to by Con. Daly at Salthill, Galway.

When policemen had been withdrawn from smaller barracks, the wives and families of Sergeants had been allowed by a slightly benevolent government to remain in residence. They had in many cases nowhere else to go. In May 1920 there were many attacks on police families living in the vacated barracks and families were thrown out onto the street. Neighbours did not dare to give them shelter. In at least one case a Sergeant's wife suffered burns when the family was burnt out by a mob.

In County Clare in December 1919 a police hut was burned by armed men. The hut had been evacuated by the policemen but was occupied by the Sergeant's wife and family. They were thrown out. The occupants of three local houses refused to give them shelter and not even a stable was open to this family in the month of Christmas. They remained in the open until they were brought to Ennis at 2 p.m. the following day.

In September 1920, the Government took over a camp in Co. Down as a refuge for the families of policemen obliged to live in barracks. It offered merely a partial solution.

And the attacks on women for any perceived contact with Police or Military continued with unabated malice. In September, four or five armed men entered the home of Sarah McKenna, a farmer's daughter aged 25, and cut off her hair. She had been talking to a policeman. In a 1 a.m. visit, armed and masked men entered the home of Mrs Fitzgerald of Newpallas, pulled out her daughters Nellie and Annie in their nightdresses and cut off their hair. They were friendly with police and military. It wasn't all one-sided. According to Leeson, in September 1920 five members of Cumann na mBan had their hair shorn by Crown forces as an unofficial reprisal for a similar attack on a woman due to give evidence to a Military Court. In the words of Black and Tan Douglas Duff, "The hooligans on both sides carried out reprisals and counter-reprisals until it seemed likely that half the girls in Galway would be bald".

Lawlessness was now an everyday condition. In December the pub of Mr B. Farrell of Balbriggan was entered by a group of eight men, all in police uniforms except one in mufti who seemed to be in charge. Everyone on the premises was searched. Then a locked desk was forced and a cashbox containing £4/5/0 was emptied. The till was cleared out and the visitors helped themselves to drink and cigarettes. The behaviour of the raiders was "most insulting" and when Farrell protested that he was a RIC pensioner, they said it didn't matter: he was still an Irishman.

As the terrible year 1920 drew to a close there were optimistic gestures towards normality. Commerce had to continue or more and more people would be out of a job. The *Freeman's Journal* of 20th December included the advertisement "BAD and all as the TIMES are you can find JOLLY FINE FARE at Findlater's this Xmas at the Right Price". Gold Flake cigarettes were available at ten for sixpence or twenty for a shilling. If you curtailed your smoking a bit, a new pair of boots was within reach from the Irish Boot Company for £1, a mere twenty shillings.

The Irish Sea: Dark skies, cold water

As a small boy, I was fascinated by aeroplanes and had no greater desire than to go up in one. My father must have felt a need to explain why he didn't share my lofty ambition.

In December 1920 the *Irish Times* carried a short item under the headline "Irish Sea Aeroplane Mishap". That splendid euphemism introduced a short account which gave few details of a dramatic tale.

RAF 100 Sqn was equipped with Handley Page O/400 aircraft for bombing Germany. About a year after the Armistice the squadron was transferred to Baldonnel Aerodrome, south of Dublin, where it was re-equipped with two-seat Bristol Fighters for a new role supporting Crown forces in their fight against the IRA. But, while surrendering its Handley Page O/400 bombers the squadron seems to have retained one. Operating out of Hendon, eight similar aircraft had been converted to carry passengers, ferrying officials to and from Paris during the Versailles negotiations. 100 Sqn's Handley Page was probably refitted in the same way.

The HP O/400 was one of the largest biplanes of its time. Its wingspan was 100 feet, almost half that of a Boing 747 Jumbo Jet. The two Rolls Royce engines mounted between the upper and lower wings could power it to a speed of almost 100 mph. Its tail assembly consisted of upper and lower tailplanes supported by three vertical stabilisers, rather like a box kite. In 1920, when few people had even been close to an aircraft let alone one of that size, it must have been impressive indeed.

The weather over Britain and Ireland in December was, according to the Met Office, generally unfavourable for flying with low cloud and generally poor visibility. It was a very cold month, with snow on the ground in Devon until the 23rd, but became abnormally mild just before Christmas. An anti-cyclone dominated Britain's weather until the 18th but from the 21st there was "very bad flying weather". There was rain and drizzle from the 17th to the 19th. An aircrew anxious to take off may have spotted a window of opportunity.

Crossings of the Irish Sea by air were still regarded as somewhat hazardous. After July 1919 it was no longer required that a surface vessel had to track each aerial crossing but there were standard precautionary measures in place. Weather at destination had to be checked and the destination aerodrome notified of the flight and the estimated time of arrival (ETA). Aircraft were generally fitted with CW radio capable of sending Morse messages and during the crossing a radio watch would be kept at departure and destination stations, Baldonnel to Shotwick or vice versa, and also at the Naval Air Station at Kingstown (now Dun Laoghaire).

Journey time in the Handley Page would have been well over 2 hours. If an aircraft did not arrive by its ETA, services were alerted, shipping notified and a search mounted.

The weather report for the morning of Friday 17th shows slowly falling barometric pressure over the Irish Sea. Weather conditions for the Isle of Man at 7 a.m. were reported as cloudy but the sea was smooth. North Wales was reported as having a "variable sky" but the sea was "very smooth". The forecast for the Isle of Man was light, southerly winds, fair or cloudy generally but with some rain or snow later. The temperature was generally rising but still low. At 10.00 that morning, the sea temperature in that area was reported at 49°F (9.5°C) and the air temperature was only 40°F (4.5°C).

On 17th December 1920, aircraft J2256 of 100 Sqn encountered engine trouble over the Irish Sea. Contemporary newspaper reports said it was on a flight from Chester to Holyhead, which doesn't make a lot of sense given that Anglesea didn't even have an aerodrome at that time and the reported ditching position was well to the northwest. As for departure from Chester, they probably took off from nearby RAF Shotwick, the standard refuelling point for military flights to Ireland. While Handley Page training flights usually took off from Andover, this flight's initial departure point may well have been Hendon, convenient for central London.

After sending out distress messages by radio, J2256 ditched in the sea. Trained airmen would have received some instruction in ditching procedures but it was a once-in-a-lifetime experience for almost all aircrew – if it ever happened at all. It was the Captain's duty to inform and instruct crew and passengers about what positions to adopt, how to don lifejackets if they were available, and which escape hatches to use. To lessen the weight, everything inessential to survival was jettisoned. Then they waited as the impotent machine dropped slowly towards the implacable sea. If both engines had stopped, the only sound was the shrieking of the wind in the rigging wires. At the moment of impact a great fountain of water engulfed the aircraft, cascading over the fuselage and all flying surfaces. The human bodies were thrown forward into their safety harness by the abrupt deceleration. And then, after checking all were alive and unhurt, came the order to evacuate the aircraft.

The SOS had been picked up by *S.S. Itajehy* of the Elder Dempster line. A substantial ship of over 4,000 tons, this vessel was originally German property but had been handed over to the victors in 1919 as part of the war reparations. Some 28 miles away from the reported location of the ditching, the *Itajehy* made for the spot.

The crew of the aircraft were experienced airmen with distinguished war service. As far as is known, the pilot was Flying Officer James J. Williamson AFC and the navigator F/O Robin Howard Haworth-Booth DFC, sometime Conservative MP for Banbury. Leading Aircraftsmen Burrows and Worsley were the two mechanics. The wireless operator was Harold Milne Aspen, then a NCO but later commissioned, who was destined to die during the Battle of Britain. There were also two passengers. J2259's descent onto the sea seems to have been a textbook ditching and the aircraft remained intact.[viii]

Some of the men on J2259 swam to the tailplane to balance the craft as it began to sink by the nose. They all spent two hours on the upper surfaces of the slowly submerging aeroplane until help arrived. Although the Irish Sea was exceptionally smooth that day in mid-December, they must have been wet, chilled to the marrow, and almost despairing of rescue by the time help arrived. What did they have to say to each other, those veteran airmen and the two men in civilian clothes? Probably not much beyond the practicalities of the situation and there was nothing to be done about that beyond keeping each other from falling into the sea. They must have watched the sky: on that date, at that longitude, sunset was almost exactly at 4 p.m. Once darkness fell, their chances of survival became very slim.

As you waited and hoped, you might reflect on your life, think of your loved ones, say a prayer perhaps, and dream of hot drinks. If they went into the sea they were doomed: at below 15°C, survival was less than an hour at best.

The airmen may have compared their situation to the fate of seven RAF colleagues back in April. Another Handley Page, taking off from Andover on a 2,000 mile proving circuit around the British Isles, had failed to gain height and struck some aerodrome buildings. The fuel tanks exploded: five of the crew were burnt to death, one survived with extensive burns and another, thrown clear in the crash, was able to walk away from it.

The *Itajehy* arrived, lowered a boat, and picked up the seven survivors. It was a close call: it was reported that within 15 minutes of the rescue the mighty Handley Page vanished beneath the sea.

The airmen identified themselves as RAF personnel but remained otherwise tight-lipped about who they were and where they were going. The passengers' refusal to give their names has led to speculation that they were Secret Service men.

One of the two certainly wasn't. He was Constable John Hennigan. The basic facts of this story tally too closely with what he told me as a child to allow of any doubt. After that incident he never went up in an aircraft again. He'd been already twelve years old when the Wright brothers made the first successful powered flight. That final take-off on J2259 may not have been his first flight but at the age of twenty-nine he'd made his last one.

Why was he on that flight? My own belief is that he was acting as a courier. The Royal Mail had long since been compromised by the highly efficient IRA intelligence service. The IRA often read official mail before it reached the intended recipient. Reliable men were needed to carry dispatches. Although John wasn't transferred to the Reserve until the beginning of February 1921, as one of the younger yet experienced policemen it's plausible that he'd be seen as a suitably bright and fit man for such duties.

This incident may be connected with John's being awarded a First Class Favourable Record on 5th March 1921. If he'd kept his head in the crisis, kept his mouth shut afterwards, and held on to his dispatches it seems the least he might have expected.

December 1920: a Postscript

Ordinary policemen knew as little as the general public but must have felt faint optimism when peace might suddenly have seemed possible. There was clear disquiet among some Sinn Fein members about the increasingly bloody and brutal conduct of the war. Roger Sweetman TD was one who wrote to newspapers advocating peace talks. More significant was the "Haverty Resolution" from a rump meeting of Galway County Council advocating peace negotiations. A letter from Fr O'Flanagan, SF Acting President, to Lloyd George, urged peace proposals. All of these unofficial initiatives were repudiated by the IRA leadership but they indicated that many in SF were separatists rather than doctrinaire republicans and not unwilling to accept Dominion status.

The real hope came with the arrival of Archbishop Clune of Perth who had been asked by Lloyd George to meet SF leaders and arrange a ceasefire. The Republican leadership was willing to negotiate but not to accept a unilateral ceasefire. Talks during December revealed the crux of the matter to be the British demand for IRA disarmament as a precursor to talks. We now know that the military chiefs including Macready and Sir Henry Wilson, and political hardliners such as Bonar Law and Hamar Greenwood, assured the Prime Minister that the IRA was on the verge of defeat. On 28th December, Clune's final proposals for a bilateral ceasefire were rejected by the Government. Ireland was condemned to another half year of savage conflict.

That dreadful year of 1920 came to its bloody end. Some Crown forces were clearly out of control. After an IRA ambush in which one Auxiliary was killed, a mob of Auxiliaries, Black and Tans and Army personnel descended on Cork city, looting and starting fires. The incendiarism destroyed the commercial centre of the city. On 17th December, Canon Thomas Magner, Parish Priest of Dunmanway, and a young man called Timothy Crowley were shot dead by an Auxiliary, Cadet Harte, who, colleagues said, was drunk and "on the verge of delirium tremens". On Christmas Eve, Police and Military mounted a raid on the Aran Islands which led to two deaths, three woundings and seven men arrested. However, although they didn't know about it in Galway, the casualties were fewer than in Sevastopol where eight thousand died at the hands of Bolsheviks that day. And on New Year's Eve, Countess Markievicz was sentenced to two years for teaching ambush techniques to seven-year olds.

Blood across Europe

To balance the enduring myth that Ireland's suffering was exceptional, and uniquely horrible, we should remind ourselves of what was happening in Continental Europe. The Armistice of November 1918 had indeed silenced the guns along the Western Front but peace had not descended quietly across all the belligerent states. The happenings on a small island off the north-west of Europe must have been of limited interest to people living their own nightmares. Between 1917 and 1923, there was a "massive proliferation" of civil wars as described by Robert Gerwarth.

The horrors that befell the Russian people after the revolutions of 1917 are well known and the casualties inflicted were enormous. By 1922, Russia had suffered 1.7 million dead through the Great War, over 3 million from the civil wars, and a further 2 million as a result of the famine in 1921-'22. A further, and an enduring, consequence of these events was the contagion of Bolshevik Communism which spread through Europe.

Following the abdication of the Tsar in March 1917, Finland had declared itself independent of Russia. But, after the Bolshevik takeover in November, the Finnish Left overthrew the country's new democratic government. In the civil war which followed, the Germans backed the Whites and the Russian revolutionaries supported the Reds. The result was 36,000 dead, 1% of the population. At the same proportion, Ireland's Troubles would have caused about 45,000 fatalities.

In October 1918 Hungary renounced allegiance to the Emperor but tensions between disorganised democrats and Bolshevists immediately split the country. In 1919, the Communist leader, Béla Kun, declared a Socialist Republic which instituted land confiscation, prohibitions and tribunals. In 113 days of "Red Terror", the Lenin Boys killed 600 of their opponents. In a counter-revolution, right-wing militias targeted Leftists, trade unionists and Jews, causing the deaths of five thousand. Adding to Hungary's problems was an invasion by Romania, whose troops occupied Budapest until 1920.

The "Protocols of the Elders of Zion" was published in 1919. Although proven to be a forgery two years later, this pernicious libel continued to feed the belief in a vast Jewish conspiracy plotting to control the world. It bolstered the anti-Semitism of the incorrigibly prejudiced. Among many extremists of the Right the Bolshevik menace was perceived as a manifestation of Jewish malice.

The experience of the Baltic States, especially Latvia, was appalling. Although made independent by the Brest-Litovsk treaty, they were re-occupied by Russian forces in 1919. Latvia offered inducements for ethnic Germans to settle there and help defend the country. Thousands of ex-soldiers arrived. This was the origin of the *Freikorps,* essentially freebooters who used extreme violence against civilians. Thousands of suspected Bolsheviks were murdered. Following a Freikorps coup, Communist supporters including hundreds of women combatants were hunted down and brutally slaughtered. After defeat by Latvian and Estonian troops, the Freikorps retreat to Germany was marked by wholesale looting, mass rape and murder.

Germany's new Liberal Democratic "Weimar Republic" was assailed from both Left and Right. In Berlin, Freikorps men were foremost in the suppression of the Bolshevik Spartacists and the deaths of leading Communists Leibnitz and Rosa Luxemburg. 1919 saw the battle for Munich where a Soviet Republic had been proclaimed. Some 600 died. In March 1920, government troops fired on workers in the Ruhr: a thousand died.

Greece was mired in an ill-advised invasion of Asian Turkey which resulted in the wholesale slaughter of civilians on both sides. Communities in which Christian, Muslim and Jew had coexisted with relative harmony for centuries were destroyed and the result was massive population exchanges of Greeks and Turks in destitute misery.

The Irish-American diaspora had, of course, deep interest and involvement in developments at home and the White Dominions within the British Commonwealth also had ties of kinship and a common language and culture. There was, among liberal democrats generally, a widespread fear of Bolshevism spreading like a bloody stain across the map throughout Europe and beyond, so interest in Ireland's woes was understandably limited.

1921: Seismic changes

As the New Year of 1921 came along some old rituals held their ground. In Dublin the Gaiety Theatre's Panto was "Sinbad". The Queen's offered "Babes in the Wood", the Father Mathew Hall "Jack and Jill", the Empire "The House that Jack Built" and "Prince Tokyo" was playing at the Tivoli.

Other aspects of life in Ireland were not so funny. In Limerick a school attendance officer Richard Leonard, aged 32, was taken out from the house he shared with his sister and shot dead. James Blayrife, an ex-soldier, was found shot dead with a piece of cardboard on his bloody chest saying "Spy". William Slattery of Emly, Co. Cavan, was shot dead by police or soldiers while trying to escape. That seemed to happen quite often.

The *Irish Independent* carried an intriguing headline: "India to be ruled by Hebrews". It seems that the Lord Chief Justice of England, the Earl of Reading, had been offered the Viceroyalty of India. (He was formerly Sir Rufus Isaacs.) Mr Montague, the Secretary of State for India was already in place. "They probably understand the eastern races better than the men usually appointed to these offices." It's a pity that the same principle hadn't been regularly applied to Ireland.

In the Sub-Continent itself, the Indian National Congress

adopted a resolution proposed by Mr Gandhi paying homage to the late Lord Mayor of Cork Mr McSwiney, and sending sympathy to the Irish People in their struggle for independence.

The *Constabulary Gazette* continued to maintain a doggedly optimistic outlook, encouraging members of the RIC and DMP to study and prepare for normal policing. On Thursday 20th January, two DIs and five other policemen were killed in the Martial Law area.

With indefensible smaller police stations having been closed, the Authorities began to look seriously at the vulnerability of larger barracks in the troubled areas. Thirty three ex-army officers were employed as Defence of Barrack Sergeants to prepare defences and to take charge if attacked. They were paid £7 per week and had no police duties. Barbed wire barriers with trip wires were erected. Obstacles were put in place at the public doorway to prevent visitors entering more than one at a time. Bombing holes were made in windowless walls to allow grenades to be dropped on attackers. Steel window shutters were fitted and doors reinforced with steel plates. Peepholes and periscopes were put in place and loopholes would allow defenders to fire out. Apertures were made in the roof and protected by sandbags; defenders could then deny attackers access to the roof. Life in an overcrowded barrack under these conditions must have been demoralising, more like being part of a besieged garrison than policemen upholding the civil law.

On 19th February the *Gazette* declared that "whatever form of government may be established in Ireland" there would be a need for disarmament if the police were to deal with the ordinary crime now rampant and to counter "the gunman malady".

In February there were dramatic changes in the leadership of the Auxiliary Division. Brig. Gen. Crozier had dismissed twenty one members for indiscipline leading to looting and civilian deaths. He was overruled by Gen. Tudor who reinstated the men. Crozier resigned in protest. Less than two years later, he would be writing a series of letters to ministers of the Free State Provisional Government seeking a commission in the new Civic Guard. His application was filed away.

February in Donegal became more violent. On the 22nd military and police were ambushed at Glen. Con. Satchwell was killed. That same day a patrol was fired on in Ballyshannon: Con. Hughes was killed. Following the deaths of Satchwell and Hughes "some houses were damaged at Mountcharles and Donegal and a creamery at Inver". Although the County Inspector put the blame on Loyalists "anxious to hit back" as the property was "owned by Sinn Feiners", it seems to be clearly a reprisal by Crown forces. The CI restated in his report that "All members of RIC in the County are doing splendidly and displaying the greatest courage". In the circumstances perhaps they were, but there could be little pretence at civil policing now.

Even in the midst of murder and mayhem, there were instances of human decency. In early February a 17-man Auxiliary patrol in two lorries was ambushed at Clonfin, Co.Longford. After a long firefight, in which four Auxiliaries were killed and eight wounded, they ran out of ammunition and surrendered. The IRA emerged from cover. Cadet Wilford later stated that the "Shin" leader shook hands with the captives and told them they'd put up a jolly good scrap. Wilford said that one of the Shinners had urged the leader to finish them off but he'd taken no notice and ordered that the wounded be attended to. The IRA commander then ordered that one of the lorries be torched and allowed the surviving Auxiliaries to use the other to take away the wounded for treatment. Later, when Sean MacEoin (John McKeown) "The Blacksmith of Ballinalee" was captured after being wounded in a gun battle, some of those Auxiliaries spoke on his behalf at the Court Martial. Nonetheless, he would be saved from hanging only by the Truce. One RIC Sergeant's son later recalled seeing MacEoin's name in his father's notebook where wanted men were listed. There was the accompanying notation "Treat with respect. He has shown kindness towards wounded men".

The *Gazette* maintained its stubbornly positive tone. The 26th February editorial referred to efforts towards a truce and wondered about the effects of the Government of Ireland Act. Would the 26 Counties be governed as a Crown Colony? In any event the RIC and DMP were to remain under the Imperial government for a period of three years before any transfer of authority. The editorial expressed the hope that an acceptable regime would be put in place "wherein the police will resume … their duties as a civic force".

Con. John Hennigan had no more appearances at Ballyshannon's Petty Sessions. On the 1st February 1921 he was transferred to the Reserve. In normal times this was a detachment of 400 men based at The Depot and under the direct command of the Inspector General. They were available for deployment to any area where police reinforcements were needed. These were not normal times and, presumably, the Reserve was under the operational control of Maj. Gen. Tudor. John could have been sent to the Depot, or possibly Gormanstown, Co. Meath, where many of the Depot functions had been transferred.

At this stage the Reserve was organised into five Companies, each commanded by a District Inspector. Transfers from Ulster were sent to No. 2 Company under District Inspector H.E. Fitzgerald. Whatever his precise location and duties may have been, John Hennigan remained with the Reserve until transferred to Ship Street, which was not a Police station but a small military barracks behind Dublin Castle, on 1st March 1922. The RIC detachment there would have been part of the Castle guard. A further posting a month later saw him attached to the Castle Clerical Company.

One impression of what life could be like in the Reserve was later given by former Constable Hugh McIvor: "Because I was in the Reserves I went in for everything. I had no more wit, I should have maybe not bothered with the Reserves but I was young and impressionable, ready to go on the road all the time… People in the Reserves were mostly from the North although there were always loyal people from the South, you see. There wasn't such a big force in the Reserves, a big lot of them was in administration but there was this section that I was in, it was all rush, rush. There was quite a few joined up and quite a few of them didn't last long because of the type of life we were living in. We were wild and rough enough."

McIvor described arriving at the Depot from Cork at 4 a.m., rain-soaked on the exposed back of a Crossley tender. Without anything to eat they were immediately sent on in the rain with despatches to Newtownards.

"Then I came back on to the Reserve Force from the Vice Regal, that meant you were rushed to every place that was in trouble. In the Reserve I'd be maybe in London at Scotland Yard today, and tomorrow I'd be away in Skibbereen".

There is no reason to doubt the truth of what McIvor recalled. However, we should take into account that he was one of the new boys who had joined up in 1920 without much education. No doubt he had a young man's broad back for the kind of soldiering work required of him at that time. An Antrim Protestant, he went on to serve with the RUC.

John Hennigan, on the other hand, was a veteran of some nine years' standing and representative of the far higher standards of the old police force. It seems more likely that he would have been employed as one of the many that Hugh noticed involved in administration.

In passing, I would say there is documentary evidence of the decline in standards. Reading letters from veterans who corresponded with Goulden in the mid-1960s, one is struck by the standard of their syntax, grammatical precision and vocabulary. Even allowing for the great differences between spoken and written English, the interviews recorded by John Brewer in the 1980s do not generally show the same precision of thought and fluidity of expression. Brewer's interviewees were of a younger cohort, some who had joined the Force in 1920 and some who were Black and Tans. Also, of course, those late enlistments were of the Great War generation and had no experience of normal, civil policing.

Perhaps some unavoidable duties in the Reserve entailed participating in joint patrols with the military. The British Army of 1921 was not the army which stood beside the French and defeated the armies of the Kaiser. Regulars had retired and the ranks were filled with raw recruits. There was an acute shortage of experienced NCOs. Officers of proven ability who'd risen from the ranks were cast aside while the Officer Corps reverted to its old conventions of caste and seemed determined to have learned nothing. In Ireland, commanders were hampered by their inability to get beyond condescension and the conventional military disdain for guerrilla warfare. Troops going on operations were left in the dark as to why they were doing whatever it was they were told to do, according to Kautt.

Policemen sent out on mixed patrols must have found the experience nerve-racking. Unlike many of the troops they were not issued with tin hats and wore their ordinary police uniforms. Motor transport, lorries and the smaller Crossley Tenders, was not altogether reliable. Driving skills were rare at the time and mechanical skills even rarer so breakdowns were frequent, with an inability to carry out repairs making things worse. Even if armoured cars were available in an area, many of those then in use were too large for all but the best roads in Ireland. The American Peerless car with twin machine guns weighed in at over 7 tons, too heavy for most bridges, and at

18 m.p.h. was too slow for rural patrols. The Army had 48 of these in December 1920 and considerably fewer of the smaller and more agile Rolls Royce machines. This meant that most military and police patrols could not enjoy the protection of an armoured vehicle. The occasional appearance of one of the monstrous Tanks on an urban street could have had no purpose except crude intimidation.

The Military did learn some lessons from bitter experience. Vehicles never travelled alone. There were four lookouts in each lorry. Beside the driver was the front lookout, an officer or NCO. There were two side lookouts and one rear lookout all with rifles ready for use (commonly with one round up the spout, safety catch on and the muzzle pointed upwards). Front and rear lookouts communicated with the vehicles in front or behind them with hand signals.

Each vehicle was under the command of a NCO. If there was only one NCO in a lorry, he was absolutely never to sit beside the driver but always in the back. If the vehicle was fitted with a tarpaulin, it was always to be rolled up. If there were no tarp, wire netting was fitted to the sides and top – despite the occupants of the lorry being then unable to jump over the side. Tailgates were always to be down or removed entirely. In the event of an ambush the wooden sides of the lorry gave no protection whatever. In early December 1920 the Army had a mere fourteen 'Tactical' lorries with one inch armour plate for protection against rifle fire in rural areas. In urban areas where pistol fire was more common a half-inch plate was considered sufficient. Desperate to give some protection to their men, officers experimented with armour plating – including the use of a barrack's steel shutters – but the extra weight reduced the speed and made breakdown more likely.

The cardinal rule was no turning around and no stopping! On 22nd August 1922, when the burden of government had fallen on the shoulders of the new regime, Michael Collins met an ambush at Beal na mBlath. The veteran soldier Emmet Dalton ordered their driver to "Drive like hell!" Collins countermanded the order: "Stand and fight!" It was Collins's first and last experience of an ambush.

A wonderfully ironic example of Crown forces' indiscipline occurred during a raid on Neary's respectable pub in Dublin. Black and Tans or 'officers'" (i.e. Auxiliaries) stole two cases of champagne along with whiskey and cigars. The champagne was the property of Lord French who didn't like the brand he'd received as a gift and, rather than give it away, had sent it to Neary's to be sold. Mark Sturgis in Dublin Castle was told in strict confidence by Macready and Tudor that "we must bring to book the Neary's robbers of wine" but that it had to be done quietly. Dublin wits would have made the most of the story, and the rank and file Constabulary might have had a good laugh while their officers ventured a chuckle or two.

March 1921 was a difficult month also, with the condition of Donegal being described by senior officers as "very unsatisfactory". Moville and Milford RIC barracks were attacked, though without casualties. On the 10th Sgt McKeone was held up, abducted and sentenced to be shot but was released unharmed except for the loss of his bicycle. On the 13th Sgt Sweeney was abducted near Falcarragh but freed. Such magnanimity did not continue: Con. McKenna was shot dead near Falcarragh on the 20th.

The *Constabulary Gazette* in its editorial of 5th March spoke of "the regard which should be had to the permanent Civil character of the force, as distinguished from its temporary and purely accidental military aspect". Published articles dealt with interesting professional points for young policemen about The Detective's Art and stressed the importance of leaving crime scenes untouched until competent detectives arrived.

In its 12th March editorial, The *Gazette* commented on the suggestion by Maj. Ormsby-Gore that all Crown forces except the DMP be put under a military chief. Hamar Greenwood had said in Parliament that the proposal would receive active consideration. The *Gazette* called for the "true civic spirit" not to be lost. Police were also concerned about the effect on promotion of extra weight being given for military expertise and experience.

The police journal also carried articles insisting on proper procedures in arresting and handling persons in custody. Regular policemen were concerned about, and frequently appalled by, the attitudes expressed and the methods used by the Black and Tans who were ostensibly temporary constables.

Pious concerns about legality notwithstanding, reprisals by Crown forces were undoubtedly occurring and extra-judicial executions were known to happen. Some may have been official reprisals, some not. On the night of 6th March George Clancy, Lord Mayor of Limerick, and former Lord Mayor Michael O'Callaghan were both shot dead in their homes. Also that night, Joseph O'Donoghue was arrested in Limerick. His body was found next day.

Around the same time, used police uniforms were at last withdrawn from sales of surplus clothing and bedding in Dublin auction rooms. Although the IRA had used police uniforms for subterfuge, it shows how the bureaucratic mind could be disassociated from reality and uncaring for the safety of the police. There were rumours that a penny-pinching civil service was trying to negotiate discounts on bulk buying of coffins for the RIC.

As an indication of how serious had been inflation during the war years and afterwards, new bicycles of the Singer and Osmond brands were being offered at prices from £12.12 shillings while the Raleigh with Sturmey-Archer gears – "The

RIC man's friend" – cost more. Back in 1913 one could have bought a new bicycle for under £4,.

Meanwhile, in Tyrone, licensed traders held meetings to oppose a scheme for Prohibition put up by the Temperance Party. That proposal did not prove at all popular. A wag said "Prohibition which took the 'merry' out of America would put the 'ire' into Ireland".

The pattern of daily bloodletting continued all through March, with policemen ambushed on patrol or individually shot down as they walked alone. There were executions by the IRA, the most notorious being that of the elderly widow Mary Lindsey and her chauffeur James Clarke. Accused of being informers, they had been held as hostages for some five weeks against the lives of IRA men under sentence of death. Her house had already been burned. When the IRA men were hanged, the lives of the hostages were forfeit. The bodies of Mrs Lindsey and James Clarke were disposed of and never found.

In March also, the Government finally gave permission for RAF aircraft to be armed during operations. However, as far as is known, their guns were never fired in anger in Ireland and reconnaissance and communications remained the Air Force's main functions.

An infectious madness seemed to be gripping the land. The Republican boycott found ever more extreme expression. In April 1921, Miss Rose A. Logue, a Donegal teacher, had her hair shorn by two men for putting a wreath on the grave of a murdered policeman. She was advised that this was a caution; if she again came under unfavourable notice she would be shot.

Nor indeed were women the only defenceless creatures to be targeted. Near Bantry, West Cork, a pony belonging to a farmer called O'Neill was subjected to multiple stabbing and died ten days later. The pony's offence was to be the property of O'Neill who had a son in the RIC. And in another incident, when a raiding party had missed their victim, before leaving they slit the throats of the family's two terriers. Fighting men of the IRA, their officers, and GHQ in Dublin may have been horrified by such actions but, given the nature of the conflict, there was little they could do to stop them.

That month also saw the nearest thing to a conventional battle in the course of the entire war. Tom Barry's West Cork flying column, augmented by locals, undertook a large-scale ambush at Crossbarry but found themselves nearly surrounded by large numbers of Military and Auxiliaries. In sporadic and protracted action, the British Army sustained unexpected casualties. After a retreat under fire which lasted some hours and an extraordinary forced march in darkness the hundred or so IRA men evaded capture and gained a huge propaganda coup for the Republican cause. Claimed casualties included 10 British and 3 IRA dead but numbers are disputed.

But hours earlier a botched attack on a train at Upton Station had caused the deaths of three IRA men and six civilians.

April 1921 offered no relief for the beleaguered Police. In Donegal the number of outrages continued to increase. It was stated at Headquarters that "the whole of Dungloe district is without police". A sixth of Donegal appeared to have become an isolated miniature republic with all roads cut, no trains running and telegraph wires severed. Like Raparees of centuries before, the Rebels sallied forth from their Dungloe enclave when it suited them.

At Ballysodare just outside Sligo town, about 30 miles south of Ballyshannon, two policemen were dragged off the train and murdered beside it. They were out of uniform, unarmed and off duty. The killings were widely condemned. Constables Thomas Kelly and James Heatherington were given a public funeral and businesses were ordered to be closed. Although the men in my mother's family were active Republicans, I was told long afterwards by one of the women of her horror and revulsion the following day at seeing the blood-soaked gravel. It has been alleged that Con. Kelly was singled out for execution as a counter-reprisal for his identifying the houses of Sinn Fein supporters in the wake of the Moneygold ambush.

With a masterly degree of self-delusion, Temporary County Inspector J. Foster reported from Donegal: "Notwithstanding the existing lawlessness, the people in general are not unfriendly towards police and it is fear of the 'gunmen' which prevents the old friendly relations being resumed".

CI Foster was not alone in his optimism. The *Gazette* on 16 April said "Peace, in short, will be brought about by constitutional means… when the old order changeth, yielding place to new, there will be no more delighted body of men than the RIC and none who will prove more loyal to the altered conditions that will supervene".

Donegal remained very disturbed in May. Roads and bridges were cut, telephone and telegraph wires were severed, and no trains ran on two of the key lines.. Forays and extensive searches by military and police in the Dungloe area were successful in recovering stolen cars and bicycles, and finding arms. Some arrests were made. But the CI considered these exercises futile as no garrison was left behind. In the north of the county at Letterkenny Con. Carter was shot dead and Sgt Maguire severely wounded. On the 17th, a Marine Corporal Williams, going by sidecar from Rosses Point to Sligo for provisions, was dragged off and murdered. May proved to be the worst month for the RIC with 53 members killed.

Anyone could be touched by violence. On the 15th May a group of two Army officers, DI Blake and his wife, and another lady were returning to Lady Gregory's house at Gort, Co. Galway from nearby Ballyturin House. The second woman was Augusta Gregory's daughter-in-law, widow of "Irish Airman" Maj. Robert

Gregory. As DI Blake opened the gates of Ballyturin House he was shot down. The two Army officers were also killed. Ordered to leave the scene, Mrs Blake refused to abandon her man As Margaret Gregory turned towards the house she heard further shots. Mrs Blake died beside her husband.

The month began badly for the police with eight members killed up to the 3rd May in Cork, Cavan and Mayo. On the 3rd, the Rathmore Company of the Co. Clare IRA executed Thomas Sullivan, an eighty year old man of the travelling people and put a label on the body saying he was "a spy and informer". "Old Tom" had been convicted by a six-man IRA court on the basis that he'd been seen talking to Black and Tans at the police barracks. Whether he'd been giving away military secrets or touching them for a few pence was not made clear. In any case, as "Old Tom" was one of the disregarded tinker class, public outrage at his execution might have been thought unlikely.

In a remarkably dispassionate statement to the BMH, Company Commander Manus Moynihan related how he decided to use Old Tom's body as a bait to draw the Crown forces into a trap. After being attended by a priest, the victim was brought to a carefully chosen ambush site and shot three times. In the morning, passers-by reported the body to the police. A mixed party of RIC and Tans arrived to investigate. Four knelt down beside the body and then the IRA opened fire. Five of the patrol died on the spot; three others later died of their wounds. One policeman dropped his rifle and escaped unscathed. Two British Army deserters who had been captured by the IRA were subsequently shot. Manus Moynihan was promoted to command the Battalion ASU.

Violence came to east Mayo also with a fierce attack on a Police patrol passing through formerly peaceful Tourmakeady on 3rd May 1921. That village which young John Goulden saw as an idyll of peace hid a darker side; it wasn't a typical Mayo settlement. All but one of the houses were owned by Protestants, remarkable in itself. Up to the 1840s the lands of Tourmakeady were owned by the Moores of Moore Hall and during the Great Famine no tenant was evicted for non-payment of rent. But the severely indebted Moores had to then sell part of their lands to Baron Plunkett, Protestant Bishop of Tuam who was Treasurer of the Church Mission Society, and an era of active proselytising began. Tenants were pressured into sending their children to Protestant schools and many were evicted for not doing so. A vile campaign of evictions reached its nadir in 1860 when the "Glensaul Evictions" saw the villages of Gortfree and Gurteensaul cleared of their tenants. As usual, Constabulary and Military had to provide protection for the crowbar men. But within four years Plunkett, excoriated in the newspapers, had sold out to an Englishman and the area settled down. With the new Century, the Gaelic Revival brought visitors to this Gaeltacht area and Coláiste Chonnacht provided a welcome new source of income. However, the fault lines of ethnicity, language and religion remained visible. The language enthusiasts attended the college were often extremely nationalistic and antagonistic to the Police as representatives of the Crown.

When the shotguns had done their work that day in May, Constables O'Regan and Power were dead, as was Constable Oakes, a Black and Tan. Sgt John Regan died of his wounds, dispatched with buckshot to the stomach at point-blank range. IRA man Padraig Feeney had been shot while escaping, while IRA Brigade Adjutant Michael O'Brien had been killed by Military pursuers. There were several wounded on both sides. Sgt Goulden was not involved that day as his Head Constable had chosen to take his place as leader of the patrol.

It is of some significance that 1921 was "an abnormally dry year" according to the Met Office. There was an "unparalleled shortage of rainfall" especially in the months of February and

June. January had been "abnormally mild" with temperatures never before exceeded and the maximum reached in Ireland was 60F (15.5 C). March was "mild and showery" although in central Dublin it was a "generally mild and favourable month". April was "sunny and dry" and Ireland overall received only 46% of its normal rainfall. Central Dublin conditions in May were "favourable". "Abnormally dry" described June, when the Valencia observatory in Kerry recorded only 2.6mm of rain, a mere inch, the lowest since its records began in 1869.

Despite the rather formulaic vocabulary of the Met Office reports, it is clear that Irish weather in the first half of 1921 was perfect for outdoor military activities. Flying Columns could move easily across country, aircraft could fly, roads were passable, and generally people were able to set about each other without hindrance from the elements. Sometimes a good storm is worth praying for.

Turning policemen into soldiers had been far from successful. Only a few days before the Truce the IG's office expressed concern about the dangers of incompetence when loading and unloading firearms. Carrying a rifle with a round in the breech was expressly forbidden: "this practice is contrary to all orders and highly dangerous to all concerned". Officers were told to point out that it took longer to release the safety catch than to use the bolt and load from the magazine. When loading a revolver policemen were warned to "keep the finger off the trigger".

On 4th June 1921 the railway goods store at Ballyshannon was entered and goods from Belfast and Enniskillen were destroyed. From Sligo it was reported that two women had had their hair cut off. On the shores of Donegal Bay, Teelin Coastguard Station was attacked and Coastguard Kennington, scarcely a combatant, was murdered.

At Culleens in West Sligo an IRA party raided Tully's shop on

1st July. The owner reported the matter to the Police at Dromore West. A party of seven policemen set out on bicycles to investigate the theft. But the robbery was only the bait and at Culleens a large party of IRA with rifles and shotguns awaited them in ambush position – having first returned the stolen money. With the first volley of shots Con. Carley fell, wounded in both arms. The leading cyclists, Constables Higgins and King, were taken prisoner. Some of the unwounded policemen commandeered a passing car and went to Easkey for reinforcements. From there word was sent to Sligo and Ballina and Crown forces were soon on their way from all three places.

Having first bandaged the wounded Constable, the IRA party had meanwhile withdrawn, taking with them the two captured Constables and three bottles of brandy from Tully's shop. They came under long-distance fire from Crown forces arriving from Easkey who had spotted the retreating ambushers. As more British forces reached the area, the IRA were under pressure but sustained no casualties. The fate of the two captives was discussed and it was decided to kill them. "We gave them a short few seconds to say their prayers" one of their captors said later. He added that both had pleaded for their lives and that the younger man, Higgins, had wept. Then they were shot and their bodies left on the mountainside. On the following Sunday the Parish Priest spoke of the "gallant young Irishmen who had been brutally murdered". There were no reprisals by Crown forces. The only one of the ambush party to be captured was taken alive by the military.

Reprisals

The whole issue of reprisals by Crown forces is contentious and emotive. That they did occur is not in doubt. However it is important to distinguish between official and unofficial reprisals. There seems little doubt that the early reprisals were carried out by regular policemen and were selective, targeting known Republicans. District Inspector John M. Regan in his memoir stated "It is a fact that those policemen quickest to avenge the death of a comrade were Irishmen, and men of an excellent type". And, again, "As the debit balance of killing grew there were those in the police force who thought that the only realistic way of correcting it was by reprisals". Reprisals by the military, as at Fermoy, were usually indiscriminate and drunken and the whole civilian population suffered. The soldiers knew little of the nuances of the situation they found themselves in. Sometimes it might be an ancient animus which motivated people. Robert Crossett, born in the USA of Londonderry Protestant parents, joined the B Specials in 1920. "Well, the trouble got worse, especially down in the South. But we, the Unionists of Ulster, we didn't let them away with it, for if they shot three policemen, they shot three policemen in Ballyronan [Co.Derry] you see, we went and shot three of theirs, do you see."

There was certainly ambivalence in government and political circles. At the highest level there is clear evidence that the reprisals were condoned and indeed encouraged as part of the policy of coercion rather than conciliation, but Government was not prepared to state that openly. Hamar Greenwood, Churchill and Prime Minister Lloyd George appeared to take that line. There was disquiet in Parliament. In the House of Lords on 20th October 1920 the Marquess of Crewe, a former Viceroy, raised the issue of reprisals by Crown forces. He said he "profoundly differed" from Sir Edward Carson's speech of the 14th October in which he "appeared to deprecate any allusion whatever to these reprisals". Viscount Bryce said he had himself observed in Ireland a "complete loss of moral authority there on the part of His Majesty's Government".

Attitudes within the Police towards reprisals obviously varied widely. Patrick Shea recalled his Sergeant father: "In the opinion of men like my father the police force was not trained or equipped or organised to deal with the situation then developing. Sooner or later the army must take over. Reprisals and all that would be involved in arbitrary retribution was outside his thinking; policemen were trained within the rule of law... The man with a gun was a self-appointed accuser, judge and executioner; the adoption of reprisals would place the policeman in the same unjustifiable role."

There was also the difference in perception regarding the killing of policemen. The IRA and its supporters saw the RIC as soldiers of the King and therefore legitimate targets to be killed at every opportunity. When questioned by the American Commission about the murder of policemen, Mary MacSwiney dismissed the possibility of such a thing. "Here it is called the shooting of policemen... I will simply take the murders of policemen by denying that there has ever been a policeman murdered in Ireland".

On the other hand, if Crown forces executed guerrillas taken in arms it was denounced as murder. Such killings and reprisals were called breaches of the laws of war. But the IRA did not adhere to the Hague Convention as they didn't wear uniform or carry weapons openly.

In this conflict none of the combatant organisations was righteous. Some policemen – and senior officers – took the view that they had no choice but to fight the IRA on its own terms. If RIC men were murdered without warning or mercy, then known terrorists would be shot on sight. If the Shinners were going to fight dirty then the Peelers would do the same. Scruples about the rule of law became less apparent after the arrival of the Auxiliaries and Black and Tans. An official Police newsletter, the *Weekly Summary* helped to promote this tit-for-tat attitude. At the very least it was ambivalent, offering IRA outrages as an excuse for police violence in response.

> Reprisals are wrong.
> They are bad for the discipline of the force.
> They are bad for Ireland, especially if the wholly innocent suffer.
> Reprisals are wrong but reprisals do not happen wholly by accident.
> They are the result of the brutal, cowardly murder of police officers by assassins, who take shelter behind the screen of terrorism and intimidation which they have created.
> Police murder produces reprisals.
> Stop murdering policemen.

If most policemen thought the IRA were essentially cowards who did not fight fairly, it is understandable. The assassins were perceived as skulking behind walls and lurking in ditches; disguised as civilians they shot uniformed men in the back. In the myths of the Wild West, particular odium was reserved for 'bushwhackers' and 'dry-gulchers' too cowardly to meet their adversaries face-to-face: when caught, they deserved summary justice at the end of a rope. Drawing parallels with the American Frontier, in the Ireland of 1920 the machinery of justice no longer functioned. Coroner's Courts were suspended, no jurors dared attend when called for jury duty, and outside the Martial Law areas it seemed that terrorists could operate with impunity. If they weren't manly enough to fight cleanly in accordance with the rules of war, they didn't deserve anything better than to be shot out of hand. There was justification enough. Or so the argument went.

Thomas Fennell was one policeman who drew a distinction, saying that attacks on barracks were generally honourable. Surrender would be followed by a handover of arms and the policemen set free. Ambushes and back-shootings of individuals and pairs, on the other hand, were not in accordance with generally accepted rules of war. Fennell attributed these to local parties acting on their own initiative. The IRA "on the run" did not engage in these acts or approve of them. "These shootings as a rule were carried out by opportunists comparable only with camp followers killing the wounded in the wake of the firing line." Citing the murder of Det.Sgt William Mulhern – shot at the Holy Water font as he entered the church for Mass, Fennell wrote "Some of these murders were carried out with barbarous malignity".

General Macready had made his opinion known:

> Formerly, in Ireland, if a police officer were murdered there was no thought of direct reprisals by the RIC. They thought only of bringing the murderer to justice, confident that he would be dealt with quickly and adequately by the courts. But now, the machinery of the law having been broken down, they feel there is no

> certain means of redress and punishment, and it is only human that they should act on their own initiative.

And yet this view of reprisals did not prevail over the greater part of the Force, at any level. Even the *Weekly Summary*, while continuing to offer justification for targeted reprisals, cautioned that the first duty of the police was the protection of the people: "The police exists for the welfare of Ireland and to lift her from the terror of the pistol. The destruction of factories, houses, and other buildings only impoverishes Ireland. Do not hurt Ireland. Put out the "murder gang" and free her from the thraldom of terror." "Arson, looting and all indiscipline are offences against the people of Ireland. Their persons and their property are sacred." The *Constabulary Gazette* never wavered from its position that the duty of the Police Force was to uphold the rule of law.

It is clear now that in some areas of the country, a "spirit of murderous self-reliance" took hold of some policemen. It could have been induced by a succession of factors e.g. the boycott and general alienation from the community, the government's betrayal of the police and of the judiciary by its release of IRA hunger-strikers in the spring of 1920, and the collapse of the courts in the summer. For some of these men perhaps all that was left was loyalty to their comrades and a thirst for vengeance. But it is equally clear that this attitude did not prevail across the country and did not afflict the majority of the RIC or cause them to act illegally. Probably most just dreamt forlornly of a quiet life and tried to keep out of trouble. Thomas Fennell would later complain that "Even the American Commission and the English Labour Commission it would seem were unable to see clearly the distinction between the RIC, and the Black and Tans and Auxiliaries".

The combined efforts of SF/IRA and the British government

succeeded in changing the character of the RIC from an evolving civil police force to that of infantry soldiers in a makeshift army of occupation. It could be said that the Republicans were doing only what revolutionaries do: marginalising the police and making them ineffective. It's the nature of revolutionary movements to destroy the organs of the state. And if you're going to isolate and murder a body of people, it really helps to demonise them first so that the general public is not too shocked. On the other hand, it may be perceived that the greater odium attaches to the British Government and its Irish Administration. They sacrificed the police in an unconvincing effort to maintain the fiction that they were dealing with civil unrest rather than an armed insurgency. It was a sacrifice doomed to futility especially as the average policeman could never be effective as a combatant soldier: an older, more settled, man than the fit young rebels imbued with revolutionary fervour.

Of course we should bear in mind that our perceptions of the period and of policemen's experiences during it may be skewed by the dramatic and horrific events in the areas of greatest conflict. Clare, Limerick, Tipperary, Kerry and Cork were counties where Martial Law had been introduced and in which it seemed that every day brought even greater bloodshed. On the other hand there were areas of relative tranquillity where normal life seemed to continue as it had been. But even where the greater proportion of the population seemed law-abiding, a policeman now had to be on his guard. Things could never be the same again.

North of the new Border

The state of Northern Ireland came into being officially on 23rd December 1920. The anti-HR, self-declared Loyalists who had signed the Covenant had now themselves been granted Home Rule – for six of Ulster's nine counties. Many would have preferred a four-county statelet where Catholics and Nationalists, who were assumed to be the same thing, would not be a sufficiently large minority to cause trouble. It was a rather surreal polity. The RIC still functioned but authority was being transferred to the new Belfast government. Because of the security situation, Sir James Craig got sanction in October for the recruitment of a Special Constabulary, in three sections, to assist the regular police. The A Specials were full timers, B Specials were part-time, and C Specials were unpaid civilian reservists. The Specials were essentially the UVF in Police uniforms. It was rather like recruiting arsonists as auxiliary firemen. And, by March 1922, they had reached 32,000 in number.

S.G. Tallents, a government official from London, reported "The Catholics regard them with a bitterness exceeding that which the Black and Tans inspired in the south and several Unionist public men told me that this purely partisan and insufficiently disciplined force was sowing feuds ...which would not be eradicated for generations".

Tallents was well informed. General Ricardo, who'd been UVF Organiser in Tyrone told Tallents he'd resigned from the Specials owing to their partisanship, lack of control and "much offensive repression". In June 1922, Major Robert Stevenson, resigned as District Commissioner of the B Specials in Dungannon. He said "There can never be any... confidence or stability as long as the B force, the ordinary Protestant countryman and in many cases "cornerboy" is supplied with arms... and authorised to use them to get on top of his Roman Catholic neighbour. The latter resents it all the time and even the most respectable and constitutional nationalist gets more bitter as the record of raids and abuses by the uncontrollable elements pile up and harmless and innocent people suffer".

Head Constable John McKenna who, to his regret had asked for a transfer back to Cookstown where he'd previously been happy, was forthright: "As to the Black and Tans, I found them perfect gentlemen in comparison to the Ulster Specials". He said that the Tans were much more easily controlled by the Police than were the Specials, who were mainly local Loyalist farmhands and labourers. "No doubt the Tans did some desperate things, but a lot depended on the man in charge of them... if I had to live that part of my life again, I would certainly prefer to live with the Tans".

T.G.S. Harbinson, Nationalist MP for NE Tyrone, had written to David Lloyd George to protest that "the coercion of Tyrone into what is called ...Ulster will be one of the most difficult propositions that any government will get set before it". Now west Tyrone, along with great areas of Derry, Fermanagh and South Armagh, had effectively been coerced into the Northern Ireland state against the will of most of these areas' inhabitants. Head Constable McKenna set down his view: "That is the irony of the way things have turned. Cosgrave, Mc Neill and Company talk of the freedom of Ireland because they got rid of the Tans in a few counties, never thinking of the plight of the downtrodden Catholics in the North who they have left to the mercy of much greater ruffians."

Mc Kenna, a Catholic serving in Cookstown during 1920 – 1922, actually feared for his life at the hands of the Specials and credited a decent Black and Tan and a decent Special for guarding him. McKenna was prompted to write his memoir in 1932, bitterly angry after the Royal Ulster Constabulary had failed to protect Catholic pilgrims on their way to the Eucharistic Congress in Dublin; they had been savagely attacked by Orange mobs as they embarked on the steamer at Larne.

HC McKenna arrived to take over Cookstown Barracks in November 1920. In July the station had been attacked by the IRA aided by Constable Denis Conway (who had allowed their entry) and passively abetted by three other policemen. All were Catholics and the affair seemed to confirm Unionist prejudices that all RC policemen were Sinn Feiners. Now the Catholic HC had to deal with his regular RIC men but also with a large local force of "B" men who were out to make his life difficult and possibly very short. The Head Constable felt that, to the Specials, he was "only a Bloody Papish". Not all Specials were behaving badly but those that did were not being held to account. They were concocting bogus outrages to justify raids and abuse of law-abiding people simply because of religious bigotry. This was not within the RIC code of conduct. "It was horrible to think that after having spent 30 years in what I thought was an honourable job to find it so rotten, and having actually to take part in such foul deeds."

With no other way to feed his family and for the protection afforded by his uniform, he remained in the RIC until disbandment in 1921. McKenna was fortunate in one way:

he had only to endure it till disbandment. Out of uniform, he obviously felt his situation in Cookstown to be untenable and, according to his son "partly for security and fear of retaliation", he went to London for work after leaving the Police while his family remained in Larne. If he was feeling under threat from both directions, his decision seems more understandable. He returned to Larne seven years later.

On 31st May 1922 the Royal Irish Constabulary was replaced by the Royal Ulster Constabulary in Northern Ireland. A and C Specials disappeared but the B Specials remained in existence, intermittently mobilised until disbandment in 1970.

Why did they stay in the job?

Unlike soldiers in wartime, members of the RIC could resign. Why then did the vast majority endure mortal danger, hardship and contumely and stick it out? There were some, usually officers, who appear to have relished the fight but they were probably a small minority and most likely returned veterans of the Great War. An example would be John M. Regan, District Inspector and son of a DI. He'd volunteered for the Army but instead of his desired posting to the Connaught Rangers ended up as one of the few Catholic officers in the 36th Ulster Division. He'd returned to the RIC with new skills, relevant to the situation then developing, and wasn't reluctant to employ them. He later stated that he had regard for the fighting qualities and bravery of the men of the Flying Columns but no respect for assassins of the defenceless and for the shearers of women's hair.

Of course 1920 brought stiffening by the Auxiliaries and Black and Tans but the majority of the "Old RIC" would likely have remained reluctant soldiers. Why didn't more resign?

There were some who saw resigners as deserters. The official

Weekly Summary called them "Rats". It declaimed "No men – worthy of the name of men – will desert their posts in the face of gangs of ditch-grovelling, hedge-hidden assassins". But those were words, not sticks or stones. Far more hazardous would be the position of those who fell under suspicion of assisting the enemy. There is evidence of several instances where resigners sympathetic to SF narrowly escaped the wrath of their former comrades and we probably will never know if there were cases where illicit retribution was accomplished. But such considerations seem rare; most who resigned simply did so and if they remained under threat it was primarily from IRA sympathisers.

In September 1920 the *Limerick Leader* carried a story about Hugh Roddy, a native of Tuam, Co.Galway, who had resigned from the RIC after the reprisal known as the Sack of Tuam. He was taken from his home by armed men in trenchcoats and caps pulled down to their eyes. Roddy was taken to a sandpit, stripped, questioned about his resignation, "and given an unmerciful beating". He then had to walk home without his shoes.

In October, the house of PJ McCooey was attacked. He had resigned from the RIC after the Tubbercurry reprisals following the killing of DI Brady. The house, occupied by McCooey and his wife, sister-in-law, and two children aged 3 and one and half, was assaulted with bombs and gunfire. Although unhurt, the McCooey family abandoned their wrecked house and left town.

While we can only speculate about the identity of the assailants in these cases, it is clear that resigned members of the Constabulary were simply not safe.

Active collusion may have been rare but it did occur. We have already noted the case of Denis Conway who had given the IRA entry to Cookstown Barracks. In his interview with Brewer, former Constable Eugene Bratton referred to the capture of Trim Barracks by the IRA at the end of September 1920. Constable

Meehan was responsible for opening the barrack door and, according to Bratton, narrowly escaped being subsequently shot. DI Egan, his brother CI Egan – who'd transferred to Meath after Knocklong – and a Tan from Gormanstown took Meehan out of his lodgings one night. Were it not for the intervention of the CI's bodyguard, Meehan would have been shot. Con. Meehan survived to become a Superintendent in the Garda Siochana. Bratton, a veteran since 1898, seems a reliable witness.

W.J.V. Comerford, son of a District Inspector, suggests that those who went over weren't very well received by those they joined, turncoats being usually regarded with suspicion and contempt. Some, he concedes, had genuine "National feeling" but some others were cowards and popularity seekers in his view.

In some cases would-be resigners who communicated their intention to Republican commanders were asked by IRA HQ to stay in place. Collins, especially, saw the value in having sympathisers in the enemy's camp. There were policemen who were known to be not unfriendly towards the rebels and there were those who simply abdicated and became useless. So much depended on the area, many places being untroubled and others ferociously violent. It's probably fair to surmise that the attitudes and actions of individual policemen spanned a continuum from violent opposition through guarded coexistence, connivance, collusion, and spying for the IRA. It seems clear, however, that the vast majority regarded the IRA as murderers of their fellow policemen.

It's curious that SF didn't make greater efforts to suborn the police. Possibly, by demonising them and instituting a punitive boycott at an early stage, SF made it impossible to woo them. The rhetoric of hatred had already etched viciousness into people's souls. As the old adage puts it: you catch more flies with honey than vinegar. When attacking police barracks in the south, Ernie

O'Malley tried to restrain his men from roaring blood-curdling threats against the besieged policemen, realising that promises of ill-treatment would make them far less likely to surrender.

Resigned policemen simply could not find employment and SF did little to help them. Jeremiah Mee tried to establish a scheme to help those without work but the Dail didn't provide enough funds or resources. Maybe there was an acceptance that blandishments just wouldn't succeed. Some senior Republicans had respect for the RIC's professionalism and disdain for the Republican Police.

Jeremiah Mee felt strongly that SF should have done a lot more to woo the police:

> While the British Government was fully alive to the danger of a complete break-up of the Royal Irish Constabulary who were in open revolt against the "new order", Sinn Fein alone was out of touch with the position because of the stupid boycott which they had been carrying on against the force for the previous twelve months. It was during this crisis that Sinn Fein showed great lack of leadership or indeed no leadership at all. The RIC who were their own countrymen were alleged to have been the great stumbling block to Irish freedom down the years and, up to that time, were the only target for attack by the Republican Army. Now with the whole Force of 9,000 officers and men a seething mass of discontent and indecision, the duty of Sinn Fein was obvious. The elaborate precautions taken by the British authorities showed that they expected Sinn Fein to do the obvious thing and extend the hand of friendship to the RIC. Had Sinn Fein been big enough to do (*so*) at that critical time the RIC would have responded and much bloodshed would have been avoided.

Referring specifically to the "Listowel Mutiny", Mee contends that SF's lack of response prolonged the conflict:

> When the crisis came in July 1920 Sinn Fein should have called off attacks on RIC and made an appeal on behalf of the Irish nation to stand firm and refuse to co-operate with the British military. This, with an assurance that the nation would stand by them, would at that time have rallied the Force and they would (*have*) responded manfully. It was the minimum that the nation should have done but it was not done. The result was that they were treated as "untouchables" and were driven back into the hands of the British Forces which they hated and from which they were anxious but unable to sever their connection.

There was some special pleading here, of course. Mee considered that "resigners" had been shabbily treated and their motives denigrated. He wrote of a Minister for Justice in the new Irish state who told such men that "they resigned because they were suffering from 'cold feet' and were lucky that they did not get six feet of Irish soil".

A report in the *Sligo Independent* of 2nd October 1920 gives an insight into attitudes:

> Dail Eireann's letter asking to have positions provided for RIC men who had resigned provoked some discussion at the Dromore West Board of Guardians. Mr M. Clarke in the chair.
>
> Chairman – We will adopt it; it is a good thing. He said he knew one man who was at home on holidays last year and during his leave he went into several public houses and said he would not be afraid to shoot any

> man who said a word to him in the discharge of his duty. That man had now resigned and he (the Chairman) would like to know if it was for the love of his country or through fear that he had left the force.
>
> Mr Kilgallon – It was to save his skin.
>
> Mr Tully said he was aware of similar cases in his parish.
>
> The Chairman said he was of the opinion that any man who did not resign after the first year of the rebellion was not a sincere Irishman, and yet he did not know of any who had resigned in Co. Sligo.
>
> Mr Tully said that several had resigned in Tully and Kilglass parishes.
>
> Mr Feeney said he knew of two who resigned in his district but they went to London to take up jobs there. They might as well have remained in the force as to have went over there.
>
> The recommendations contained in the letter were adopted.

Following his own resignation, J.J. Mc Elligott had made representations to an apparently sympathetic Michael Collins. Mee was sent to Constance Marcievicz, then the Dail Eireann Minister for Labour, and they appealed to public bodies and large private employers but had no success in finding work for the men.

While overtures from SF might have swayed fewer policemen than Mee had hoped, no doubt a successful campaign to find employment for ex-policemen could have influenced more of the younger, single members who could forego stability and pension entitlements. Older members with family responsibilities and who were halfway or more towards the pension would not be so readily seduced.

So why did the Roberts keep going? The Government had treated them shamefully so it's unlikely to have been blind obedience, adherence to the uniform. There was probably an element of sheer stubbornness – they were Irish too – and contempt for those Irishmen they perceived as cowardly murderers. Coupled with the lack of options, there was also the real issue of vulnerability outside the Force. They would be helpless in the face of those who sought easy targets for their grievances. Also the concept of duty, unfashionable today, was very real a century ago. Not easily defined, it held men and women to a commitment, a moral or legal responsibility, to the requirements of those they were bound to in the social contract be it family, employer or state. One had a duty to one's parents and greater family, to the school, church, sports team, regiment or monarch. If duty was the concept, honour was the ideal to which one aspired. To do one's duty was honourable, to neglect one's duty was dishonourable.

In contrast to people in many other jobs, police men and women have always had more than one loyalty. In the case of a RIC member in 1912, he had his loyalty to his immediate superior, to his colleagues, and an over-arching loyalty to the community he served. In normal times these loyalties could be complementary and in balance. During the Land War period, when police had to participate in actions that were inimical to the community and repugnant to themselves, policemen sometimes had to suppress their loyalty to the community and simply obey orders without question. In the decade after 1912 things became a great deal worse. By 1920, loyalty to the community in disturbed areas must have been tenuous indeed.

When Dorothy Macardle asserted in *The Irish Republic* that "no body of men ever served their paymasters with more loyalty than the Royal Irish Constabulary", the veteran policeman Thomas Fennell was moved to a rebuttal in his memoir although

Macardle had in fact conceded "That loyalty was always in conflict with their own natural feelings". Fennell wrote: "The RIC were anything but loyal to the English Government. They were loyal to themselves and those depending on them".

Probably the greatest single factor in holding the Police together was loyalty to each other. This is not the Regimental Spirit which inspired generations of soldiers, the deeds of the unit's past members providing an ideal for the present. It is the bond of men who share similar backgrounds, experiences and aspirations and must depend on each other for survival. They would not let each other down.

Truce 1921

The *Constabulary Gazette* of 2nd July 1921 carried the optimistic message: "We have never wavered in our belief that once the bright day dawns, the Irish police will soon regain their former position in the esteem and neighbourly regard of the citizens."

On the same date, the *Sligo Independent* carried the story of Con. Patrick Clarke of Cliffoney Station who went out to buy cigarettes at a village shop and was shot to death from the cover of a lock-up premises close by; someone had been waiting to kill a policeman. It was a callous postscript to the killings at Moneygold: now Cliffoney had lost five Patricks.

On 11th July the Truce came into effect and active hostilities ceased. Actual implementation of the ceasefire was uneven. Whereas in many areas Crown forces ceased operations over the previous couple of days, some IRA units remained active up to the deadline. Two policemen were killed on the 11th itself.

The 16th July edition of the *Sligo Independent* reported on the cheerful weekend atmosphere: "The very air held a new lightness and irradiated, not only with sunshine, but with hope." Crown forces were seen relaxing at Rosses Point, Strandhill and Lough Gill. Town dwellers could go to the seaside by the new char-a-banc and motorboat services. For the IRA, the day was marred by the drowning of Michael Marren, O/C of their 3rd Sligo Battalion, who was obviously unfamiliar with the dangers of swimming at Strandhill.

A frequently bizarre co-existence between Republicans and Crown forces began. In some areas it was almost amiable and cooperation was constructive; much really depended on the attitude and character of those who were appointed as liaison officers. In Limerick, Acting CI John M. Regan found his IRA opposite number a "most decent man" and gave him a German automatic pistol and ammunition as a souvenir. Regan would not be the only one on either side who noted the difference between seasoned IRA fighters and those now joining up once the gunfire had stopped: the swaggering "Truciliers". A question worthy of scholarly consideration is the extent to which those post-Truce Volunteers influenced the IRA attitude to the Treaty of December 1921.

James Comerford, chronicler of the Coon Company of the Kilkenny IRA, gives us a clue. He wrote that most of the pre-Truce men, 86 in all, had mixed emotions about the Treaty. Michael Collins was their hero, regarded with admiration and respect, so the majority supported the Treaty. Of the 62 who had joined after the Truce, including fourteen and sixteen year old boys, the majority opposed the Treaty.

Comerford also offered an unusually balanced Republican view of the RIC:

> The Royal Irish Constabulary, abbreviated to RIC, were much more than policemen. The dictionary definition of that word did not explain them. They were political spies for the English Government. That is why, as a police force, they found themselves opposed to Irish patriotic people...

> An RIC man in those days had a respectable occupation. He had status. He was looked up to as a symbol of goodness. In the villages and small towns of Ireland, the five leading men – accepted as such by the residents – usually were the Parish Priest, the Protestant Minister, the RIC Sergeant, the Doctor and the School Master. Where there was no Protestant Minister or Doctor, then there were only three. Members of the RIC were well liked as men.

Policemen could have respect for IRA men who'd been on the run, risking their lives and enduring the hardships of cold, hunger and the "Republican itch". But as one RIC man put the question, where were the assassins and bushwhackers when the Auxiliaries and Tans were roaring around the countryside?

As for feelings within the police, one former Constable offered a rather jaundiced opinion: "When the Truce came the officers of the RIC were almost crying. They realised that their good days were over and they had good days before the trouble began. They were kings in their own areas. The ordinary rank and file of the RIC were generally pleased that Ireland at last had succeeded in getting somewhere. As far as the Black and Tans were concerned, they did not give a damn, they were soldiers of fortune". The opinion of this witness may be somewhat prejudiced as, before the ceasefire, he had already transferred his allegiance to Sinn Fein.

In the week following the Truce some green shoots of normality became visible. The restrictions on private motoring imposed under the Restoration of Order Act were lifted. Women searchers were allowed to return home to Britain on leave, but were warned they could be recalled if needed.

While we may never have conclusive numbers, it is certain that up until the Truce the RIC had lost well over 400 members killed with nearly 700 wounded, a huge loss in proportion to their numbers. British military casualties, by comparison, were 150 killed and 345 wounded. The ratio of fatalities to wounded is telling. Policemen were callously shot down, often from behind, whereas off-duty soldiers were far less likely to be harmed. Military casualties were more often the result of shooting affrays than assassination. The trials of the police were not yet over. Between the Truce and December 1922, twenty-eight more would die. These included two Sergeants who were lying ill in their beds in a Galway nursing home and were murdered in cold blood.

The number of attacks on policemen diminished but did not stop. In the week ending 10th July, just before the Truce, there were 25 police deaths. In the week ending 27th July there were three. There is variation in the casualty figures cited by different authorities, partly because of injured men subsequently dying of their wounds. Abbott, in "Police Casualties in Ireland", gives a breakdown year by year: in 1919:15 fatalities, in 1920:178 dead, in 1921: 241, in 1922: 59, with an overall total of 493 dead men. The worst month had been May 1921 when 56 police deaths were recorded. Eighteen were listed as missing. Adding the losses in 1916 brings the total well over 500. Whatever the precise number, it was appalling.

On the 1st July a circular from the IG's office stated "No member of the RIC will be permitted to leave barrack in plain clothes and then only with a party of not less than three." On the 27th those restrictions were lifted generally but continued to apply in the Martial Law areas.

Abuse of the civilian population by self-styled Republicans continued. On 16th July Margaret Dawson, a domestic servant in the house of Walter Malone of Co. Carlow was taken outside by ten armed and masked men. They cut off her hair and told her it was punishment for being on friendly terms with the police.

The following day Mrs Maria Valentine, working as a barrack servant at Gorey, was threatened: "We request you to leave the RIC Barrack at once or you will be doomed by order of the 'IRA Soldiers'". She'd been in the job only two weeks and probably badly needed it. IRA GHQ and responsible commanders may have been utterly sincere in implementing the Truce but they seemed to have little enough control over local bullies and recently converted shirkers anxious for belated glory. As Black and Tan Douglas Duff put it: "For these both we, and the men of the real IRA, had nothing but contempt and many were the surreptitious kicks in the pants they received both from ourselves and the men of the 'flying columns' when their actions became intolerable".

Battalion officers would have wanted to build up their numerical strength in case of renewed hostilities and to bolster their own prestige. It's said that all politics are local and in Ireland that's demonstrably true. There is also plenty of evidence to suggest that, freed of the constraints of active service, many experienced IRA fighters over-indulged in alcohol. The fawning adulation and tide of free drink in pubs could have turned anyone's head.

The RIC also continued to recruit Temporary Constables, mainly from London but also from other major British urban areas. Total strength of the Force at the beginning of October was 13,974, reaching 14,067 by the end of the month. Attacks on members and those who associated with them continued. At Loughrea Co. Galway, Julia Cannon and Norah Ryan were abducted and had their hair cut off. Their offence was walking out with young policemen. One unarmed policeman, visiting his family in Tipperary, was having a drink in a pub when a man rushed in and opened fire. He was lucky to escape with a slight scalp wound. A bizarre discovery was made in Sixmilebridge in Co. Limerick on 22nd October. Inside a coffin in the Catholic church was the body of a policeman who'd been abducted the previous March. It is unclear how long he'd been dead.

Pressure was exerted to force people to move out of an area. Armed men attempted to enter the home of Mrs Johnston and her four daughters in West Cork. She was a police widow and her son had been murdered the previous February. The Constabulary had to evacuate the family to Cork.

In Donegal, there were many recorded breaches of the Truce. Most involved the IRA flexing its muscles with threats rather than direct violence, and SF expanding its grasp of the civil administration. In September young men were warned to withdraw their money from Ulster Bank and other Belfast banks. Threatening notes were sent to Ballyshannon traders demanding compliance with the Belfast Boycott. Notices were sent out prohibiting payment of rents, Land Commission annuities or payments to the Congested Districts Board. Publicans were warned to observe the licensing hours as defined by the IRA. The County Inspector saw it all as "the beginnings of Bolshevism".

As, in many areas, there was no functioning court system, publicans' licences could be officially renewed at the discretion of the local police.

At Carrigart on 5th Sept, three RIC Sergeants and three Constables attended a SF Court. They were asked to remove their caps but refused. The Court Chairman then said that the business of the court would not proceed unless they removed their caps or left the premises. After a while the policemen left. However, in some other locations, police did acknowledge the Court's authority by removing their caps and simply observing proceedings.

SF Courts were a delicate area requiring liaison. Under the Truce terms, Arbitration Courts were legal – if there were no intimidation. Dealing with crime or enforcing penalties were not legal. The RIC was instructed to tolerate Republican Police looking after IRA members and enforcing the Truce but the Constabulary was not to permit the RP to interfere in police duties.

On 2nd Sept the IRA unit at Carrick village issued a proclamation on licensing hours: Weekdays 7am to 10pm, Fair Days 7am to 8pm and closed on Sundays to all except Bona Fide travellers.

On 14th October, Fair Day at Carrick, publicans were told by the IRA that they must cease trading at 8pm. When asked by Mr McShane, a publican, Head Constable Duffy assured him he was legally entitled to remain open till 10pm. Joseph Cunningham of the IRA "in a loud voice" ordered McShane to shut the pub at once or "the IRA would deal with him afterwards". McShane and the other publicans complied.

Shopkeepers held to be in breach of the Belfast Boycott were publicly named and a heavy fine of £20 imposed. A substantial £5 IRA levy was imposed on all shopkeepers.

In the fishing village of Killybegs on 20th October, two men cut 5 inches off a girl's hair. Her father was a shopkeeper of Unionist sympathies.

Although Donegal was riven by historic sectarian and ethnic tensions, there, like all along the western seaboard, the national question for many was in fact the land question. Land hunger had sparked and fuelled the "Land War" and many in Twentieth Century Republican colours saw themselves as fighting for the actual fields which they regarded as their ancestral birthright.

The Treaty and its aftermath. December 1921

From 6th December 1922 the first phase of Ireland's Civil Wars was over.

Representatives of Dail Eireann had gone to London to negotiate with representatives of the Imperial Government. There's no need to repeat here what has been said and discussed in lengthy detail over the years about the peace talks. There are however a couple of points that perhaps should be borne in mind as affecting John Hennigan and the entire population of this island.

The credentials and instructions given to the Dail delegates were contradictory. On the one hand, they were referred to as plenipotentiaries i.e. people who have authority to conclude an agreement. On the other hand, they were told to report back to the Dail before concluding an agreement. The Irish delegates were not skilled or experienced negotiators, nor were they backed up by a legal team. It is generally agreed that Michael Collins was the most competent of the lot but he was essentially a brilliant bureaucrat, an organiser, rather than a negotiator. This task required more than charm; it would be better served by guile.

On the other side of the table sat men like David Lloyd George, Winston Churchill, and F.E. Smith – Lord Birkenhead, all of whom had many years of experience in running an empire and who were supported by the full resources of their Civil Service.

The Irish Party, founded by Butt, forged by Parnell and latterly led by Redmond may have been middle-class and middle-aged, complacent and venal but at least it had some competence in politics beyond the local. Imperial politicians such as Churchill may have had brute force as their default position but they could be inveigled into compromise if they were persuaded of its advantages. SF / IRA had no negotiating strategy, just a line in the sand. There was no possibility of Britain's conceding the status of Republic even though the settlement which emerged offered its substance. It's hard to avoid the conclusion that De Valera realised that, and avoided taking a role which would inevitably have entailed compromise. Pure principle was exalted beyond practicality and in consequence people like John Hennigan who had served the Crown, the Southern Unionists and the supporters of Home Rule, were now to be pushed beyond the new Pale.

What did the revolutionaries understand by a republic? For the more intellectual elements of the movement, the only models they had were the USA and France. The former had declared the separation of Church and State a fundamental principle. The latter was decidedly anti-clerical. The great majority of revolutionaries were Catholic by upbringing and conviction, some very committed to their Faith, so neither model could have been very appealing. The old Gaelic tradition had been monarchist, from the native kingship which had gone under in the 14th Century, through allegiance to the Catholic Stuarts in the 17th Century. There had been symbolic offerings in the 18th and 19th Centuries of the Gaelic Crown to those O'Connors who were lineal descendents of the last Kings of Connacht and All Ireland. There are unsubstantiated stories that in the revolutionary period The O'Connor Don was approached with a view to restoration of the Gaelic monarchy.

Historically, republican ideology had appeared in Ireland with the United Irishmen of the late 18th Century; the leadership was predominantly Protestant. A contemporary may have referred to Tom Paine's *The Rights of Man* as "the Koran of Belfast" but rank and file secular republicanism seems to have been largely confined to Ulster. The Wexford uprising of 1798 seems more of a peasants' revolt and decidedly sectarian. While the conduct of the predominantly Protestant Yeomanry was appalling, the massacre of 200 Protestants by burning alive at Scullabogue and the hangings at Wexford Bridge were hardly the expression of the secular Enlightenment. These in turn gave further excuse for the pitch-cappings and half-hangings carried out by Milita and Yeomanry.

The Young Irelanders of the 1840s with their leadership of educated middle-class idealists were inspired by Continental revolts aimed at over-throwing reactionary monarchs. They had no hope of gaining many adherents among the dispossessed Irish in the middle of the Great Famine.

It's possible to see Sinn Fein as a millennial movement, defined more by what it was against that what it was for. Once the British were out of the picture, wrongs would be righted, justice for all would be assured, and Ireland's saints and scholars would prosper. The observations of an outsider, Roger Chauviré, Professor of French at UCD, are interesting. As cited by Charles Townshend, Chauviré explained to a French readership that Sinn Feiners were determined "to ignore what is, and to take account, nay to admit the very existence, only of what ought to be". For the Irish, he thought, "there is between justice and might, not a harmony to be realised in the long run, but immediate and substantial identity". Sinn Feiners were "millenarians as sure of their triumph as tomorrow's sun". Patrick Lyons put it more caustically: "It came to be assumed that if the British could be got rid of, every Irishman could have his harp, his woman (maybe more than one of these) and his crooskeen of wine".

The military side of the movement, the IRA, concentrated on the means rather than the ends. Beyond winning what they saw as their battles, the fighters and activists put the task of defining their objectives on the long finger. This neglect of clear political targets would cost them dearly in the near future.

In 1921 there was neither time nor opportunity for debate on the subject. Probably for many of the fighting men, the republic was a synonym for independence. But how do you define independence? Did it mean no further role for the King? Would there be an end to the privileges of the Anglo-Irish gentry? Was it an end to landlordism and ranching?

One possible outcome was discussed by Joseph Plunkett, Patrick Pearse and Desmond Fitzgerald in the GPO during the 1916 Rising. With the support of a victorious Germany, an independent Kingdom of Ireland might be established. Prince Joachim was mentioned as a possible candidate. An advantage for the ultra-nationalists would be that a German king would favour a process of de-anglicization and the promotion of the Irish language. The triumvirate of thinkers thought further into the future. In Fitzgerald's account:

> For the first generation or so it would be an advantage in view of our natural weakness to have a ruler who linked us with a dominant European power, and thereafter when we were better prepared to stand alone, or when it might be un-desirable that our ruler should turn by personal choice to one power rather than be guided by what was most natural and beneficial for our country,

the ruler of that time would have become completely Irish.

As contemplated by these visionaries, the future seemed more monarchical than republican. Concerned with "moral rectitude", they also "each brought forward every theological argument and quotation that justified that Rising". Tellingly, referring to a subordinate officer who had taken to dating his notes by 1st, 2nd , 3rd Day of the Republic and so on, Fitzgerald wrote "that method of dating seemed to associate the Rising with the French Revolution, an association that was utterly repugnant to me".

At the time of the East Clare by-election in 1917, the victorious candidate, Eamon De Valera – only surviving Commandant from the Easter Rising – declared that, while he wanted an Irish republic, he would "not put a word against" another form of government provided that it was an Irish government. The Dominion status which was offered by Britain in 1921 was an enormous concession in comparison with the Home Rule measure of 1912.

Perhaps much of the confusion around the definition of independence can be traced to a blind adherence to the dogma of Wolfe Tone that all Ireland's ills resulted from the connection with England. If that simplistic proposition is accepted, the corollary is that the Irish must burn everything British except their coal. The IRA would split on the symbolism of an oath rather than the substance of the new constitution.

On 6th December 1921, a treaty was signed between representatives of the British Government and plenipotentiaries of Dail Eireann, the SF undercover parliament. The Dáil was to adopt a constitution in accordance with the Treaty terms and establish a provisional government to which power would be officially transferred. That government decided that the RIC must be disbanded and replaced by a new police force. The

Dublin Metropolitan Police would be retained in the service of the new state, the Crown deleted from its badge and the words "*Poliní Áth Cliath*" substituted on their helmets.

The first considerations of RIC disbandment had begun with the Truce. Now the matter was urgent. Eventually pension entitlement was calculated at service years plus eleven years at the same rank added. For John Hennigan that meant 10 + 11, which would have given him a pension entitlement of 21 years.

Even now there was no respite for the RIC. After the Treaty, attacks on the Police increased. In Thurles on 9th December shots were fired at two unarmed policemen emerging from a tailor's shop. The following day in the town a Police patrol was fired on. There were no casualties in either case. In the week ending 18th December the weekly total of outrages against police increased from 5 to 9, including three deaths. On the 14th in Kilmallock, Sgt Thomas Enright was shot dead and Con. Timoney wounded. Both were from Thurles but in Kilmallock on leave. The previous day in Ballybunion, Co. Kerry, Sgt John Maher was shot dead and Con. George Callow severely wounded. Both cases look like a settling of old scores when the policemen were off guard. That seems likely considering how other policemen were threatened. Sgt Commins of Carrick on Suir was threatened with death similar to that meted out to Maher and Enright.

As the last RIC convoy left Tipperary town on 2nd March 1922, it met an IRA roadblock. HC Christopher Davis and Con. Williams were killed in an exchange of fire. Survivors, including several wounded, were taken prisoner but later released. Their arms and vehicles were seized.

There were also incidents where attacks on police were clearly inflamed by alcohol. And there were many robberies of policemen's houses.

Author Seán O'Faoilán, himself a militant Republican, was the son of Denis Whelan who served as a policeman in Cork. "Men like my father were dragged out in those years and shot – so be it. Shot to inspire terror – so be it. But they were not traitors – they had their loyalties and they stuck to them."

1922: The New Order and Disorder

Entering the new year of constitutional change and the emergence of rickety political structures, the general population of Ireland had little time to appreciate literary innovation or theoretical physics. Books published in 1922 which would prove of enduring significance included Joyce's "Ulysses", Eliot's "The Waste Land", and Einstein's "Meaning of Relativity".

In The Castle and Dublin's City Hall the Provisional Government set up shop. Kevin O' Higgins described it:

> Simply eight young men… standing amidst the ruins of one administration, with the foundations of another not yet laid, and with wild men screaming through the keyhole. No police was functioning through the country, no system of justice was operating, the wheels of the administration hung idle, battered out of recognition by the clash of rival jurisdictions.

The widening division between those revolutionaries who accepted the Treaty and those who did not can be seen in differing terms depending on the perspective of the observer. One view is that it was a division between pragmatists, those who wanted to get on with constructing a state within the current constraints, and those who pursued a unrealisable ideal of a totally independent republic, immediately established and purged of British influence. The English writer V.S. Pritchard, reporting for the *Christian Science Monitor*, saw the Republican side as wild in rhetoric, romantic and violent, compared to those who wanted to get on with nation-building, the practical people. "De Valera has not tried to make them pay rents, and taxes and rates…" Dev was acclaimed and elected in Clare.

While the DMP continued to police Dublin, beyond the city limits the 26 County area had no organisation maintaining law and order. The RIC had ceased to function. The Republican Police, under Austin Stack's ineffective Dept of Home Affairs could not be relied on. Armed criminality dominated many rural areas. The Provisional Government's emergency response was the creation of a special unit drawn from the IRA, equipped with Ford cars and machine guns which could be dispatched to areas of extreme lawlessness such as the Arigna Hills. This small CID force, which became known as "Oriel House" after its headquarters in Westland Row, was ruthless and violently efficient. Initially responsible to the Dept of Defence it was later transferred to Home Affairs and was disbanded at the end of the Civil War.

In January 1922 the Auxiliaries began to demobilise. The RIC was officially disbanded on 31st March and the process wasn't completed until August. It was an uneasy period for the RIC members. Mark Sturgis noted in his diary "The rebels are using them as an Aunt Sally in the whoop up campaign". Smaller barracks were evacuated and the police concentrated in larger centres pending disbandment. In some cases they took refuge in military barracks. Special groups were formed from the

Reserve to organise the logistics of evacuation and protect the men in transit. It was not a simple task, given that many roads were still impassable and rail links cut, especially in Munster. In Republican areas of the South the usual procedure was to carry the police in lorries accompanied by armoured vehicles to the nearest port. They would then be taken by ship to Dublin. From the port they were escorted to either Gormanstown or Collinstown Camp to be paid off. The precautions were necessary: too many "eleventh-hour gunmen" were keen to take pot-shots at the departing police in the hope of bagging a sitting duck. Between December 1921 and February 1922 alone there were eighty-two attacks on the RIC resulting in twelve deaths and twenty seven people being seriously wounded. Many of the murdered policemen were unarmed and defenceless. In Clonakilty Co. Cork, DI Michael Keany was shot dead as he left a hotel with his teenage son who was also fatally wounded. On 15th March, former Sgts John Gilmartin and Tobias Gibbons were slaughtered in their beds in St Bride's Nursing Home, Galway. The heroes who murdered them also killed a male civilian, Patrick Cassidy, and wounded another ex-policeman.

This was in some ways the worst phase of the torments of the RIC. Policemen were being murdered out of hand with not even the veneer of military necessity to justify the killings. It was a vicious succession of seemingly random attacks on often defenceless men. A Truce had been in effect since July 1921, a Treaty had been signed in December and yet some elements of the IRA seemed possessed of a purposeless blood lust. GHQ was clearly unable to control large sections of the Republican army and local commanders failed to stop the madness. Resigned and retired members of the Force were not spared and assassinations could occur in any circumstances. It was despicable, it was dishonourable, it was pointless and yet some thought themselves great fellows for the killing. Once unleashed, hatred is a genie almost impossible to contain and as the IRA moved towards an open split, the venom of the thwarted was directed towards former adversaries as well as former comrades.

On leaving their barracks, the policemen removed the heavy metal Station Badge from over the front door and carried off all firearms and military equipment. Each RIC member carried his personal firearm and personal belongings. Fittings such as the steel window shutters and furniture such as the hard wooden forms remained in place and could still be seen in older Garda stations decades later. The premises were usually handed over to IRA detachments. Those supporting the Provisional Government would hand them over to the new police force; in extreme Republican areas many barracks were burned to prevent that use. In some cases the handover was friendly and even accompanied by the exchange of presents and a drink.

If one were in the mood for symbolism, it's worth looking at the RIC evacuation of Clones barrack. In Patrick Shea's account, the menacing machine gun which poked from an upstairs window and commanded the Diamond was revealed to be nothing more lethal than a length of iron piping. For irony, look no further than a bizarre firefight at Clones in 1921 when the RIC had intervened after a party of B Specials crossed the *de jure* border apparently intent on reprisals and looting. One Special was killed.

On the 4th April 1922 an official "standing-down" parade was held at the Depot. General Tudor, about to leave for his new job in Palestine, addressed the three hundred or so RIC members present and thanked them for their loyalty. The RIC Band played and the Depot Commandant replied to Gen. Tudor. In the afternoon a similar ceremony was held at Collinstown Camp (which later became Dublin Airport).

Discharged on 24th August at Dublin Castle Yard, John Hennigan must have been one of the last to go. He had been transferred to Ship Street Barracks in March. It was not a regular police station but a military post situated at the rear of Dublin Castle and the police had been there as part of the Castle's security arrangements. Once demobilisation was decided upon, Ship Street had a new role and John a new superior officer. DI Victor Henry Scott had served with the Army from 1914 to 1919 and been wounded. In September 1920 he was made Adjutant at the Depot. In February 1921, Scott was appointed as Commandant of Dublin Castle with the rank of Temporary CI, responsible for its defence and the preparation of Ship Street for the reception of policemen before their discharge. Members of the station party were sent around military barracks to scrounge Soyer Cookers[ix], palliasses, blankets etc. in preparation for the arrival of policemen from around the country.

John may well have been present when Commissioner Michael Staines entered the Castle on 17th August at the head of a party of the Civic Guard, the new police force, and officially took over. A colleague in the Clerical Company at The Castle, Sgt Jack O'Mahoney, was certainly there when Collins took it over and on the day Jack left the place the Civic Guard marched in.

In its leader of 18th August, *The Irish Times* wrote:

> …With the Castle, the Royal Irish Constabulary passes into history, and there can be few men of Irish blood who do not feel a pang for the disappearance of this splendid force. Irishmen differ in politics, but they are at one in their admiration of human bravery, and the steadfastness of the Royal Irish Constabulary throughout the most terrible ordeal to which a force of its kind was ever exposed will stand for all time as an expression of Irish valour. Our country is on the threshold of a new era. For better or worse Irish destiny is in Irish hands

> and the future will be of our own making. If the new Ireland is served by a force which upholds the best traditions of the Royal Irish Constabulary she will be fortunate indeed.

In a fine gesture, the officers of the Royal Irish Constabulary presented a splendid silver cup to Timothy Healy KC, the first Governor General of the Irish Free State. Engraved with the RIC badge, this became known as the Cup of Peace. It was later given by the Healy family to the Garda Siochana in the person of the Commissioner.

A more sour note was struck in thirteen verses of doggerel accompanying the gift of a silver snuffbox from the Officers' Mess to the King. The final verse reads:

> So it may hap when we are dead
> And rebels drink their toasts instead
> That Your Majesty, over a pinch of snuff
> May give a thought – one thought enough –
> To the loyal corps that used to be –
> The Royal Irish Constabulary.[x]

To replace the RIC, the inaugural meeting of a police foundation committee had taken place on 9th February under the chairmanship of Michael Staines. On the 17th, the Provisional Government received their report on establishing the Civic Guard. On 21st February, recruitment began with IRA Brigade officers being asked to send suitable recruits to the RDS premises in Dublin. Candidates had to be 5ft 9 ins in height, unmarried and aged between 19 and 27. They had to sit examinations in Reading, Spelling and Arithmetic. The speed of organisation was commendable but entailed a risk that not all recruits were really suitable for policing.

It was inevitable that the new force would share many of the characteristics of the old one. Michael Staines had been advised by a committee largely composed of ex-RIC men so it's hardly surprising that the new force was so closely modelled on the original. In the first place, it would be a centralised, national force rather than made up of local constabularies on the British model. Initially the Civic Guard was equipped with Webley revolvers, whistles and belts from RIC stores. Rifles were also held in the Guards' armoury. However, an official willingness to make use of the old expertise by accepting a number of former RIC men as officers or recruits outraged some of the former guerrilla fighters. This led to a crisis, the "Kildare Mutiny" as a result of which the force was reconstituted as an unarmed service: *An Garda Síochána* – Guardians of the Peace.

Ostensibly the cause of the revolt was IRA veterans objecting to the presence of RIC veterans but that problem was at least exacerbated by growing divisions over the Treaty. Attitudes to the Treaty may well have been the underlying cause. In any event a group of leading mutineers decamped with the contents of the Kildare armoury and joined the Anti-Treaty IRA who had occupied the Four Courts in Dublin. A statement issued by the mutineers in July 1922 expressed a view which was probably common enough among active Republicans and their supporters:

> The hatred of the ordinary Irishman for the organisation known as the Royal Irish Constabulary is understood by everyone and condemned by few. That being so, it was only natural that there should be trouble of some sort once it became evident that the Civic Guard had begun to take on a definite RIC complexion … these RIC have received a certain training in a machine invented by English and anti-Irish brains for the

> purpose of holding this country in subjection. The mentality of men who have been pulverised and re-created in that machine is of a particular type and possesses particular attributes.

Though unsigned, the statement was taken as representative by the authorities. However, after reassurances most of the Guards accepted the Treaty and remained loyal to the elected government.

On the 28th January the last issue of the *Constabulary Gazette* appeared:

> We therefore welcome most heartily the coming of the new National Police of the Irish Free State. And, hoping that present causes of bitterness will evaporate in the dawn of happier days, we look forward to seeing the ranks of the future guardians of the peace in Ireland reinforced by many of our present friends of the RIC whose knowledge and experience, bravery and resourcefulness would be invaluable to the general organisation and to the Authorities.

In fact, 180 former members of the RIC joined the Garda, 160 of them in 1922. Of those 160, fourteen were directly admitted as officers with the rank of Superintendent or above. Five of these had been DIs. The new force took over not only many of the old barracks with furnishings and equipment but a great deal of the structures and ethos of the former Constabulary. An old RIC man visiting a Garda station in the 1950s did not feel at all out of place. Looking back, it seems fair to say that the unarmed *Garda Síochána* was the embodiment of what the majority of the RIC had hoped to become.

In a memorandum quoted by Gregory Allen, Collins in

June 1922 referred to the need to establish a Garda presence in the areas where it could now function. "The nucleus must be the Garda Siochana organisation… We do not want a casual police force without proper training… It is not necessary for me to illustrate this by pointing to the wretched Irish Republican Police system and to the awful personnel attached to its ranks. The lack of construction and control in the force have been responsible for many of the outrageous things which have occurred throughout Ireland".

Desperately short of skilled leadership the new force even offered a Cadet entry in 1923, the only one in the history of the Garda Síochána.

Staines had submitted his resignation after the mutiny. His farewell address as Commissioner in August 1922 was inspirational:

"The Garda Siochana will succeed not by force of arms or numbers but on their moral authority as servants of the people."

There were echoes of the old Constabulary in the appearance as well as the practices of "The Guards". The high tunic collar remained until the mid-1950s when it was replaced by an open collar and tie. Rank and file *Gardaí* and their Sergeants wore a dark blue uniform but officers were resplendent in a pale blue uniform with Sam Browne belt. One difference from the RIC system was that Inspectors were now dressed as officers rather than wearing a sort of Warrant Officers' badge like the old Head Constables. Only in 1987 was a new uniform of an intermediate shade of blue introduced, common to all ranks, and the Sam Browne belt was relegated to formal occasions.

When the DMP was assimilated into the Garda Siochana in 1925, badges and buttons were changed but not all the metropolitan policemen were happy to relinquish the historic title of Constable. Although the DMP Station Sergeant's sleeve badge of three crowns was exchanged for one of three castles, for decades later older members of the public would refer to "the Crown Sergeant".

One of the earliest recruits to the new police force was John Hennigan's future brother-in-law, Timothy O'Connell from Sligo who was soon to be promoted to Sergeant. His photograph shows a young man beaming with pride. He later became Sgt O'Connell of the New York City mounted police and carried the flag at the St Patrick's Day parade, with a new set of chevrons on his sleeve. Another early Garda recruit was Patrick Flynn of Leitrim who would later marry Tim O'Connell's sister and become my uncle by marriage. Pat, a sinewy giant with a gentle heart, retired in 1966 with an "exemplary" record. Another sister, Helena, would marry Garda Martin O'Connell whose service was also exemplary.

Timothy's story illustrates some of the difficulties faced by the new state and its police. With his brother Michael, Tim had been involved with the Sligo IRA. I don't know what activities they were involved in but as a child I found the wooden case they'd constructed to hide two rifles in the dunghill, and some other scraps of military equipment. The brothers accepted the Collins view of the Treaty but Sligo Brigade as a whole took the anti-Treaty path. As the situation became more fraught the O'Connells apparently decided to take no active part in any internecine hostilities. In early May 1922, Tim was driving a horse and cart along an open stretch of the old Dublin road when rifle shots rang out. Realising he was under fire and without any cover he threw himself backwards into the bed of the cart, and lay as if mortally wounded. The ruse worked. Tim was convinced that the would-be assassin was Johnny ----, a former comrade.

Soon after, one of his sisters cycled into Sligo town and bought a cheap suitcase. After dark it was strapped onto the bike and brought back to the house. Tim packed his bag and walked through the night to Ballysodare Railway Station in time to catch the early train to Dublin. He was inducted into the Civic Guard on 10th May 1922. Timothy could have been one of those who marched into Dublin Castle on 17th August.

The enlistment of Martin O'Connell within a couple of days of Timothy was also with hazard. A native of Craughwell, Co. Galway, he'd travelled by train discreetly from Athenry. Approaching the recruitment centre in Dublin, Martin and another man thought it prudent to walk on opposite sides of the street. The other man was shot down.

It soon became clear that a substantial minority in the Dáil would not accept the Treaty terms. The situation deteriorated until overt civil war broke out and the country was again in flames. The destruction of infrastructure was far greater than that sustained in the previous phase of conflict and many areas of the new state were utterly lawless. The Republican policy of cutting transport links led to an orgy of destruction which paralysed the country. Railways were a favoured target. The irremediable destruction of the picturesque Kerry Monorail was one event among many in which bridges, engines, rolling stock and tracks were wrecked. At Sligo on 14th December, a commandeered locomotive had the throttle opened and was left to hurtle towards the buffers of Sligo Station – a runaway bomb. Fortunately, railwayman managed to change the points so that the engine was derailed. On 11 January 1923, the station was mined and totally destroyed by armed men. Seven engines were sent down the line to the goods yard. One ran towards the Deepwater Berth at Sligo port where it smashed though the sea wall. Some wheels were still visible at low tide in the 1950s. What rationale could justify putting hundreds of Irish civilians at risk and derailing the country's economy?

The new Guards were sorely tested but their unarmed status spared them the murderous violence suffered by the RIC. Gen.

Eoin O'Duffy who'd taken over as Commissioner spoke to massed recruits – and the press – in November:

> I trust that when you go to your stations you will not let down the Civic Guard and the people by abandonment of your post at the behest of any armed coward who would shirk from meeting you in combat on an equal footing. Far better the grave than dishonour. Don't be alarmed at the sound of a rifle shot. You've heard it before and you were not subdued because you had right on your side and gunmen had only might.

It was a huge demand to make of inexperienced young men, a challenge not too far removed from that which had faced their predecessors. In November 1922, a young Guard named Harry Phelan entered a shop in Callan, Co.Kilkenny, to buy a box of matches. It seems his mission in the village that day was to buy equipment for a hurling team he was organising. He was seized by three men, two of whom held him to the floor while the third put a rifle to his head and blew his brains out. He was the first Garda to die by political violence. A month later, the same village of Callan was occupied by anti-Treaty IRA, part of a unit commanded by none other than Dan Breen. Garda Sgt Thomas Kilroy and his men were lined up in the street and publicly humiliated. Sgt Kilroy believed that their lives were spared because of previous IRA service.

However, although Republican leaders such as Liam Lynch regarded the Guards with contempt, it was clear the public would not countenance the murder of unarmed men. On the 12th December, an IRA General Order forbade firing on unarmed Civic Guards.

The words of playwright Thomas Kilroy, the Callan Sergeant's son, describing what he found when researching into the years which formed his parents, serve to describe the whole bloody span of years from 1919 to 1923.

> In the newspapers, reports of relentless ambushes and killings of police and military throughout the countryside are placed alongside the results of games of golf from the local links. Masked men drag out victims from their homes on a nightly basis and shoot them while the well-named local theatres, the Empire and the Victoria, continued to do brisk business in comedies and farces. A buy Irish campaign sits uneasily on the page near reports of the more lethal activity of Irish nationalism.

The Civil War would drag until the spring of 1923 in the South-West. In Sligo, where the most of the local IRA opposed the Treaty, fighting was bitter in the summer of 1922. At Rockwood on the shores of Lough Gill a National Army patrol was ambushed by Republican forces and suffered three immediate fatalities. Many years later I heard an elderly man, a relative by marriage, chortle into his pint when recalling how "the Staters", with the roads cut, had to bring their dead back to Sligo by rowboat. Some time after the ambush, my mother's brothers Timothy and Michael erected a wooden cross at the site but it had vanished by the time I was a boy. On the slopes of Ben Bulben in September six Republicans were killed, possibly executed, by the National Army. One of them, Brian MacNeill, was the son of Eoin MacNeill, former commander of the Irish Volunteers. Brian's father and brother took the pro-Treaty side. Those two local incidents alone can serve to illustrate the raw and brutal intimacy of all civil war.

The cycle of atrocities in 1922-'23 gave a savage irony to the term *Sinn Féin*. The movement had turned on itself. The Free State's 77 official executions far exceeded the British total of 24 during the pre-Truce period. The anti-Treaty side was guilty of its own appalling acts. The legacy of bitterness would echo down the decades.

Confronted by naked might, the new Guards suffered intimidation and hardship. Forced to rely on passive resistance and dogged perseverance, they did in general refuse to abandon their posts and gradually won acceptance even among people who bitterly opposed the Treaty.

Commissioner O'Duffy expanded the policy of earlier RIC Inspectors General in encouraging his policemen to embrace sporting activities in the community, telling them they could "play their way into the hearts of the people".

In gaining acceptance, it also helped that the Guards eschewed the political policing role. They avoided confrontation with the anti-Treaty forces and confined their activities to dealing with ordinary crime. Until the establishment of the Garda Special Branch in 1926 the task of watching political malcontents and dealing with subversives was left to the National Army. There was also an intermediate counter-subversive section of DMP officers under David Neligan which operated on a national basis.

Among the new policemen and their political masters, there was probably a growing recognition by many of the professionalism of the former force and an understanding of the difficulties those men had faced. Kevin O'Higgins said of the RIC "Let us not forget that it was the height of ambition of most young fellows who happened to be 5 foot 9 or thereabouts".

In one important respect, the Garda Siochana differed from its predecessor. Whatever the religious composition of the upper ranks, the rank and file RIC had been a proudly non-sectarian force. Religious tracts and symbols were prohibited in Constabulary stations. On the 1st April 1923, a ceremony was held at The Depot in which the Garda Siochana was solemnly dedicated to the Sacred Heart. Commissioner Duffy and Chief Supt McCarthy assisted Rev. Patrick McAuliffe, Chaplain to the

Force, in the religious ceremony. On the parade ground, drawn up in a hollow square, 1,500 Gardai repeated the Apostle's Creed. Whatever the depth of the men's religious convictions, it was clear that the new State and its institutions would not worry too much about the sensitivities of religious minorities. The Sacred Heart emblem in the form of the Pioneer Abstinence badge could be worn on the uniform. The Catholic Church was establishing its dominance in the Free State.

The following day the *Irish Independent* reported on the ceremony. It said that the new Guards "went through different evolutions of foot drill in the most creditable manner". The report also said "This was the first time in Irish history that an Irish police force, constituted in accordance with the wishes of the Irish people, have (sic) been consecrated to the Sacred Heart, to work for Ireland, similarly consecrated". That surely was identifying both the State and its police force with the Catholic interest.

The same issue of the paper carried a photograph of the funeral of Sarah Bernhardt, France's most celebrated actress. A report from the occupied Ruhr told of the shooting dead of ten German workers in a Krupp factory after they had attacked French troops enforcing war reparations. Bolshevists were persecuting priests in Russia. In south-west Ireland, National Army troops were still being fired on and dozens of Irregulars were being arrested. In County Offaly rate collectors were promised "the extreme penalty" if they collected rates, taxes or annuities. At Hawlbowline Island the Royal Navy handed over its base to the Irish board of works and Irish troops moved into the quarters vacated by the Royal Marines. Most interestingly, it was reported that His Majesty's light cruiser *Caster* departed the jetty with the last batch of RIC under the command of Head Constable McGonigle. That is fully seven months after we thought the last Constabulary members, John Hennigan among them, had been discharged.

In September 1922 a Sergeant and four Guards arrived in Collooney. The Republicans had been expelled from the town after a noisy but largely bloodless battle in July. The new policemen sought the help of Sgt King in getting themselves sorted out. This he was glad to give and monitored them for some weeks. Locally, there was no animosity shown towards the King family.

Discharged RIC men found it difficult to find alternative employment. They were certainly not encouraged to join British police forces. In the words of the Chief Commissioner of London's Met to the Under-Secretary at the Home Office, "we cannot make the Metropolitan Police a place of refuge for RIC men". Britain's colonies were politely unhelpful: Australia, New Zealand and South Africa gave negative responses. As for Canada, in Toronto "the Belfast of North America" the police force was dominated by Irish Protestant Orangemen and offered no welcome to Catholic Irishmen.

The Palestine Police was activated in April 1922 under the command of General Tudor. He was joined by many former Auxiliaries and Black and Tans to make up the bulk of the new force taking over from the Military in the maintenance of order. They'd tried the formula out on Paddy; maybe it would work better on Mohammed. John Fails, a Limerick Protestant and son of a policeman, served in the First World War before becoming a Black and Tan. He went to Palestine: "There were bits of riots, you know, the same as in Ireland. There was some of the policemen there that knocked them Arabs about a bit. Oh, they were rough, yes".[xi]

The majority of discharged RIC men stayed in Ireland but between 1919 and December 1923 a total of 1,436 ex-RIC emigrated. Of these 219 went to America. John Hennigan travelled to New York, his occupation listed in the British passport as "motor mechanic" despite his utter ignorance of the workings of the internal combustion engine. John Gilmartin also crossed the Atlantic but would remain much longer in New York. He did not return to Ireland until the 1950s, unmarried and too old to adjust to the Ireland of that time.

As they were demobilised, men of the RIC said their farewells to one another and dispersed. Men who had depended upon each other for their very survival touched each other for the last time. There would be no public get-togethers for the veterans, no Regimental reunions. Like many others John Hennigan burned the photographs which showed him in uniform. Only one photo survived; cut from a group photo, it was a head shot which showed the tunic collar with its crowned harp. That postage-stamp-sized picture is now missing.

In 1922, after enduring some of the most appalling years any police force ever had to face, members might have found it impossible to reconcile their present status with that of the policemen twenty years before – as described by Arthur Griffith:

> The Royal Irish Constabulary is a body of Irishmen, recruited from the Irish people. They are bone of their bone, and flesh of their flesh. The typical young constabularyman is Irish of the Irish, Catholic and (as the word goes) Nationalist; the son of decent parents; his father a Home Rule farmer; his uncle a patriotic priest; his cousin a nun; his sweetheart the daughter of a local Nationalist District Councillor and patriotic publican; her uncle being chairman of the local "league" branch and a friend of the eloquent and patriotic member for the Division, who asks questions on the floor about the young constabularyman's prospects and grievances. The young constabularyman subscribes liberally to the Church; he is smiled on by the Irish clergy; he is smiled on by the Irish girls; he is respected by the young fellows on the street corner and the country crossroads.

That view of the policeman had not entirely vanished, even among Republicans. In his book *My Kilkenny IRA Days,* James J. Comerford had this to say: "Describing them in general terms, the Royal Irish Constabulary men as individuals were good fellows. They were nice men. They were good family men. It was the RIC 'as an organisational entity' that was bad".

And so the RIC passed into history. The passing was not attended by the solemnity of occasion as when the Colours of the southern Irish infantry regiments were taken into the personal care of the King at Windsor Castle. There was no monument raised to honour the fallen. Only in the hearts of men and women would their sacrifices be recognised. Some former opponents and their hangers-on would denigrate the old police and it could be unwise to speak in their defence but less biased people might see things in shades more subtle than black and white. Policemens' children – "Peelers' gets" – learned to hold their counsel but some would later try to balance the record. Patrick Shea offered his comments: "The men of the Royal Irish Constabulary had not the background or the disposition or the training which produces heroes. They were quite unfitted for the part they were called up to fill by those who saw a resort to violence as the way to the attainment of the Ireland they wanted". The revolutionaries thought the RIC would disintegrate "but they knew nothing of the deep loyalty of those simple men, one towards another... the comradeship which bound them together". Shea was unequivocal: "I am quite sure that there were in the Royal Irish Constabulary more good men than my children or my children's children will meet in any company anywhere".

Perhaps the finest, if the only – and the unintended – monument to the Royal Irish Constabulary is *An Garda Síochána*, a truly civil police service.

1923: Emigration to America

On 2nd March 1923, John Hennigan embarked at Southampton on *RMS Majestic* bound for New York. At least he was travelling in style. The sparkling-new *Majestic*, flagship of the White Star Line, was 10,000 tons greater than its predecessor Titanic. The previous August, the new ship, about to enter service, had been visited with considerable pomp by King George V and Queen Mary. But what must have intrigued John most was the fact that *Majestic*, like *S.S. Itejahy* which had plucked him from the sea just a couple of years before, was a German ship handed over to the British as war reparation. The hull had been launched as *S.S. Bismarck* in 1914 but had lain unfinished due to the war. She would remain the largest ship in the world until 1935 but on that March day in 1923 was sailing for America with fewer than half the full complement of passengers. If the weather was fair it could have been a most pleasant voyage but a former RIC man would still have been on his guard.

This was an era when, to many at home and especially in western areas, New York and Boston seemed like parishes in a faraway Irish county. Although still disdained by the predominately Protestant elite, Irish Catholics were becoming more prominent in American business and local government. I know nothing of John's life in the USA other than that he worked, for a period at least, for the Woolworth corporation. His sister Mary, Mrs Johnson, had been resident in New York for years. To Irishmen of enterprise the big city offered ample opportunity. Former Irish policemen were literate, numerate, English-speaking and accustomed to giving and following orders; they would have been particularly suited to middle-management. No doubt there were many Irish haunts and Irish-American circles which did not offer a welcome to former Peelers but by-and-large people in America had to rub along together. From 1923 onwards, America was host to many former IRA men who'd been on the losing side in the Civil War and had left the Free State in disillusioned frustration or through prudence. Ernie O'Malley was a notable example. Is it really fanciful to think that in exile some of these men might have found fellow feeling with their former adversaries? Both groups had been cast out of their familiar society. It could have been that Irish emigrés who had witnessed lethal violence, as opposed to those Irish-Americans always ready to fight to the last drop of someone else's blood, were more open to reconciliation. Perhaps that's just a wishful notion.

However, it's true that Arthur Shields, actor, and brother of the better-known Barry Fitzgerald, was a Republican and veteran of the Easter Rising who migrated to Hollywood. So did the director Rex Ingram, the brother of Major Francis Hitchcock MC, author of "Stand To". Another Hollywood resident was actor John Loder, husband of the highly intelligent and stunningly beautiful Hedy Lamarr. He played opposite Maureen O'Hara in *How Green Was My Valley*, a movie which won five Oscars. As John Lowe, a junior officer on leave from France, he'd stood beside his father when General William Lowe received Patrick Pearse's surrender in 1916. It's not fanciful to imagine all their paths crossing. But that was Hollywood and John was in New York.

This was the era of Prohibition, of speakeasies and the Charleston. Hemlines and share prices rose to dizzying heights as the United States began to discover its economic strength, displacing an exhausted Europe as the centre of world power. Ford cars rattled off production lines in prodigious numbers while the new Californian movie industry began to deliver an image of America to the world. Ordinary Joes wanted their slice of the economic boom and put their pennies into the stock market. As share values continued to increase by the day, they bought more stock. There was a restless energy in the air. As the song put it: "How ya gonna keep them down on the farm, after they've seen Paree?"

In New York while subway trains transported thousands of travellers beneath the streets, the elevated railroad clattered around overhead. Rich white folks made forays into Harlem to see black folks perform. And they needed suitable lubrication. Some Irish immigrants discovered that their ancestral expertise in making *poitín* was now a very marketable skill. I don't believe John Hennigan had anything whatever to do with the illegal alcohol trade – he was just too straight – but there were whispers that John Gilmartin may have been involved.

It seems John Hennigan did not fall for the allure of the stock market. Whatever mattress he kept his earnings under, they were obviously secure when The Crash came. In 1929 the house of cards collapsed with catastrophic results. But John was able to return to Ireland with sufficient money to set up in business.

The auguries probably looked good. After the assassination of Justice Minister Kevin O'Higgins in 1927, the new Garda Special Branch was taking a tougher line with Republican activists. In that year too the Cumann na nGaedhael government had seen off an electoral challenge by De Valera's new Fianna Fáil party backed by Labour. (It was the mysterious absence of Sligo's John Jinks from the crucial vote that saved the day for the government.) The Free State seemed to have survived its chaotic beginnings and developed into a stable democracy with conservative elements in charge. It seemed safe to return.

All New York's Irish community, of whatever political persuasion, must have felt pride when Wall Street hosted a ticker-tape parade in April 1928 for the gallant aviators Fitzmaurice, Von Hunefeld and Koehl. They had made history by the first crossing of the Atlantic east to west against the prevailing winds, having departed from Baldonnel military aerodrome outside Dublin. The flight, in their single-engined Junkers monoplane *The Bremen* had lasted over 36 hours. A former RAF officer, Major James Fitzmaurice wore the uniform of Ireland's National Army with its cap badge identical to that of the Irish Volunteers. In Ireland songs were composed in their honour and Fitzmaurice was promoted to Colonel. Germany was still a democratic republic and on excellent terms with Ireland. Rather shocking to some, the 1927 contract for the great Ardnacrusha hydro-electric scheme had been awarded to Siemens rather than a British firm.

Not all the exiles in New York were willing to brush recent atrocities under the carpet. From New York at Christmas 1930 we have a poem entitled "RIC Reminiscences" dedicated to "my dear friend and best man CN" by an anonymous author. In fifteen stanzas he recalls the Constabulary's peacetime routines and expresses strong emotions about what happened to the force. A few verses give the flavour:

II

How joyous was the outlook when on tour
How wondrous was wood and vale and sea
From Sixmilebridge to Burren's upland dour,
And down again from Scariff to Kilkee.
And round about, and in and out, and back
Each weather–beaten weighbridge for to test
The standards you dumped down beside the track,
And the local ex-officio did the rest.
And after that good liquor flowing free-
Great souls they were, those weights and measures men,
With minds alert, and physique good to see,
And skilled technique to back them where and when
Requirements of the merits of a case
Incumbent meant a court of law to face.

IV

The RIC are gone but nevermore
Shall Ireland own or see their like again,
A force of regal worth – a royal corps –
To duty's dictates staunch through thick and thin
How great they were when in the golden prime
The peace they kept in storied Inisfail,
And greater still when through the slush and slime
Of crime and blood they trudged without a quail
Deaf to the tempter's lure – the traitor's wile –
By threats and death and terrror undismayed
Cheap sneers and ribald jest – assassin's jibe –
Without result – they stuck it fast –
With pluck and grit and nerve – trustworthy to the last.
And murder's foulest malice were arrayed.

IX

And thou, my poor Mulhern, pure and brave,
And clean of heart, what tragic fate was thine,
Struck down where law and custom ever gave
Surcease of woe – like Beckett at the shrine.
To those who knew thee well, Oh, what a shock
    That human fiends could sanctuary defy,
And God's divine decree deride and mock
His temple desecrate – his will defy
And saddest thought of all, no sage rebuke
    From those whose duty bound them to condemn
The wretch abhorred, who traitorously took
    Thy young life, scarcely budding at the stem: –
Nor one regret, nor scarce a passing prayer
    From the ungodly crowd assembled there.

XIII

And in a summing up – of what avail
    The crimes, the tears, the blood that has been shed,
The cruel deeds that blaze the crimson trail
    That took its gory rise in Solohead?
Where are the gains predicted to accrue
    The harvest rich, resultant of the strife

The happy homes, where wealth and comfort strew
    Content and peace, adown the way of life?
You have them not – but a dismembered red land
    Torn and scourged, disgruntled to the core,
With burdens crushing, and the fairy band
    Of revolution, looming evermore –
Till the message has become a thing accursed,
    And the country's last condition is the worst.

"Poor Mulhern" clearly refers to D/Sgt William Mulhern, aged 39, who was murdered when going into Mass at St Mary's Church in Bandon. If any among his executioners were troubled about the sanctuary of a church being violated, the precise theologians among them may have argued the nice distinction that it didn't apply in the church porch. More importantly perhaps, a man with his right hand dipping into the Holy Water font was a defenceless target.

Curiously, the now defunct RIC would continue to have an influence even beyond the British Empire. Post-war, the RIC and RUC were involved in organising a new Greek Gendarmerie amid Greece's political turmoil consequent on that country's invasion of Turkey. The first RIC presence was that of Major Rigg, appointed as advisor after the Great War. He was followed by Sir Charles Wickham, former District Commissioner in the RIC and then the RUC's first Inspector General. Informed observers claimed to see in the Greek force many recognisable characteristics of the Irish Constabularies.

EPILOGUE
The Publican Settles In

For years after the Treaty, there was still residual animosity and occasional violence prompted by politics. It may not have been mere levity which caused Patrick Lyons to write to G.H. Orpen in December 1931: "But that it would not be safe I would live in a cabin among the mountains – with a few goats to give me milk. But this pastoralism would not be safe for an ex-RIC man".

After returning from New York, John Hennigan spent a year in Dublin, having married Bridget O'Connell of Sligo – known as Della. The ceremony took place in the Catholic church on Arran Quay and they lived briefly in Fairview. They returned to Sligo and bought the Midland Bar in Wine Street from Stephen Carroll who wore a bowler hat and a droopy moustache like a character in a silent movie.

John Hennigan's name went up over the door. This, however, was to be no ordinary public house. It was a whiskey house catering for a discerning clientele. There would be no draught beer on sale and the absence of the pint of stout guaranteed a near-absence of working class customers. The speciality of the house was John Jameson's Ten Year Old whiskey from the Dublin distillery. It was delivered periodically in great wooden barrels. The cask was mounted on a wooden trestle and the next task was to tap it with the brass spigot. This was a critical skill because too gentle a blow from the wooden mallet would not insert the spigot into the bunghole properly and result in loss of the precious golden liquid. Too forceful a blow could be disastrous. The aroma seeped into the timbers of the building and the sense memory of a child.

The manual skills my father displayed spoke of the self-reliance of a generation which had known hardship. He'd built the trestles on which the barrels rested, he'd sawn and hammered to create kitchen cabinets and, when school shoes needed new soles, the cobbler's last emerged.

The whiskey was dispensed into clear glass bottles: five-naggin bottles, each a sixth of a gallon. Then the labels were affixed – numbered labels bearing the information John Jameson & Sons' Dublin whiskey, bottled by John Hennigan of Wine Street Sligo. At the time, Jameson's produce was not distillery-bottled, unlike Power's, and was shipped in bulk to wholesalers and selected retailers. Consequently, quality varied around the outlets and people who took their whiskey seriously sought out certain vintners. Reputation was all and John Hennigan's whiskey soon earned a high reputation.

In 1932 Mr De Valera's Fianna Fáil party, "a slightly constitutional party" according to Sean Lemass, achieved parliamentary power. Despite widespread fears, the transition went peacefully and smoothly with the Army and Garda accepting the authority of the new government. Given that it was under a decade since the "dump arms" call had ended the Civil War, it was a remarkable achievement and demonstrated that the Irish Free State had found maturity as a constitutional, democratic state. Despite its shaky beginnings, it proved to be one of the few European states where Fascism never took hold in the 1930s. The durability of the Irish state is the more impressive when we look at the fate of other new states which emerged from the Treaty of Versailles. However, it probably would have been a different story if the North East had been coerced into a unitary state. It's not hard to envisage the island being engulfed by violence of a Balkan scale and ferocity. Some considerations are still valid in the 21st Century.

But stability came with its own price. Revisiting Ireland in the late 1920s, V.S. Pritchett wrote "One could smell the coming reaction and the dullness of growing religious obduracy". In the 1950s, George Seldes would write that a thing of beauty had been "altered and perverted into a shoddy middle-class stupid conservative uninspired unpoetic unromantic Free State and finally an independent Republic devoted to nothing more noble than the perpetuation of middle class respectability and the *status quo*". In the first heady days of self-government, the franchise was extended to all women – ahead of their British sisters. In following decades, Ireland's male politicians seemed determined to limit women's political involvement to using a pencil every few years.

Still, it was nice having one's own flag even if many of the citizens confused the colours with those of Kerry football.

There was a further price to stability. That took the form of a silence which denied the possibility of earlier wrong-doing. To demand truth and justice would have meant rocking a boat which had achieved a precarious equilibrium. Probably few would have risked that. In our Irish way we can believe that if we don't put it into words, it didn't happen. Some who had acquired land and property at gunpoint during the civil wars went on to prosper; there was no appetite to reopen old wounds. Others, more idealistic, were reduced to penury. Whatever you say, say nothing.

I suspect that in the decades after the ceasefire of 1923, the deep and enduring wounds of the post-Treaty Civil War tended to obscure the divisions between Loyalists and Sinn Fein, between former Crown servants and the IRA. There was certainly tacit agreement to leave things unspoken; it was the only way to maintain a tolerable society. In any case, there were so many connections as well as divisions within families and among friends when it came to membership of the various organisations, both established and revolutionary, that silence offered the best medium for society to function. There was a web of connections between the RIC, the Garda Siochana and the IRA; acknowledgement of this could foster instability.

Attitudes could mellow. In an interview with Desmond Rushe in December 1968, Dan Breen again: "I had no grievance against the ordinary Tommy or RIC man. He was only in it for the job. The poor devil was there and poor Tommy was even worse than the RIC man. But, of course, looking back on the RIC man, the economic position made him do things he didn't want to do. He had this bit of security in the RIC and a pension, and it was a hell of a thing for an Irishman, and you'd want to be very strong to resist it."

Conservative elements were still nervous about De Valera's populism and some of his new measures seemed to justify their fears. A decision to withhold payments of Land Annuities to the British Exchequer led to the "Economic War" when Britain imposed retaliatory tariffs on Irish exports. That hurt larger farmers who responded by withholding rates.

The Authorities in turn seized cattle. Republican attacks on Cumann na nGaedheal election meetings led to the forming of the Army Comrades Association, better known as the Blueshirts. Street violence developed into pitched battles and again the police were in the middle.

There were major changes in the Garda Siochana. David

Neligan was replaced as Head of the Special Branch by his old DMP colleague Eamonn Broy. Shortly afterwards, Eoin O'Duffy was replaced as Commissioner. Eamonn Broy took over the job in February 1933.

Poachers and gamekeepers could exchange roles. In his new incarnation as leader of the Blueshirt movement, more fantasy than fascism, Eoin O'Duffy announced a great rally in Dublin in 1934. Fearing a *putch* on the lines of Mussolini's March on Rome, the government proscribed the event and all available police were drafted in but there were some worries about divided loyalties. Broy took drastic steps: former IRA members who'd come around to De Valera's way of thinking were drafted into the Garda Siochana as a sort of armed special constabulary. In the event they weren't needed: O'Duffy backed down and the Garda proved as resolute as the RIC had ever been. The new men, however, were inducted into the regular police's Special Branch. In tribute to another pack of hounds, the wits dubbed them the "Broy Harriers". Irregular as the procedure was, the result was probably beneficial in that it introduced greater balance into the Garda with the anti-Treaty persuasion now represented.[xii]

In Sligo, as in most places, politics settled into a perennial contest between Fianna Fail and Cumann na nGaedhael, later rebranded as Fine Gael. Labour with some small urban support was peripheral. Fine Gael, depending on one's point of view, stood for conciliatory policies and prudent, Christian values or it represented the business class and large farmers and was West British in outlook. Fianna Fail could be seen as representing the poorer classes, "the fellow with no arse to his trousers" and upholding Republican ideals, or it could be perceived as a bunch of wild men in suits, still with a whiff of dynamite about them. It all came down to Eamon De Valera really. The great equivocator, he was a political chameleon whose greatest trick was to give the impression of unwavering principle.

Most importantly for many, Fine Gael seemed the broader church. It embraced pro-Treaty Republicans, constitutional Nationalists, former Unionists, and other convictions. Lacking the ideological basis of Fianna Fail, and De Valera's expressed commitment to the National Aims of ending Partition and making Ireland Gaelic, Fine Gael thought itself the more pragmatic party. The FG supporter might have questioned the likelihood of Belfast's Shankill becoming a *Gaeltacht*. Beyond the rhetoric, the fundamental need for peace and security was the over-riding consideration. And Michael Collins, the Laughing Boy, was acknowledged as one who had known when to stop the terror and had given his life in doing it.

To those of any wider vision it must have been a depressing era as the island of Ireland transformed itself into two ideologically opposed camps. Active hostilities ceased but attitudes became entrenched. For the Unionist Home Rule state, the watchword was "What we have we hold". The new Customs posts along the Border opened for business on 1st April 1923, which many thought an appropriate date. The physical barriers to cross-border traffic and the accompanying tariffs were physical manifestations of the new Free State policy of protectionism. That ethos would soon be extended to the moral sphere as well as the economic one.

The Boundary Commission collapsed in farce in 1925. (Spike Milligan's interpretation of The Border in "Puckoon" seems no more surreal than the actuality.) Roman Catholic dogma began to inform the Statutes of the Free State with the abolition of divorce, a ban on artificial contraception and the Censorship of Publications Act of 1928. In vain would Senator WB Yeats defend Irish Protestants as "no petty people"; in the Irish Free State members of minority religions learned to keep their heads down and their mouths shut. The small gentry class had suffered disproportionately in the Great War, leaving many families without a male heir. It is undeniable that there was an exodus of Protestants from Southern Ireland in the 1920s. Robin Bury adduces a figure of almost 42,000 "exceptional emigrants" but warns the figures are uncertain. Some 20,000 may have gone to Britain. Those who remained may not have shared the ideal of a neo-Gaelic Ireland structured by Catholic doctrine but many served the new state with quiet loyalty and served it well.

Public religion and private politics

Two events of 1932 signal the division across the island. Both northern Nationalists and southern Unionists had good reason to believe themselves betrayed as the new states promoted homogeneity in their respective ways. Dublin hosted the Eucharistic Congress in which the State played a key role. It was a great event for Catholics indeed, but it was a case of no others need apply. Belfast saw the grand opening of the impressive new Parliament Building at Stormont by King George V. A bronze Carson looked over his achievement and working-class Catholics found themselves regarded as less than loyal citizens. Even senior policemen, like John M. Regan, knew that as Roman Catholics their career prospects in the Royal Ulster Constabulary were blighted.

New allegiances and alliances south of the border saw the stately lodges of the former Chief Secretary and Under Secretary become residences for the Papal Nuncio and the American Ambassador. Also in the Phoenix Park, the Vice-Regal Lodge was occupied by the Governer-General, Timothy Healy. It would eventually become the Presidential residence.

Sometimes the zealotry of the self-appointed custodians of culture became farcical. In 1929 the Gaelic League banned "foreign dances". In other nations still reeling from the mass slaughter of the war years, a younger generation often embraced an apparent hedonism. In the Irish Free State the social laceration of political violence, mass unemployment and wholesale emigration seemed to Church and State of less concern than the danger to sexual morality induced by modern music. North of the Border, hotel pianos may have remained locked on the Sabbath but south of it there was pressure to impose Nationalist and Catholic orthodoxy in the musical sphere.

Leitrim emerged as the centre of resistance to the invasion of foreign music. In 1932, Fr Peter Conferey P.P. led the defenders, denouncing jazz and urging people to listen only to Irish music and wear home-spun clothing. Jazz, he claimed, was "borrowed from the language of the savages of Africa". In Mohill, a demonstration by several thousand people, some of whom carried signs reading "Down with Jazz" and "Out with Paganism", was organised by the Gaelic League. Cardinal McRory described jazz dancing as "suggestive…demoralising [and] a fruitful source of scandal and of ruin".

Fr Conefrey's language was restrained compared to that of a contributor to the *Leitrim Observer* in January 1934: "Let the pagan Saxon be told that we Irish Catholics do not want and will not have the dances and the music that he has borrowed from the savages of the islands of the Pacific". The writer urged the people of Leitrim to "rush forth again to expel the last and worst invader – the jazz of Johnny Bull and the niggers and cannibals". [xiii]

In that year my father was still in New York and must have had some awareness of jazz. In Sligo in the Thirties there was little opportunity to hear jazz music but I know that on his return there he at least occasionally attended the Elsinore Ballroom in Rosses Point. I'm sure he would have regarded the anti-jazz campaign with the same contempt he had for zealotry of all other kinds.

As the Sligo publican, Jack Hennigan took no active part in politics. However, at some point he became an outright supporter of Fine Gael and his premises hosted many a small gathering. The larger snug became the town clinic for Martin Roddy where the TD met his constituents and offered advice and help. Martin served in the Dail almost continuously from 1923 to 1948. After Martin's death, his brother Joe was elected in his stead and served from 1948 to 1957. After defeat in that year's General Election, he became a Senator until 1961. During the Roddy years John Hennigan conveyed numerous messages to and from constituents on their behalf.[xiv]

There was another political connection. A cousin, another John Hennigan, had served from 1914 as a Farmers' Party member of Sligo County Council. In January1918 he attended a meeting at Maugherow to establish a Sinn Fein club. In August that year, Councillor Hennigan spoke at a meeting to protest against the banning of Sinn Fein. Arrested, he was taken to Galway and in September sentenced by a Court Martial to two years in prison. The sentence was later commuted to one year and on his release in September 1919 he was given a big reception in Sligo. [6]

On the SF ticket, Councillor Hennigan headed the poll in the Local Government elections in May 1920. Nominated as Chairman of the County Council, he declined the office but proposed that the Council pledge allegiance to Dail Eireann.

In the General Election of 1923 Hennigan won a seat as

---

6 Coincidentally, another sentenced at that time for making a seditious speech was my future mentor, Bertie Anderson of Calry, Sligo. He later told me his stance was that of a non-violent Sinn Feiner. Whilst doing his time in Derry Jail, Bertie, graduate of Queen's University Belfast and literate in five languages, kept the minutes at meetings of the warders' trade union, presumably the NUPPO.

a Pro-Treaty candidate. He went on to serve several terms as a Cumann na nGaedhal T.D. alongside Martin Roddy until defeated at the 1933 election. His parliamentary career was over just when his namesake returned to Sligo. After divergence in 1918, the political views of the two Johns converged by 1933.

The Free State settled gradually into a new political order which wasn't all that different from the old one – in practice as opposed to symbols. A feature of Sligo's social life in the 1930s was the annual Garda Ball. I learned long afterwards that my parents used to regularly attend. There was social continuity between the new and old custodians of the law.

John Hennigan must have had good political connections. As a child of about six, I was brought by my father to Leinster House. Queen Victoria, Empress of India, was still on her plinth inside the gates. Many years later, in the company of my son and daughter, I would meet her again where she sits now in the Victoria Shopping Centre in Sydney.

The story of how the statue got there is revealing. After having been removed from public gaze in 1948, the statue sat in the shadows of Public Works repositories until the government was approached by the Australians in 1986. At Cabinet the only voice opposed to sending the embarrassing lady into exile was that of John Bruton: "the monument is representative of one of the many traditions of Irish history. It is part of our heritage in no less a way than Norman or Viking remains". The Director of the National Museum, John Teahan, also expressed opposition: "If we are deemed not to be mature enough to distinguish between the art-historical merits of Hughes's Victoria and a symbol of authority, which does not or at least should not apply, I advise that such a figure should be retained and protected until we have grown up sufficiently to look that Queen, long dead, straight in the eye".[xv]

From 1932 onwards, good whiskey was being appreciated in

Sligo. On the outside wall of Hennigan's , a mural about five feet high was painted depicting a bottle of "Jameson TenYear Old" and the legend "Our Speciality". The artist was W.J. Heuston, a Republican who'd been a close friend of Countess Markievicz. He once told me that she and he had concocted a plan to steal the Lane Pictures at gunpoint from the Tate. Clearly the plan never came to fruition. Every year or two, Mr Heuston , whose day job was painting landscapes, came by to touch up the mural, especially the delicate gold lettering. I was fascinated by the technique of applying gold leaf. Using his artistic licence, he'd amalgamated the correct label with the more ornate elements of the Seven Years Old one.

Apart from Jameson Ten, the shelves bore Jameson Seven Years' Old and some Power's Three Swallow whiskies. Hennigan's also stocked some blended Scotch for those with an undeveloped palate. Soda syphons stood ready for the splash. Some Gordon's gin was available for golfers and other eccentrics. Among the occasional lady visitors, usually country women on a market day, the most popular tipple was sherry and these ladies usually sat in the small snug along the front window. That window was a work of art. Apart from the upper quarter the plate glass was frosted with a baroque design of swirling branches and, in large florid letters, the name: "The Midland Bar". It had been etched, not by crude sandblasting, but with hydrochloric acid in the old difficult, dangerous and expensive process. On a summer day, tobacco smoke and dust motes drifted in the sunshine above the frosting.

Lower shelves held bottles of beer and stout, ready to provide a chaser. The most memorable beer was Smithwick's No.1, a bottle-conditioned natural brew that had to be carefully decanted off the lees. The shelves were stocked once or twice a week by Jack McDermott, John Hennigan's cousin. Jack had been a regular soldier before war broke out in 1914, having enlisted underage, and survived the war without a scratch. This was much to his regret as he was ineligible for help from the British Legion in his declining years. His wife Mary had eloped with him on an ass cart in the night and they remained a devoted couple into old age.

The Midland Bar carried a six-day licence so Sunday was sacrosanct as a private, family day. My parents both owned fine bicycles, her Raleigh and his Humber, which Da kept in perfect condition. Weather permitting, Sunday was an outdoor day. There were occasional family visits to the Gaiety Cinema; the very first film that I remember seeing was full of aerial warfare which seems an odd choice but I think I enjoyed it.

It was well into the 1950s before I became aware of the clientele in Hennigan's. The regulars were a diverse group, coming from a variety of backgrounds. Tankey Henderson had earned his nickname from driving a tank during the First War; it left him permanently deafened so he spoke very loudly. A devout Protestant, he observed the Lenten fast by "going on the tack"; for him, that meant he eschewed whiskey and made do with beer for forty days. Ronald Harper Campbell Perry was a scion of one of Sligo's old merchant families but had chosen to go on the stage and was a veteran of Dublin's Gate Theatre. Jack Mooney, with a Dublin accent O'Casey would have envied, was old IRA and unswerving in his views. Pop was another old IRA man who'd taken the anti-Treaty side in the Civil War. Dermot did something vague but, it was said, had a wife with means enough to keep him in style. Though distrusting zealotry of any persuasion, John Hennigan showed an understanding of Unionism in the sense that he thought that Ireland was just too small to contain its population and too weak in its resources to go it alone. There was the notion that Ireland's people needed wider fields for their abilities and two obvious areas of opportunity were the USA and the British Commonwealth. Home Rule would have fitted the bill nicely. Sometimes, if annoyed by some particularly irritating example of parochialism, he would mutter darkly about the "cabbage patch of a country". But only in private. A cultural duality – not a dichotomy – was heard too from the big cabinet wireless: Radio Eireann alternated with the BBC. The unique tones of Alastair Cooke as he read his Letter from America were as familiar to me as the soulful piping of Leo Rowsome.

Even in the 1950s, Sligo was a divided place. Its population was not just stratified by wealth and privilege, as obvious in every country town; the fissures of religious division ran deep. There were Protestant businesses which didn't employ Catholics; there were Catholic businesses to which no Protestant need apply. There seemed to be two of everything: Catholic Boy Scouts and 'Baden-Powell' scouts; YMCA and CYMS; two tennis clubs; Knights of Columbanus and Freemasons; different areas of the town cemetery. Socially, Sligo was a Kaarst landscape, as tricky for a child to negotiate as The Burren.

I suspect John Hennigan felt more in sympathy with the Protestant minority in Sligo than with the Roman Church triumphant. For religious observance, he preferred to attend the Dominican Priory rather than Sligo Cathedral, the episcopal seat of Elphin Diocese. I know that he detested the strident expressions of the majority religion such as Corpus Christi processions through the streets when craw-thumpers with solemn faces showed public piety.

I don't know how he reacted to the extraordinary announcement by Taoiseach John A. Costello in 1948 that Ireland was about to leave the Commonwealth. This precipitate decision, made on an official visit to Canada, has never been satisfactorily explained and seemed to be the antithesis of traditional Fine Gael attitudes. John Hennigan must have been horrified. Ireland was already isolated enough from the wider world.

In the period 1939 to '45 the Irish state had an Emergency while most countries were enduring a world war. Cereals now being needed for food, distillation of spirits was suspended and public houses were given a whiskey quota from bond. This was based on their recorded purchases over the preceding three years. Accordingly, John Hennigan received a very large quota. With American troops arriving in Northern Ireland and spirits almost unobtainable in the U.K., whiskey could fetch very high prices on the black market. It was a once in a lifetime opportunity. But he would have nothing to do with profiteering and chose instead to help out his less fortunate publican colleagues. It was who he was. With foresight born of the previous war, he'd laid in supplies of tea, sugar and coal before those essentials were rationed and so his family never lacked them through the lean years. Prudence was fine but profiteering was despicable. Having prosecuted the profiteers in the earlier war, he wasn't going to become one of them in the second.

The regulars in Hennigan's were a diverse group in religious background and political conviction, but voices were never raised in dispute. There was one absolute rule in conversation: no politics and no religion. That little establishment was a model of tolerance and mutual respect and the affection which developed between the men was unstated but real. Loyalties which were apparently in conflict could be reconciled within the individual too. When Hitler's war began, Ronnie Perry was one of the many who joined the Local Defence Force, Ireland's Dads' Army, and stood ready to defend his little country from any aggressor – German or British. Later, when the threat of invasion had receded, he joined ENSA and went on tour entertaining British troops behind the lines. Few would have seen anything strange in that. Petty Officer the Hon. Patrick Campbell, future Lord Glenavy, was then a volunteer in the Maritime Inscription and searching ships in Dublin Bay "for any sign of Hitler". In other families, one brother battled Fascism in khaki while another, usually the elder, wore the green uniform at home. One of my mother's sisters tended to Allied soldiers in Gibraltar as a nurse in Queen Alexandra's Nursing Corps. Who is entitled to define the parameters of patriotism as opposed to blind nationalistic fervour?

But still there were dark secrets in the Ireland of the Fifties. In my childhood, I heard occasional mention of Michael Joseph, my father's young brother, who had died young. There were confusing and seemingly contradictory references. Several times I was told by my mother that Michael Joseph had been beaten up by "Black and Tans" so severely that he'd never been right in the head afterwards and had died as a consequence. Once she told me that he'd worked in a shop in Ballina and was cycling home for the weekend when stopped by the Tans. They found the dirty laundry he was bringing home for his Mammy to wash and were convinced that he was an IRA man on the run. He possibly could have avoided the beating if he'd convinced them that his brother was a policeman. Maybe he was too proud to plead like that. Maybe it wouldn't have made the slightest difference to the Tans or Auxies. They could as easily have shot him.

My father never offered information about Michael Joseph. Many years later I was told by an older cousin that he had not then in my childhood been dead, but had been a patient in St Columba's Mental Hospital in Sligo all along. His big brothers, John and P.J., visited him every Sunday. What deep hurt did John suffer, I wondered, especially in relation to his own employment at the time of the assault on Michael Joseph? He wasn't to blame but he and the Auxies had ostensibly been on the same side and it must have weighed on his conscience. In 'Fifties Ireland mental illness in a family carried a stigma and only the rich could afford home care. So poor Michael Joseph's continued existence remained in the shadows through the years.

The story also illustrates the brutal legacy of a civil war and the abuse of state power, and it was not unique.

It's a revealing narrative except that it wasn't true. Whether or not Michael Hennigan ever had a bruising encounter with "Black and Tans" we will never know, but he died in Dublin, at No. 16 Upper Mount Street, on 13th May 1928. His employment at the time was given as shop assistant. If he had been a psychiatric patient it could only have been for a relatively short time. Why would his family have concocted stories around this young man? What dark secret was darker than mental illness?

The answer is in the cause of death: pulmonary tuberculosis. He had also been suffering from cardiac syncope – fainting spells – for six months before his death. Tuberculosis, TB, Consumption, whatever you choose to call it, was the scourge of Ireland and half the world until it was brought under control in the 1950s. It is an infectious disease and it thrived in the crowded conditions most people then lived in. Having T.B. in the family background was enough to destroy any young person's marriage prospects. Mental illness was a lesser admission.[xvi]

So, two months short of his 26th birthday, Michael Joseph Hennigan from Grange died in the house of K.A. Walsh, adjoining the Elphis Nursing Home. Number 16, Upper Mount Street in Dublin is a large Georgian house, four stories over a basement. It seems probable that the building formed an adjunct to the Elphis, housed in Nos. 17 – 20. With its dull yellow pointed brickwork and splendid facade adjoining the Pepper Canister church, it's not a building which had ever fallen enough in status to be lodgings for a humble shop assistant.

Michael Joseph's older brother John was then three thousand miles away in what was really enforced exile. By the time I had arrived on the scene and grown old enough to ask questions, the cover story was more or less in place. But I didn't hear it from my father. I now think that John Hennigan simply didn't know how to lie convincingly and preferred to say nothing, leaving the fabrications to others. But I did sense that his lost little brother was very dear to him. And it must have hurt him that Michael Joseph had not died at home by the sea but in an unfeeling anonymous city.

Around the same time as the visit to Leinster House, my father brought me to Glasnevin Cemetery, "the dead centre of Dublin". There I was brought to the grave of Daniel O'Connell "The Liberator", who was clearly revered by my Da and many, many others. But he was belittled by the Brothers in school and derided by nationalists of the physical force tradition because he'd set his face against patriotic bloodshed. In the crypt under the majestic round tower, I could put my small hand through and touch the coffin but it seemed really creepy when Da told me that O'Connell's heart was buried separately in Rome.

Parnell was also referred to with admiration and my attention was drawn to the inscription on the obelisk of his Dublin monument: "No man shall have the right to fix a boundary to the march of a nation. No man has the right to say to his country thus far shalt thou go and no further".

Love of country and one's people finds diverse forms of expression. In 1947, the remains of W.B. Yeats were brought back to Ireland from France. My bedtime was delayed while my Dadda brought me, aged five, around the corner to the Town Hall to be present when the cortege arrived in Sligo. This was a historic occasion that he wanted me to witness. There was a military guard of honour. All I can really remember is asking my father why the soldiers had their guns turned upside down. Though it has taken me a lifetime to realise it, that innocent question must have evoked painful memories of earlier funerals.

Even though my memories of him cover only a short period, it was clear that he was trying to educate me about my country, its history, and its place in the world. I remember his bringing me into to the dark recesses of Sligo Cemetery's older section to find a particular headstone. "Captain Edward Doherty, the Brave Avenger of President Lincoln" read the epitaph. I can't recall his explanation on the day but years later I did rediscover the story of Lieut. Doherty, US Army, who'd led the cavalry troop that cornered John Wilkes Booth.

Like so many of his generation, if John Hennigan had been given the opportunity of further education he would have made full use of it. But he did well with what he'd been given. He took enormous pride in his appearance, a taller and broader man than I became. He was conscious of how he faced the world, paying great attention to his clothes. Most afternoons he took his constitutional, a walk that usually involved striding out along "The Line", the Markievicz Road, previously the Albert Line. His route took him by Ash Lane and Ballytivnan, across Asylum Road and back into town by The Mall. Sometimes, coming down The Mall he would drop into his brother's shop but usually P.J. was off in the daylight hours touring the countryside in his red travelling shop. Always well turned-out, in the cooler months in a well-cut overcoat, Jack was, as they said, a fine figure of a man. Hats were his special affectation; his small but select collection included the Homburg or "Anthony Eden" and various softer hats. Meeting a lady of his acquaintance, the hat was raised in old style courtesy. Owning several pairs of gloves, in cooler months he wore the ones appropriate to the outfit of the day. I suppose he could have been called a Dandy but it wasn't a term I encountered till long afterwards. Looking back, I suspect it was a wordless riposte to the style of the hairy- tweeded new masters with their lapels bristling with *Fáinne* and Pioneer pins. Some of his clothes came from Kennedy & McSharry, the Dublin drapers who had for years advertised themselves as Constabulary outfitters.

The same sense of style was shown in his choice of timepiece.

He never wore a wristwatch but sported an American-made pocketwatch, gold with silver inlay on its face. This sat in one fob pocket of his waistcoat and was joined by a fine gold chain to an antique little silver matchbox. The matchbox housed a couple of sovereigns. It's good advice to always have a couple of bob in your pocket but the sovereigns were something of an over-statement. I heard him ascribe his premature baldness to having to always having to wear headgear as a young man and also to a habitual use of brilliantine then but, sadly, implacable heredity cannot so easily be denied.

John Hennigan never appeared in public unshaven. The bowl of hot water and shaving brush appeared every morning and, sharpened by a quick strop on the leather, the selected straight razor was employed. After a small boy's curiosity had resulted in blood everywhere, the box of glamorous cut-throats was supplanted by a mere safety razor.

From my present perspective, I realise that my father wasn't merely fastidious about his appearance. He liked order and structure and embraced the values of the RIC as expressed in the Code, valuing honesty and fair-dealing. It's clear to me now that he'd been an ambitious young policeman. Of course he would have wanted to emulate his uncle Sergeant Bartley but I suspect that his horizons stretched beyond the three stripes. At least into 1916, a successful Constabulary career was his for the making. Head Constable rank was attainable through intelligence and application. In Ballyshannon he would have had the constant example of District Inspector Tyndall, the 'P' man. Perhaps young Jack aspired to such heights and groomed himself accordingly. I don't believe it mattered a jot to him whether the helmet harp had a crown over it or not.

Like so many men of his generation, Jack smoked a pipe and regarded cigarettes with disdain. The pipes came from Kapp and Petersen in Dublin, elegant, functional and treasured. His chosen tobaccos were aromatic ready-rubbed brands, far from the bitter pungency of the plug and coil tobaccos favoured by outdoor workers. I remember how, on being presented with boxes of cigars from America, he'd smoke one or two for politeness then later chop up the remainder and puff them in the pipe.

Loyalties in the new Ireland could be seemingly contradictory but not necessarily in conflict. Even after the independent state was established, Sligo continued to provide soldiers to the British forces. Outsiders may have sneered at the "garrison town" but the reality for many was a family tradition of soldiering – for most, in British uniforms. Ireland's tiny army offered little opportunity so they did as their fathers and grandfathers had done and took the King's shilling. That tradition really only began to die when The North erupted in violence in 1968. Up until then old soldiers of the First War, reinforced by veterans of the Second, pinned their medals on their breasts every Armistice Sunday and marched in commemoration up the Pearse Road to the Memorial Cross, ignoring public indifference.

Looking back on the events of 1912 to 1922, who had the right to call themselves patriotic Irishmen? Did anyone or any persuasion have an exclusive claim on patriotism or righteousness? Was Sir Horace Plunkett, a Unionist and founder of the Agricultural Cooperative movement who became a Free State Senator, any less of a patriotic Irishman than Count Plunkett, SF Dáil Deputy and father of an executed 1916 leader? As bitter reward for his work on behalf of small farmers Sir Horace had seen over a hundred vital local creameries destroyed by Crown forces and then in 1922 his fine house and its contents were burnt by Republicans.

For far too long, one official narrative dominated Irish life. Church and State colluded in shaping a version of events which was forced into the ears of every schoolchild. Reality is always complex, however inconvenient that may be. When in

1966 Fianna Fail organised the Jubilee commemorations and victorious survivors took the reviewing stands, some observers not of that political persuasion wondered about sowing dragons' teeth. Although it seemed a great joke to many, the demolition of Nelson's Pillar by a timer-activated mine – not a remotely controlled explosion – showed an utter contempt for the citizens of Dublin going about their nocturnal business. It could easily have resulted in multiple deaths but The Boys didn't worry about that. It was keeping their hand in for the years to come..

There were some sporadic attempts to balance the historical books. In September 1962, there was a discussion in the letter columns of the *Irish Times.* A correspondent calling himself "1922" made his point: "How many Irish lives did they [the RIC] take in this century down to 1919? None. How many Irish lives did they take directly from then until disbandment? Very few." On the 22nd a letter over the signature of Dan Breen was printed:

> "Of course Alison Philips of Trinity College should know more about Soloheadbeg than I do. He was not there. I was.
>
> Dan Breen TD.
>
> p.s. Why don't these apologists for the RIC, 'Fair Play', '1940 – 1945', etc. come out from behind their hedge of anonymity and fight fair?"

Clearly Mr Breen had no sense of irony.

At primary school we learned that Pagan England was the ancient enemy but most of the boys in my class emigrated there. They may not have wanted to take the Mail Boat with a cheap suitcase but there was nothing for them at home. No doubt the religious responses and *cűpla focail* which had been drilled into them at school proved a comfort as they offered their bodies for labour in the pre-dawn chill of Kilburn. But perhaps there was also a sense of freedom even as they accepted servitude to the gangers instead of the authorities who had ruled body and mind through childhood and adolescence.

John Hennigan died in October 1957 after a very short illness. He took his secrets and his painful memories to his grave. He did not live to see the celebrations of 1966 nor the atrocities which would be visited on Ireland and on Britain in the decades to follow. He had already experienced his share of horrors.

As I stood at his funeral, an uncomprehending fifteen-year old receiving the condolences of people I did not know, the word I heard repeatedly was "gentleman". I couldn't quite understand how this austere man who rarely showed emotion could inspire so much obvious respect and affection. And yet I'd seen him show compassion and indeed sentimentality, qualities not always appreciated by an adolescent. It needed the influence of my own son, and the pain of losing my own son, and many years of life to gain an imperfect comprehension.

It has taken me a long time to give him and his comrades this small recognition. Let us commemorate all who behaved honourably, whatever their convictions.

Appendix 1

SIR JAMES SHAW-KENNEDY, first Inspector General of the Irish Constabulary

In 1805, at the age of seventeen Glasgow-born James Shaw began his military career as an Ensign in the 43rd Light Infantry Regiment. Becoming a Lieutenant, he served during 1807–1809 under Sir John Moore, the pioneer of Light Infantry tactics. Moore was distinguished also for having shown exceptional restraint during the ferocious suppression of the 1798 Rising in Ireland. He showed uncommon appreciation of the value of the common soldier, concerned not only for his men's physical welfare but believing them to be more than cannon fodder.

The Light Infantryman was allowed to show initiative and flexibility. A key element was Moore's concern to avoid breaches of discipline rather than punishing them once they'd occurred. Such notions would not find ready acceptance throughout the Army but Light Infantry troops were better disciplined and demonstrated greater efficiency in action than ordinary infantry.

Shaw became ADC to the commander of the Light Infantry Division and edited the unit's *Standing Orders*. He was briefly employed at the Royal Military College before serving under

Wellington in the Netherlands in 1814 as Deputy Assistant Quartermaster of the Light Infantry.

In 1815 he got the chance to test his theories, when he used "complex and unorthodox formations" against cavalry at Waterloo. He impressed his superiors, was promoted to Major and given command of Calais during its military occupation. This was a job which needed considerable diplomatic skills as he dealt with a French administration with no reason to love the English occupiers.

In 1819, on the recommendation of Wellington, Shaw was promoted to Lieut. Colonel; he married Mary Kennedy the following year. He then became Shaw-Kennedy on inheriting an estate through her family.

From 1827 to 1831, he served as military commander in the Manchester area. It was a time of great labour unrest and demonstrations quickly became riots. Unrest was exacerbated by magistrates constantly calling out the military. Shaw-Kennedy developed a more considered approach.

In 1829 he was invited by Sir Robert Peel to become one of two Commissioners of the New London Metropolitan Police. Shaw Kennedy declined the offer. He continued to develop his ideas on using troops as a sort of unobtrusive reserve police. He wrote that the commander should "hold in readiness such a force as can instantly support the civil power... only showing the military when the civil force is evidently inadequate".

In June 1836, he was appointed Inspector General of the new Irish Constabulary, consolidating the four pre-existing provincial forces. He clearly shared Under-Secretary Thomas Drummond's enthusiasm for establishing disciplined, restrained, non-sectarian policing, and encouraged Catholics to join. "I wished that men of all classes and parties should have an equal chance of appointment."

The Act establishing the new force stipulated that the members had to be literate and bear a magistrate's certificate of good moral character; this would be checked. A physical examination was followed by a competitive examination in literacy and numeracy skills. Only on appointment would an applicant be asked his religion. Station parties were to be denominationally mixed.

Potential officers were interviewed by Shaw-Kennedy to ensure their fitness to command. Appointments to all ranks were conditional on satisfactory completion of training. Some of the half-dozen Army officers drafted in as Sub-Inspectors were, according to Curtis, "not at home in policing". The IG's view was that the force's civil duties made it "very objectionable to be too military" and the military aspects of training were modified towards maintaining discipline. Clear procedures were established to deal with breaches.

The Regulations stated: "In the performance of their duty as peace officers they are distinctly to understand that their efforts should be more principally directed towards the prevention of crime, which will tend far more effectually towards the security of persons and property than the punishment of those who have broken the laws".

Shaw-Kennedy left his post on 15th March 1838 after disagreement with the Irish executive in Dublin Castle. Officials there had wanted to promote certain officers against his recommendations and refused to sanction the dismissal of another. The IG considered his authority undermined and resigned.

Whatever banner waved overhead, Nineteenth Century Ireland needed a police establishment. The country was fortunate in getting a system which, despite its faults of rigidity and excessive discipline, was generally efficient and impartial. In 1922, with firearms and the Cadet system removed, the

Constabulary would be the model for policing an independent Ireland. Shaw-Kennedy, as a thoughtful and progressive chief, deserves credit for that.

Appendix 2

Oath of Office, Royal Irish Constabulary 1836

I do swear that I will well and truly serve Our Sovereign Lord the King in the office of constable without favour or affection, malice or ill-will; that I will see and cause His Majesty's peace to be kept and preserved and that I will prevent to the best of my power, all offences against the same; and that while I shall continue to hold the said office, I will to the best of my skill and knowledge, discharge all the duties thereof, in the execution of warrants or otherwise, faithfully according to law; and that I do not now belong, and that I will not, while I shall hold the said office, join, subscribe or belong to any political society whatever, or to any secret society whatsoever, except the society of Freemasons. So help me God.

Gárda Síochána, Form of Declaration 1923

I ___________ do solemnly and sincerely before God declare and affirm and my word and honour pledge that I will be faithful to the utmost of my ability in my employment by the Ard-Chomhairle of Saorstát Eireann in the office of __________ in the Gárda Síochána and that I will render good and true service and obedience to Saorstát Eireann and its constitution and government as by law established, without favour or affection, fear, malice or ill-will, and that I will see and cause the peace to be kept and preserved; and that I will prevent to the best of my power all offences against the same, and that while I shall continue to hold the said office, I will to the best of my knowledge discharge all the duties thereof faithfully according to law, and that I do not now belong and that I will not while I hold the said office, join, belong or subscribe to any political society whatsoever, or to any Secret Society whatsoever.

Constitution of Irish Free State 1922, Oath of Allegiance

I (name) do solemnly swear true faith and allegiance to the Constitution of the Irish Free State as by law established, and that I will be faithful to H.M. King George V, his heirs and successors by law in virtue of the common citizenship of Ireland with Great Britain and her adherence to and membership of the group of nations forming the British Commonwealth of Nations.

Manuscript Sources

Bureau of Military History (BMH), Witness Statements, Cathal Brugha Bks, Dublin

Census of Ireland 1901 & 1911, National Archives of Ireland (NAI)

Chief Secretary's Office memo re. J.Henegan, RIC Dungannon – pension, and supply of artificial foot by grant from Royal Bounty Fund, 1916 National Archives, Kew, London (NA)

Circulars to RIC, 1921 – 1922, NA London

W.J.V. Comerford, unpublished m/s: *Harp, Sheds, Crown* Manuscripts Dept, National Library of Ireland (NLI)

Correspondence of Patrick Lyons with G.H.Orpen, NLI Manuscripts Dept

Official diary of W.H. Bodley, NLI, Manuscripts Dept

Papers of Jeremiah Mee, Garda Museum, Dublin

R.I.C. General Register, NAI

Records of Petty Sessions Co. Donegal, NAI

Registry of Births, Deaths and Marriages, Dublin

RIC County Inspectors' Reports 1912-1922, Colonial Office 904 "The British in Ireland", NLI

RIC Pension Rolls – disbandment. NA

RIC Weekly Outrage Reports 1920-1921, NA

The Papers of J.R.W. Goulden, Trinity College Dublin, Library – Manuscripts Dept

Reference

Dictionary of Irish Biography Dublin, Royal Irish Academy
Dictionary of National Biography London, Royal Academy
Thom's Directory

Periodicals & Newspapers

The Constabulary Gazette 1912-1922
The Irish Times
The Irish Independent
The Freeman's Journal
The Sligo Champion
The Sligo Independent
The Donegal Democrat
The Donegal Vindicator
The Tyrone Constitution
Mayo News

Bibliography and further reading

Abbott, Richard *Police Casualties in Ireland, 1919-1922* Cork 2002

Allen, Gregory *The Garda Siochana: Policing in an Independent Ireland* Dublin 1999

Allen, Gregory *The Passionists and the Policeman* Dublin 1993

Ambrose, Joe *Sean Treacy and The Tan War* Cork 2007

Andrews C.S. *Dublin Made Me* Dublin 2001

Anon *Tales of the RIC* Edinburgh 1921

Bennett, Richard *The Black and Tans* London 1964

Brady, Conor *Guardians of the Peace* Dublin 1974

Breathnach, Seamus *The Irish Police* Tralee 1974

Breen, Dan *My Fight for Irish Freedom* Dublin, Anvil Press 1969

Breen, Dan *My Fight for Irish Freedom* Dublin, Talbot Press 1924

Brewer, John D. *The Royal Irish Constabulary: an oral history* Belfast 1990

Buckley, Donal *The Battle of Tourmakeady: Fact or Fiction* Dublin 2008

Bury, Robin *Buried Lives: the Protestants of Southern Ireland* Dublin 2017

Butler, Peter *Constables, Peelers and Civic Guards* Cahir 1997

Comerford, James J. *My Kilkenny IRA Days* Kilkenny 1980

Coogan, Tim Pat *Michael Collins* London 1990

Cooper, Bryan *The 10th (Irish) Division at Gallipoli* London 1918

Curtis, Robert H. *History of the Royal Irish Constabulary* Dublin/London 1869

Dagg, George A. de M. Edwin *"Devia Hibernia": the road and route guide for Ireland of the Royal Irish Constabulary* Dublin 1893

Dalton, Charles *With the Dublin Brigade – espionage and assassination with Michael Collins' intelligence unit* London 1929

Duff, Douglas V. *Sword for Hire: the Saga of a Modern Free Companion* London 1934

Farry, Michael *Sligo 1914 -1921: a Chronicle of Conflict* Dublin 1992

Farry, Michael *The Aftermath of Revolution, Sligo 1921-28* Dublin 2000

Farry, Michael *The Irish Revolution 1912-23: Sligo* Dublin 2012

Fedorowich, Kent "The problems of disbandment: the Royal Irish Constabulary and imperial migration 1919-1929" *Irish Historical Studies* May 1996

Fennell, Thomas *The Royal Irish Constabulary: a History and Personal Memoir* Dublin 2003

Fitzpatrick, David *Terror in Ireland 1916-1923* Dublin 2012

Fitzpatrick, David (ed.) *Revolution? Ireland 1917-1923* Dublin 1990

Fulham, Gregory J. "James Shaw-Kennedy and the Reformation of the Irish Constabulary 1836 – 1838" in *Eire/Ireland* Vol. XIV

Gannon, Sean "Sure it's only a holiday": The Irish Contingent of the British (Palestine) Gendarmerie, 1922-1926 *Australasian Journal of Irish Studies* 2013 Vol. 13 pp. 64-85

Garrow-Green, G. *In the Royal Irish Constabulary* London 1905?

Garvin, Tom *Preventing the Future* Dublin 2004

Garvin, Tom *The Birth of Irish Democracy* Dublin 1996

Gaughan, J.Anthony *The Memoirs of Constable Jeremiah Mee* Dublin 1975

Gregory, Vere R.T *The House of Gregory* Dublin 1943

Griffin, Brian *Sources for the Study of Crime in Ireland 1801-1921* Dublin 2005

Hart, Peter *The IRA and its Enemies* Oxford 1998

Herlihy, Jim *The Royal Irish Constabulary – a Short History and Genealogical Guide* Dublin, 2nd Ed. 2016

Herlihy, Jim *The Royal Irish Constabulary- A Complete Alphabetical List of Officers* Dublin 1999

Higgins, Tom *Mr O: the Life and Times of an Irish Policeman* Amazon 2016

Hopkinson, Michael (ed.) *The Last Days of Dublin Castle –The Diaries of Mark Sturgis* Dublin 1999

Horne, John *Our War* Dublin 2008

Kautt, W.H. *Ambushes and Armour: the Irish rebellion 1919 – 1921* Dublin 2010

Kautt, W.H. *Ground Truths: British Army operations in the Irish War of Independence* Dublin 2014

Keane, Fergal *Wounds* London, 2017

Kearney, Felix et al *Drumquin "you're not a city, but..."* Omagh1979

Kee, Robert *The Green Flag vol.lll: Ourselves Alone* London 1972

King, Cecil A. *Memorabilia* Ballyshannon 1989

Kingston, Diarmuid *Beleaguered: a history of the RIC in West Cork during the War of Independence* Cork 2013

Lawlor, Pearse *1920-1922 The Outrages* Cork 2011

Leatham,C.W. *Sketches and Stories of the Royal Irish Constabulary* Dublin 1919

Lee, J.J. *Ireland 1912-1982* Cambridge 1989

Lohan, Máire *An Antiquarian Craze: the life, times and work in Archaeology of Patrick Lyons R.I.C. 1861-1954* Dublin 2008

Lowe W.J. & Malcolm, E.L., 'The Domestication of the Royal Irish Constabulary 1836-1922' *Irish Economic and Social History* Vol. XIX 1992

Lowe, W.J. 'The War on the R.I.C. 1919-1922' *Éire-Ireland: a Journal of Irish Studies 2002,* p.79ff

Macardle, Dorothy *The Irish Republic* London 1968

McCall, Ernest *The Auxies – a Pictorial History* Newtownards 2013

McCall, Ernest *Tudor's Toughs* Newtownards 2010

McCullagh, David *De Valera: Rise 1882-1932* Dublin 2017

McDowell, R.B. *The Irish Administration 1801-1922* Toronto 1964

McKenna, John *A Beleaguered Station: the Memoir of Head Constable John McKenna 1891-1921* Belfast 2009

McNemara, Conor "Rebellion in Ballymacbritain: conservative Nationalist responses to the 1916 Rising in the west of Ireland" *Journal of the Galway Archaeological and Historical Society* 2016 Vol. 68

McNemara, Conor *War and Revolution in the West of Ireland 1913-1922* Kildare 2018

McNiff, Liam *A History of the Garda Síochána* 1997

Maguire, Fiach *Peeler and Patriot: one man's journey from enemy to patriot* (Amazon) 2016

Mukhopadyay, Surajat "Importing Back Colonial Policing Systems" *European Journal of Social Sciences* Sept. 1998 Vol. 11, Issue 3, pp.253-265

Myers, Kevin *From An Irishman's Diary* Irish Times, Dublin 2000

Myers, Kevin *Ireland's Great War* Dublin 2014

Myers, Kevin *More Myers* Dublin 2006

Neeson, Eoin *Civil War in Ireland* Cork 1996

Neligan, David *The Spy in the Castle* London 1968

O'Brien, Paul *Havoc – the Auxiliaries in Ireland's War of Independence* Cork 2017

Ō Duibhir, Liam *The Donegal Awakening* Cork 2009
O'Donoghue, Flor *No Other Law* Dublin 1986
O'Malley, Ernie *On Another Man's Wound* Dublin 1979
O'Malley, Ernie *The Singing Flame* Dublin 1978
Ō Ruairc, Pádraig Ōg *Truce: Murder, Myth and the last Days of the Irish War of Independence* Cork 2016
O'Sullivan, Donal *The Depot* Eugene OR, USA, 2007
O'Sullivan, Donal *The Irish Constabularies 1822-1922* Dingle 1999
Reed, Sir Andrew *Standing Rules and Regulations for the Government and Guidance of The Royal Irish Constabulary* Dublin 1888
Reed, Sir Andrew *The Irish Constable's Guide* Dublin 1912
Reed, Sir Andrew *The Liquor Licensing Laws of Ireland and Innkeepers' Guide* Dublin 1907
Reed, Sir Andrew *The Policeman's Manual* Dublin 1887
Regan, John M. *The Memoirs of John M. Regan: a Catholic officer in the RIC and RUC* Dublin 2007
Reid, Myles *Royal Irish Constabulary Memories: The Forgotten Irish* Dublin, Foxrock Local History Club 2013
Reynolds, John *46 Men Dead: the Royal Irish Constabulary in Co. Tipperary 1919-22* Cork, 2016
Scanlon, Mary *The Dublin Metropolitan Police* London 1998
Senior, Hereward *Constabulary – The Rise of Police Institutions in Britain, the Commonwealth and the United States* Toronto/ Oxford 1997
Shaw, G.B, eds Laurence, D. Leary, D. *John Bull's Other Island - Prefaces, Vol. 1* London 1993
Shea, Patrick *Voices and the Sound of Drums* Belfast 1981
Sheehan, William *British Voices from the Irish War of Independence 1918-1921* Cork 2005
Sinclair, R.J.K. and Scully, F.J.M. *Arresting Memories: captured moments in Constabulary life* Belfast 1982, RUC Diamond Jubilee Committee

Stewart, A.T.Q. *The Shape of Irish History* Belfast 2001
Sullivan, A.M. *Old Ireland* London 1927
Sullivan, A.M. *The Last Serjeant* London 1952
Townshend, Charles "Policing Insurgency in Ireland 1914 –'23" in Anderson, D. M. & Killengray, D. (eds) *Policing and Decolonisation – politics, nationalism and the police 1917 – 1965* Manchester 1992
Townshend, Charles *The British Campaign in Ireland, 1919 – 1921* Oxford 1975
Townshend, Charles *The Republic: The Fight for Irish Independence 1918-1923* London 2014
Walsh, Maurice *The News from Ireland* London 2008
Younger, Carlton *Ireland's Civil War* London 1968

USEFUL WEBSITES

Garda Museum: www.garda.ie/en/About-Us/Our-History
Garda Historical Society: www.policehistory.com/garda
Northern Ireland Police Museum: www.psni.police.uk/inside-psni/our-history
Harp Society: www.irish-police.com/the-harp-society-constitution
Royal Ulster Constabulary George Cross Foundation: www.rucgcfoundation.org

LITERATURE

Art can bring us to the heart of a matter more precisely than mere facts. Poetry is especially helpful. Irish poetry in English is perhaps the best medium for expressing the complexity of the interaction between the Irish and English peoples. It can reveal how individuals address ideas of multiple identity and sometimes conflicting loyalties. These are just a few suggestions; the dramatists, novelists and poets mentioned here have other relevant works and there are many other writers who have much to contribute to our understanding.

Richard Murphy: *The Battle of Aughrim*

AE (George Russell): *On Behalf of Some Irishmen not Followers of Tradition,* and *Salutation – to the memory of some I knew who are dead and loved Ireland*

W.B. Yeats: All the poems relating to 1916 and to Casement, and *Meditations in Time of Civil War*

Tom Kettle: *To My Daughter Betty, The Gift of God*

Francis Ledwidge *Lament for Thomas Mc Donagh.* and *Soliloquy*

John Hewitt: *Neither an Elegy nor a Manifesto*

George Bernard Shaw: *John Bull's Other Island* (the play and the preface)

Sean O'Casey: *The Plough and the Stars*

Brian Friel: *Translations*

Augusta, Lady Gregory: *The Rising of the Moon*

Sean O'Casey: *The Raid*

Frank O'Connor: *Guests of The Nation*

Liam O'Flaherty: *The Informer, The Sniper*

J.G. Farrell: *Troubles*

Roddy Doyle: *A Star Called Henry*

James Plunkett: *Strumpet City*

Kevin Mc Carthy: *Peeler*

Sebastian Barry: *The Whereabouts of Eneas McNulty* and *A Long, Long Way*

Conor Brady: the DMP novels - *A June of Ordinary Murders, The Eloquence of the Dead, & A Hunt in Winter.* (While these novels are set in the 1880s, they give a very vivid impression of contemporary society and policing in Dublin.)

Endnotes

i) This same light-hearted policeman has also left a puzzle in his notebook:

P R V R Y P R F C T M N V R K P T H S P R C P T S T N

The addition of a single vowel can turn this into a readable sentence.

A clue might be that it's a sentiment that both priest and parson would endorse.

ii) William Gibson succeeded to the title as 2nd Baron Ashbourne but was effectively disinherited because of his nationalist leanings. He had converted to Catholicism as had Violet. His Unionist father's estate of some £100,000 (worth some £10 million today) went mostly to his younger brother. Willie received only £800.

Willie would die in 1942 at his house in Occupied France, having been briefly interned by the Germans. He lived surrounded by Irish cultural artefacts and was buried in his habitual green kilt and cloak.

iii) Historian Goddard Henry Orpen remains best known as the author of *Ireland Under The Normans* originally published in four volumes between 1911 and 1920. His proposition that the Normans brought order and progress to an Ireland in thrall to tribal traditions which kept the land in a state of comparative anarchy, offended many. It continues to offend many. One of Orpen's bitterest critics was Eoin McNeill then

Professor of Mediaeval History at University College Dublin. Despite its controversial aspects, Orpen's great work, republished in 1968, remains the definitive study of the topic.

iv) The story of Patrick Lyons exemplifies the opportunities offered by the RIC to an intelligent young man of limited prospects. Born into a landless Tipperary family which had suffered eviction, he had to leave school aged ten and by his early teens was working as an agricultural labourer. He was fortunate in that the family which employed him also tutored him in the evenings.

As an adult, Lyons continued his studies, prepared for the RIC tests, and was accepted in 1886. By 1896, as a 'P' man, he'd been promoted to Sergeant. In 1913 he became Head Constable in Ballyhaunis, Co. Mayo. There his ambition rested, having no wish to subject himself to the snobbery of many Cadet Officers, who, he thought, were "not real policemen at all".

Besides, HC Lyons had another secret life beyond his Constabulary duties. His discovery of an Ogham stone sparked an interest in archaeology and antiquarian matters. He entered into correspondence with Sir John Rhys at Oxford University and became the unacknowledged collaborator with H.T. Knox in nineteen academic papers. Although he'd been made a member of the Royal Society of Antiquaries in 1905, his field research remained covert. He retired in 1920. Unfortunately, "the suspicions of the gunmen compelled me to relinquish research and virtually terminated my antiquarian career". His correspondence with Orpen began in 1907 and continued intermittently into the 1930s.

v) In Ireland as in Britain, there was a rush to enlist. There was a variety of motives but one such was the martial romanticism which gripped young men who craved adventure. There had been no widespread conflict in Europe since the defeat of Napoleon Bonaparte a century before and war had taken on a mythic status. General Sir Ian Hamilton, who would command the 10th (Irish) Division described this spirit in his diary:

> Once in a generation a mysterious wish for war passes through the people. Their instinct tells them there is *no other way* of progress and of escape from habits that no longer fit them. Whole generations of statesmen will fumble over reforms for a lifetime, which are put into full-blooded execution within a week of a declaration of war. There is *no other way.* Only by intense sufferings can the nations grow… Should the fates decree the whole brave army may disappear during the night at least we shall have lived, acted, dared.

As we look back now, it seems obvious that Rupert Brooke wasn't the only poet inspired by this sort of sentiment; Patrick Pearse's notion of the soul of Ireland being revitalised by blood sacrifice was no different. And young men who donned khaki in 1914 in a longing for excitement were matched by many of those who joined the Irish Volunteers.

The quotation from Gen. Hamilton is borrowed from Christopher Robbins's delightful memoir: "The Empress of Ireland".

vi) Many years later, John Hennigan's big sister, by then little Sr Zita of the Ursuline Convent in Sligo, referred to Winston Churchill when she expressed concern about the danger that excessive reading might pose to my faith. The link, though she didn't know it, was Wells's book.

vii) In the year 2015 when it was proposed to erect a monument to Shackleton in his native Athy, there were "Republican" objections on the grounds that he'd once stood for Parliament there as a Unionist.

viii) There was a precedent for the successful ditching of a Handley Page bomber. On 17th September 1917, a HP O/100 piloted by Naval airman John Alcock, (who had earlier that day, whilst flying a Sopwith Camel, shot down two German aircraft) suffered an oil leak over the Gulf of Xeros after attacking railway yards near Constantinople. The crew survived the ditching and remained prisoners in Turkey until the end of the war. In June 1919, Alcock, accompanied by Arthur Brown made the first successful trans-Atlantic flight which ended with an undignified touch-down near Clifden, Co. Galway. On 19th December

1919, John Alcock died after a crash in France.

Ditching an aircraft successfully requires skill and a great deal of luck. With some power at his disposal, e.g. with one of two engines still working, the pilot can maintain control longer. The trick is to fly as slowly as possible without stalling – which means a crash – and to hold a flying attitude which keeps the nose higher than the tail. If the sea is calm, the ideal procedure is to descend into the wind. If there's a swell, the pilot may have no choice but to land crosswind; hitting a wave is like flying into a solid wall. The machine must be level at the moment of impact: if one wingtip hits the water first, the aircraft will slew around and crash into the water. With a fixed-undercarriage aeroplane like the Handley Page, the problems are compounded by the wheels hitting the water first. The nose will pitch forward violently and the whole machine can end up in a vertical attitude. If it goes completely over, there is little chance of anyone getting out.

ix) Soyer cookers were named after their inventor Alexis Benoit Soyer, a French celebrity chef and social progressive who lived in England. During the Crimean War, the poorly equipped British Army cooked their rations on open fires, a practice extremely wasteful of scarce firewood, and badly cooked food contributed to the army's notorious ill-health. Soyer designed a simple cylindrical oven which did the job efficiently and thoroughly. The British Army's reliance on Soyer cookers really only came to an end in 1982 when the Argentinian Air Force sent almost their entire stock of them to the bottom of the sea.

ix) During Ireland's Great Famine, Soyer designed and set up a free soup kitchen in Dublin.

x) Preceding stanzas refer to the rebels:

> Further, on information good,
> We mislike their present attitude,
> Having detected their intent
> From a certain captured document –
> Which is – more from revenge than gain –
> To murder such of us as remain.

This not improbably they will do,
Although we claim it is strictly true
That one of our Constables could beat
Six of the cornerboys off their feet,
Yet as they have arms which we are without
The result is hardly open to doubt.

xi) Sean Gannon's informative paper sheds some light on the plight of those former RIC men who were forced into involuntary exile. The lives of some had been directly threatened; others knew themselves to be under threat at a time when old scores were being settled. While it appears that the majority of "Old RIC" eventually resumed their lives peacefully in Ireland, several hundred were effectively forced into permanent exile.

Gannon computes that the original draft of the Palestine Police's other ranks included 80 of the "Old RIC", along with 473 Black and Tans and 139 Auxiliaries. Among its officers were 9 RIC and 21 Auxiliaries. Another calculation is that 7% of the officers were Irish-born as were 38% of the other ranks. The Assistant Commandant was Gerald Foley, former Mayo County Inspector.

xii) Ireland is indeed a small country. After serving in three police forces, David Neligan's policing career was over but he was given a sinecure in the Land Commission. My future father-in-law Thomas Lavin was alone at his desk in a small office when a new face appeared and announced that one of the three desks was his. Surveying the room, the stranger asked if Lavin knew who he was. "Yes, you're Neligan." The new man then commandeered the desk opposite the door and with a wall at his back. Opening the drawers, he pulled pistols from his pockets and placed them inside, one at each hand. A lot of scores were being settled and wise men took precautions. A few years before, Thomas's own brother had departed suddenly and inexplicably to America and disappeared for many decades.

xiii But Louis Armstrong got his retaliation in first. In 1926 he had recorded "The Irish Black Bottom". His lyrics could win no prizes but he had fun with the notion of the Irish adopting Black music. That little laugh was sheer devilment.

> All you heard for years in Ireland was the 'Wearing of the Green'
> But the biggest change that's come in Ireland that I have ever seen
> All the laddies and the cooies laid aside their Irish reels
> And I was born in Ireland (ha, ha)
> So imagine how I feels.
> Now Ireland's gone Black Bottom crazy,
> See them dance,
> You ought to see them dance.
> Folks supposed to be related even dance
> They play that strain
> Works right on their brain
> Now it goes Black Bottom
> A new rhythm's drivin' the folks insane.

xv) My sharpest memory of that visit is of a green-clad soldier with steel helmet and rifle at the slope marching slowly backwards and forwards in front of that elegant building. Then I was introduced to the legendary Alfie Byrne who had been repeatedly elected Lord Mayor of Dublin. I saw an old man with white whiskers and twinkling eyes. He knew exactly how to intrigue a little boy. I was brought down a spiral staircase into the bowels of the earth where a tunnel ran into the darkness, a fairytale cavern. This I later learned, was the tunnel which linked Leinster House with Government Buildings on Merrion Square, dug during the Civil War when members of the Government had to be protected from sniper fire. At the time of my visit it was being blocked up.

xvi) Consumption, a common name for it, aptly describes the effect of the bacterium as its victim wasted away. At its peak in 1904, it claimed some 12,000 young people in Ireland according to Red Cross estimates.

In 1922, records show 4,614 Irish deaths from TB. Erroneously referred to as "the poor people's disease", it affected all classes. The difference was that the rich could be treated in Alpine clinics while the poor just died. However it was romanticised in literature and opera, it was still the silent killer. In 1928, the great Alice Stopford White was just developing her career as a paediatrician: it would be 1948 before she initiated the BCG vaccination campaign in Ireland at the request of Health Minister Noel Browne.